LEBANON
A Shattered Country

LEBANON
A Shattered Country

Myths and Realities of the Wars in Lebanon

ELIZABETH PICARD

translated from the French by Franklin Philip

HOLMES & MEIER
New York / London

Published in the United States of America 1996 by
Holmes & Meier Publishers, Inc.
160 Broadway
New York, NY 10038

Originally published under the title *Liban: État de discorde*,
copyright © 1988 Flammarion, Paris. Expanded and revised by the author for the
English-language edition.

Book design by Linda M. Robertson
Typesetting by Stephanie True Moss

This book has been printed on acid-free paper.

Library of Congress Cataloging-in-Publication Data

Picard, Elizabeth.
    [Liban, état de discorde. English]
    Lebanon, a shattered country : myths and realities of the wars in
  Lebanon / Elizabeth Picard : translated from the French by Franklin Philip.
      p. cm.
    Includes bibliographical references and Index.
    ISBN 0-8419-1233-5 (alk. paper)
    1. Lebanon—Politics and government—1946–   I. Title.
DS87.P5213 1996
956.92—dc20   94-30521
                                                CIP

Manufactured in the United States of America

La vérité est mystérieuse, fuyante, toujours à conquérir. La liberté est dangereuse, dure à vivre autant qu'exaltante. Nous devons marcher vers ces deux buts, péniblement, mais résolument, certains d'avance de nos défaillances sur un si long chemin.

Truth is mysterious, elusive, ever to be earned anew. Liberty is dangerous, as hard to live as it is exciting. We must journey toward these new goals, painfully but resolutely, sure in advance that we shall weaken and flinch on such a long road.

ALBERT CAMUS
Discours de Suède, Speech of Acceptance upon the Award of the
Nobel Prize for Literature, Delivered in Stockholm on December 10, 1957.
Translated by Justin O'Brien (New York: Alfred A. Knopf, 1958).

الحرب بالنضّارات هيّن

Seen from afar, war seems easy

MICHEL FEGHALI
Proverbes et Dictons Libanais (Paris: Institut d'Ethnologie), 1938.

Contents

Maps

Preface

A short while ago Lebanon seemed nearby, a familiar and attractive country enjoying an exceptionally positive image in the West. Today it has come to stand for desolation, a hostile universe painfully conjuring up the deaths of thousands of civilians, and the intolerable disappearance of close friends. It is therefore very tempting to claim that we now have nothing in common with it, admitting that from crisis to battle, from murder to assassination attempt, hemmed in by the cynical lusts of its neighbors, Lebanon has exhausted our understanding and solidarity.

Alas, this Lebanon has remained as close to us as the Lebanon of light. In our global village, wasn't the massive stock of arms of the local militiamen expending thousands of cartridges on the concrete walls of an abandoned apartment building a miniature image of the nuclear force capable of destroying our planet dozens of times over? Didn't the ceaseless inflow of weaponry making for the conflict's indefinite prolongation reflect the logic of arms production and sales which the Western powers claim indispensable to their economic recovery? Wasn't the scandalous wealth of the "warlords" and the speculators betting on the collapse of the Lebanese pound a caricature of the universal domination of the logic of finance? In Lebanon, terrorists kidnapped and murdered civilians; elsewhere, democratic governments ordered the bombing of a capital with the avowed intention of "bringing down" an enemy head of state. Weren't battles between militias, the self-defense of communities, the rejection of equality, contempt for the rule of law in this tiny country just so many guises of the intolerance and exclusion poisoning our world in the name of religions, identities, and ideologies, that all have in common the rigidity of their certitudes and fear of and exclusion of the Other?

We were more and more tempted to forget Lebanon as, one by one, foreign interventions failed, costly for the reckless who risked themselves and mostly calamitous for the populations subjected to them. France in particular has had the bitter experience: well-intentioned interventions through its role in the Multinational Force under the aegis of the United States, its air attacks in the Bekaa and the frustrating mission of the United Nations troops in southern Lebanon. Western policy failed, trapped in conflicting loyalties, outworn interests, selfish calculations, and murky prospects. The more than twenty-year absence of long-term thinking bears much of the responsibility, and also the sheer complexity of the Lebanese conflict, which bordered on the absurd. Lebanon exhausted our compassion and discouraged our solidarity, for from one event to the next, reflection and analysis lost their way in a mindless and bloody turmoil. Nothing made any sense or fit our understanding: the obscene reversals of alliance; the carnages between two valleys or two villages or two families; the serial assassinations of political figures; the systematic destruction of its patrimony; the declarations, as radical as they were vacuous, of its political leaders marking each stage of the deterioration; and today, an interest mainly in state operations while the country is still occupied.

Clichés and inherited ideas shamelessly rush into this vacuum of reason. For more than a decade, many Lebanese who owe their prosperity to their country's external relations, to the circulation of commodities, money, and persons between the Arab East and the West have clung to the certainty that their misery had been inflicted from the outside, that they were the innocent victims of a drama that did not really involve them, and that they were the object of conspiracies hatched by neighboring nations or even the superpowers for the purpose of plunder and subjection. According to this logic, salvation can once again come only from the outside, the breach is opened to arms, the money of manipulation, the entry of foreign troops, and the contempt and hatred of compatriots.

This confusion gives rise to explanations and interpretations of the most ideological kind—simplistic for propaganda needs and extremist for justifying the degree of armed violence. Today we can get samples of this in the talk of the combatants allied with Iran, for example—those who call on all of Lebanon's populations to turn Muslim and to rally under the banner of an Islamic republic. But in the information disseminated in condensed form by the Western media, the propaganda slogans and clichés put out to satisfy our sensibilities are no less false and dangerous. Yesterday, reactionaries were fighting progressives: the privileged Maronite Christians were exploiting the poverty-stricken Muslims. Today, Lebanon has become Christendom's front line of resistance against Islamic conquest. And what can we say about the widespread nonsense that, in Lebanon, "Arabs" fought "Christians" other than that it fuels the racist fantasies and painful memories of those who peddle it? Some of these contradictory interpretations have ready access to the Western media, if only because they are better able to speak our language or use more effective networks; but the opposing positions ought not to be suspect on that account, nor certain victims more pitiable than others.

Yes, the Lebanese conflict is indeed complex. No more so, however, than the war in Yugoslavia or the international trade crisis. In any event, it did not result from some mysterious thunderbolt out of a tranquil sky, but from internal and external historical processes whose protagonists, Lebanese, regional, and international, are identifiable and in no way ingenuous. The causes of the Lebanese conflict are simultaneously strategic (the Arab-Israeli conflict), social (the hegemony of conservative sectarian elites), economic (the choice of liberalism [unbridled laissez-faire in the extreme] privileging the service sector). They can be identified, analyzed, and need to be taken into account in the search for peace, for the complete independence of the country, and a new constitutional system.

A look at the history of the Mediterranean Near East reveals the significant features of its populations, the importance of regional differences, and the severity of the tensions between the various groups as well as the competition between their elites. It also indicates the signs of the birth of new relations of force from community to community, from region to region, from government to opposition. Mount Lebanon in particular both points up and exacerbates the principles of a social and political organization based on precarious balances between confessional communities, the end point of the fragmented, eventful history of the Mountain and the product of a dynamic intermixing in the coastal cities. Paradoxically, though of all the countries of the Near East, Lebanon seems the closest to liberal parliamentary democratic regimes, it is the one whose politics has most strongly preserved the imprint of the social organization of the Ottoman regime.

Moreover, because of Lebanon's size, the makeup of its populations, and especially its geographical location, the colonialist designs of the European powers had a heavy influence on the modeling of the society's political structures, the carving out of the country's territory, and the orientation of its economy—more than in any other area of the Mediterranean Near East. Even before the breakup of the Ottoman Empire, the stakes represented by the control of this trading coastline and its hinterland produced a competition for influence with local effects of devastating proportions. Today the West loves to recall its old solicitude for Lebanon. Nevertheless, one must put Western cultural and political activity in the Near East together with the strategic aspects and economic dimension of the competition between France and Great Britain. Above all, the responsibility of France, as the mandatory power for close to twenty years, must be acknowledged, for it headed toward an explosive situation in a seemingly peaceful evolution: it was under France's authority that the highly fragile, externally oriented liberal economy was set up; it was under France's inspiration that Lebanon adopted a communitarian political regime; it was under France's protection that the Maronites came to consider themselves the sole agents of the state; it was under France's influence that an independent Lebanon broke its close and indispensable economic ties with Syria. France's solicitude for Lebanon today should also involve the knowledge of this formative period.

When we grasp the specific historical, ecological, and cultural conditions of the country and its differences from and also its resemblances to its neighbors, when we take account of the heavy heritage of the colonial period, we confront an independent Lebanon fashioned by its populations and directed by its elites. For some thirty years, under the admiring commentary of experts ("I can't understand it," said the Belgian economist Van Zeeland, "but keep it up"), the liberal merchant republic sailed on triumphant; it took admirable advantage of the currents and the winds; it dangerously ignored the shoals. In any case, the knowledge of being embarked together on the good ship "Lebanon" grew stronger in the country's various populations while the contradictory views on the direction to take became more sharply divided.

When the tranquil ship cruised into the storm-tossed waters of the Near Eastern conflict, the crisis of Arab nationalism, and the oil recession, its crew mutinied and its officers argued about where to steer. Some lowered the lifeboats, and as panic broke out, it grew harder and harder to keep events in mind, and to understand them, to recompose the puzzle of a shattered country, and to take into account the myths and the complex reality.

In the final years of the war the slide into the underworld seemed unstoppable — down to the terrible fratricidal warfare between Christians and between Shi'is. *Lebanonization* had become a generic term for shelling and destruction the world over. Suspension of the hostilities was made possible only by the 1991 Persian Gulf War and the opening of negotiations between Israel and the Arabs, and, above all, by the exhaustion of the Lebanese people. Syria, the iron-fisted arbiter, controls the larger part of the territory while Israeli occupation of southern Lebanon continues to this day. How can Lebanon be reconstructed under these conditions? How can the security indispensable to its commercial activities be recovered? How can the sovereignty of the state and especially the confidence of the Lebanese in each other, be renewed?

This book was written with the friendly and critical support of Pierre Allix, Louis Audibert of Editions Flammarion, Nabil Beyhum, Jean-Luc Domenach, director of the Centre d'Etudes et de Recherches Internationales, Carolyn Gates, Alain Gresh, Eric-Olivier Stemer, and the Centre for Lebanese Studies, Oxford. May it be a milestone in the search for peace, however small in comparison with the suffering in Lebanon, and with my anger.

LEBANON
A Shattered Country

Topography and Transportation Routes

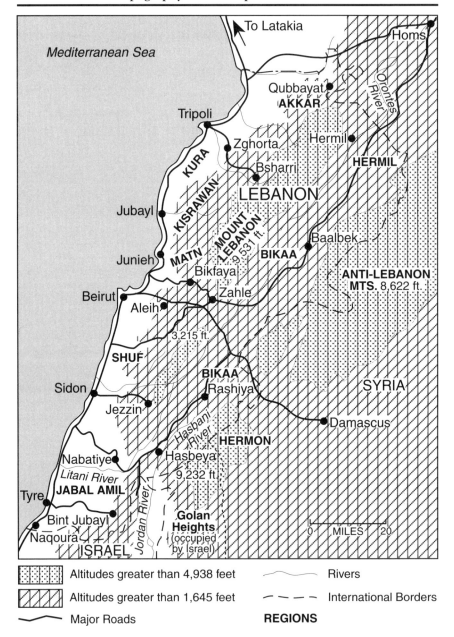

Mediterranean Sea

To Latakia

Homs

Qubbayat

AKKAR

Orontes River

Tripoli

Zghorta

Hermil

HERMIL

KURA

Bsharri

LEBANON

KISRAWAN

Jubayl

MOUNT LEBANON 9,531 ft.

Baalbek

Junieh

MATN

BIKAA

ANTI-LEBANON MTS. 8,622 ft.

Bikfaya

Beirut

Zahle

Aleih

3,215 ft.

SHUF

BIKAA

SYRIA

Sidon

Rashiya

Jezzin

Damascus

HERMON

Hasbani River

Nabatiye

Hasbeya

9,232 ft.

Litani River

JABAL AMIL

Tyre

Jordan River

Golan Heights (occupied by Israel)

Bint Jubayl

0   MILES   20

Naqoura

ISRAEL

	Altitudes greater than 4,938 feet		Rivers
	Altitudes greater than 1,645 feet		International Borders
	Major Roads		**REGIONS**

1

The Search for Origins

DURING these war years, as Lebanon has been collapsing, the social fabric tearing, and the political factions hardening, one special category of combatants has advanced to the front: Lebanese historians setting out to write their country's history. They chase after manuscripts in forgotten corners of Mountain monasteries, search out lost chronicles of the leading families, scrutinize the least tract left by enthusiastic intellectuals from the nineteenth-century political and literary renaissance.

On some things there is unanimity. No matter that the country is held by enemy armies, occupied, divided by unbreachable front lines—these historians don't despair of the country's existence. No one doubts the importance of its past or present reality, but all are betting on its future. Lebanon exists, and to grasp the meaning of its experiences, one has to discover its contours, illuminate its history, identify its protagonists.

On other things there are disagreements. Thus a prewar study of Lebanon's educational system showed that it had nine different types of primary and secondary schools, of which the "official" public schools served only 46 percent of the pupils. These schools used twenty different history texts, and the minister of education exercised his authority over their content only in cases of extreme abuse. After decades of existence as an independent state, Lebanon permitted the young to be educated using highly selective and contradictory versions of its history, a history that the researchers concluded was "dissociative" and "mystifying" in content.[1] What is true of popularization and civic education is also true of historical research and the formation of ideologies to back up political positions: the origin of the country's populations, the identification of the victors and the vanquished, allies and enemies, in past conflicts in the Near East and Mount Lebanon—

all this served primarily as arguments for those who wished to gain a hegemonic position in the battle. So it is not surprising that the progress of scholarship has done little for the coherence of these analyses: in Lebanon, history too is in a state of war.

So it is not a concern for details that prompts these researchers to inquire about who inhabited the Lebanese mountains in the fourth century, or whether the emirs of the seventeenth century reigned over a principality or a nation. What is at issue is a heritage, a heritage to reinforce or undermine the legitimacy of the protagonists today. In volumes 4 and 5 of his erudite survey *Histoire des Maronites*, published in the midst of war, Father Butros Daw[2] sets out to prove the historical continuity between the Amorites of the third millennium, the Mardaites who fought the Arabs and the Byzantines in the seventh century (whom he takes care to specify were not Semitic and whom he calls "the founders of the Lebanese entity and independence"), and the Maronites in the current war. True, history is not neutral, and to retrace the significant stages in Lebanese history eventually means taking a stand about today's conflicts. One has to try, however, and one might as well begin with a geographical perspective.

The Middle Eastern isthmus lies at the hinge of three continents, running along a sea that for thousands of years has been the most heavily trafficked in the world, giving onto the caravanned steppes of Asia. In Lebanon itself there rise two high mountain ranges (more than 9,000 feet behind the Cedars to the north of Mount Lebanon, and at Mount Hermon toward the south of the Anti-Lebanon Mountains), whose westernmost slope runs into the Mediterranean and whose easternmost slope overlooks the oases and desert of Syria. The climate, the vegetation, and the natural regions are reminiscent of Corsica: in the Mountain, olive trees, grapevines, and mulberry trees are cultivated; along the coast, citrus fruits; on the interior plain, grains. But the country is most comparable to the Greek islands, with their blend of audacious ventures and fierce isolation.

Since the time of the Phoenicians, a branch of the Canaanite Semites urbanized in the third millennium and symbols of the first tendency, trading and human influxes have unceasingly modified and enriched the populations of the Lebanese plains, both the coastal plain and the interior plain of the Bikaa Valley: the sea peoples in the twelfth century B.C.; Assyrians and Persians; Greeks led by Alexander in 332 B.C.; Romans, then Byzantines for close to five hundred years; Christian Arabs from Hauran; Omayyads who came from the Muslim empire at Damascus beginning in the seventh century and who made Lebanon the frontier of their western province of Syria and installed Arab garrisons in its ports; Frankish Crusaders in the twelfth and thirteenth centuries, and Mongol conquerors (both groups driven out by Mamluk armies); the Ottoman sovereign who imposed himself in 1516, and then his ambitious vassal from Egypt who stormed and occupied South Lebanon in 1831; and finally Western "pacifiers" or colonizers in the twentieth century.

Transformed and enriched by these highly varied material and cultural infusions, Lebanon's populations in turn scattered all over the world. From the splendor of Carthage to the daring skyscrapers of São Paulo, the toiling exiles in Cairo, Douala, or Detroit, more people outside the country are of Lebanese origin than inside its compact 4,015 square miles. These are outposts or annexes of a country regretfully forsaken, but to which many Lebanese-born or their children return, accentuating the cultural diversity of the Lebanese identity and also the society's openness and mobility. The Lebanon adjoining the sea or the steppes is essentially the Lebanon of the cities: the northern coast on which Tripoli, the rich port of central Syria, flowers; the narrow sahels of Jubayl (Byblos), Beirut, and Sidon, and the rich orchard-strewn littoral of Tyre; and, in the interior, Zahle and Baalbek, both agricultural centers and stopping places for caravans. A prewar image of Lebanon became known throughout the world: that of a liberalism exuberant almost to the point of wildness. It was a country of prosperity, free enterprise, contempt for agriculture, and little interest in modern industry, one where commerce and finance, services and communications, flourished. The exceptional openness to the surrounding areas gave the Lebanese a boldness, an endurance, an incomparable talent for overcoming obstacles, for daring new enterprises. The society was tolerant and hedonistic, cordial to the foreigner, curious to learn, indifferent to religious quarrels, excited by debates over ideas; pluralism and the anonymity of the cities were the guarantor of individual freedoms. Hence also its adaptability to circumstances, its ingenuity in solving problems, its flexibility in dealing with many and varied interlocutors. On the other hand, during the nineteenth century the cities were the home of a modern political consciousness in which support for the idea of a national state was born, grew, and took shape; an unobtrusive state certainly, but one that could be differentiated from the regional surroundings, a state defined simultaneously by its exact territorial extent, its necessary trading with neighboring regions, and the pluralism of its populations—a state for a both diverse and open society. The distinctively Lebanese culture was often held to be the culture of the cities, especially Beirut, so much so that it is puzzling how one day it abruptly yielded to a surge of violence and excommunications.

But the Mountain stamps its other image on Lebanon, that of a haven of refuge—conservative and on the defensive. It was a refuge for the ancient Aramaic population which was driven back by Arabic-speaking nomads, and also for Arab farmers, woodcutters, charcoal-sellers[3] who resisted the Roman conquest: a refuge for the Maronite Christians in the valleys of northern Lebanon, who abandoned the Orontes River valley in Syria around the seventh century; a refuge for the Shi'is in the Jabal Amil in the south after they were expelled from Kisrawan in the fourteenth century; a refuge for the Druzes in Wadi Taym at the foot of Mount Hermon during the reign of the Mamluks and the first Ottomans. The successive upheavals caused by the foreign conquests and the local conflicts radically changed the demographic balances of these isolated communities, these fortress villages: one valley would be abandoned, another settled; one group would flee the region while another collectively converted to another religion in order to stay put. On the whole, however, in this limited area with its extraordinarily tight compartmentalization, we find the same features forming the cultural identity of the Mountain from north to south.

In first place are family solidarities, which are closely connected with the organization of the peasant farmers, the distribution of farmland, and the type of agricultural exploitation, both when small properties were on the increase (up to the eighteenth century) and later, when the growing indebtedness of the peasant farmers favored the accumulation of private land by the tax-collecting notables. Agricultural labor and the functioning of economic units are organized according to the kinship system, and shape the Mountain's fiscal and administrative structure: for centuries, from the Ottoman conquest in 1516 to the mid-nineteenth century, the Mountain depended on a category of notables who collected taxes at a lump-sum rate for the tax authorities,[4] just as in the neighboring regions of Syria and Palestine, but with the difference that in Lebanon prominent families were considered hierarchically superior to other families. Finally, from generation to generation, prestige and political power were maintained and transmitted independently of economic power, through the channel of familial lineage.

I am of course speaking of extended families, rather like tribal clans with multiply branching relationships. Being born in the same area of the village, having the same patronymic, brought even closer by endogamous marriage, family members recognize the strength of the family bond that has withstood great waves of rural exodus. These family solidarities are clearly alien to the egalitarianism and anonymity implied by the idea of citizenship in so-called modern societies; in addition, though even now the Lebanese electoral system still requires that each person vote in his native village, while half the country's population lives in the capital, isn't that because the family-based political decisions are collective and depend more on the balance of power in a rural setting than on the new social dynamics of an urban one? These solidarities are also alien to ideological constructions and the programs of political parties. They form around an individual, a leader with whom a complicitous kinship is felt; they work within the same religious denomination, which is both the framework of social organization and a *brander* of identities: the community. The solidarities make for the strength of a system for redistributing material or symbolic goods and a system of allegiance networks constructed on personal exchanges between patrons and clients—a possibly unequal system, but one eminently effective and far more alluring than an anonymous bureaucracy. Finally, these solidarities are the source of a conservative and inward-looking worldview in which the stranger is seen as a threat.

A second feature of Mountain culture is violence, with cyclical developments in the conflicts between rival groups. A Mediterranean culture par excellence, the Lebanese Mountain is especially prone to the defense of honor, honor concerning women of course, but more generally anything that involves the whole patrimony. Here it is a matter of self-defense that scorns an appeal to any authority external to local interests—the police or the army—and demands that each household be armed so as to exact justice for itself when necessary. Honor has been an essential value in this region for millennia; only the arsenal for defending it has changed. Each attack produces a cycle of vengeance and reprisals that subsides only after involved negotiations. These reprisals tend to intensify, and the cycle of vengeance is prolonged through the interplay of antagonisms and alliances. From the local level to the structure of the whole, the society is permeated by divisions that split its segments into opposing pairs: lineage against lineage within an extended family, one part of a town against another, one mountain slope against another, region against region, to the point where people are considered as belonging either to the Qaysis or to the Yamanis, the two great rival bedouin tribes dating back to before the first Islamic era, identification with which serves as a sign of nobility for Arab families.

This Mountain culture formed by a solidarity of clans politically organized by family hierarchies combines with the culture of the cities that it both fears and scorns, to form an explosive mixture described by the historian Albert Hourani. How then could there have come about the alchemy of a Lebanese identity and a single and independent political community? Certainly, at least since the sixteenth century, the mountain and the plain, the interior and the coast, share a common language: scholars, chroniclers, and the Muslim clergy write in literary Arabic; all speak the dialect of El Sham, the Syrian region between the Taurus Mountains and the Sinai Desert; the Arabic language and the predominance of a Semitic strain over the complexity of ethnic origins are objective factors for unification, but these must be overlaid with a divided historical consciousness. Political unity requires primarily a form of authority—that of a prince or prefect or president—who, whatever his origin, would place himself above the interests of particular groups; political unity also calls for some agreement about the distribution of power and the objectives guiding the exercise of that power, particularly in the relations between Lebanon and its neighbors.[5] Did any such authority exist in Lebanon before a colonial power imposed one in the twentieth century? Or did the country have up to that point only an intermingling of ethnic, religious, political, and military groups between truces and conflicts and at the mercy of outside powers? We see that the question of the territorial and administrative unification of Lebanon by the Mountain emirs in the seventeenth century forms the first great theme of a national history and a founding myth of the Lebanese state.

Echoing Jouplain,[6] the first historian of "Lebanonness," many twentieth-century studies take a particular interest in the reign of the Maan emirs and especially Fakhr al-Din II (1590–1635). Through the mediation of a local military administrator, the pasha, the Ottoman rulers dominated the Syrian province's agricultural plains, cities, ports, and means of communication. The Ottomans had, however, relinquished direct control of tax collection by the prominent families, thus strengthening the latters' traditional domination. One of these families, the Maan, known as "the emirs of the Druzes," succeeded—thanks to its strong structure and skillful encouragement of agricultural colonization by the rapidly growing Maronite peasantry—in establishing its preeminence over other rival families. Fakhr al-Din II in particular federated the Mountain's Qaysi factions under his authority and victoriously fought the great tax-collecting families that resisted him. To do this, he raised a small band of mercenaries, the nucleus of an army committed to the defense of the areas he controlled. Up to that time no local leader had extended his territorial base in this way: the emir won the allegiance of the great families of the north up to the Khabur River; he encouraged the Maronite peasants to migrate to the Akkar; he vanquished the Harfush emirs at Hermil. On the coast he controlled the ports of Beirut and Sidon. In the south he made himself master of the Jabal Amil and Galilee as far as the Palestinian town of Nablus. He also concluded an alliance with the dukes of Tuscany whom he visited and who offered him both an economic opening to the West, technical assistance—for the development of agriculture, the construction of palaces, and the organization of his small administration—and, most important, diplomatic guidance in his disputes with the representatives of the Ottoman Empire. According to historians of Lebanonness, however, the essence of the entity created by the emir lay more in the local symbiosis between the populations of the Mountain and its environs: a "national unity," consciousness of which had just been stirred and for the first time was represented by a single power rising above the divisions in civil society.

In summary, "this emir laid the cornerstone of the Lebanese entity that took form after him. In turn, that entity was the foundation of the Lebanese idea so marvelously depicted by the legend growing up around the name of Fakhr al-Din."[7] A legend indeed—for historical research has shown that many features of the Lebanese entity born during the period of Fakhr al-Din were partly mythical, particularly those suggesting that, before he was strangled at Constantinople in 1635, the emir had conceived of and was setting up a Lebanese state independent of the Ottoman Empire. In reality, his accords with the dukes of Tuscany can scarcely be understood as treaties between sovereign powers. And even though in recognition of his conquests the Sublime Porte bestowed on him the title "sultan barr Arabistan," he still remained a mere vassal.

Historians are dubious not only about Fakhr al-Din's independence from the Ottoman Empire and the pashas of Damascus, but also about his ability to found a state overcoming the rivalry between the local social groups, a doubt that reflects the Lebanese questions about their own state today. Were Fakhr al-Din and, years later, the emir Bashir II Shihab (1789–1840), another unifier of the Lebanese Mountain, able to get beyond the narrow interests of their own group? In other words, could there exist yesterday, could there exist today, a Lebanese state whose politics is independent of the logic of the Lebanese society, one that neutralizes the segmented structure of this society, and presents itself as a secular space in which all equally recognize they have an equal interest?

Though the efforts of Fakhr al-Din and Bashir II toward unification promoted the interests of one faction, were these interests those of their religious community? This question has sparked an engrossing debate about the religion of each of the emirs. The Maan are Druzes, but some writers cite evidence that Fakhr al-Din was a Sunni Muslim; other writers present evidence suggesting that he converted to Christianity under the influence of his Maronite counselors and allies. As for Bashir, his family was Sunni Muslim and had been at the head of the government of the Druzes since the start of the eighteenth century, and the Druzes consider him theirs; eventually, some members of the family converted to Maronitism. The confusion surrounding the religion of both emirs may in some way help to substantiate their image as unifiers of Lebanon: their exact religion is unimportant, since the main issue is a state to which all can belong. Most often, however, religious identity is the focus of conflicting demands by several groups, and even of rejection by certain groups which do not see themselves adequately recognized in the project and politics of the emirs of the Mountain. For though the origin of the autonomous and even independent Lebanese entity is problematic, the question of rivalries and conflicts between the communities structuring civil society, and especially the question of their relation to political power and hence the state, is even more crucial today.

2

A Land of Communities

Besides the question of who may legitimately lay claim to the Lebanese heritage and within what borders, Lebanese historians are divided on yet another question: how their society's organization into confessional, or religious, communities should be translated into politics. A community is more than an allegiance to a shared faith. It is a social, political, and even economic structure; for the stormy, centuries-old debates about the divisions in the Eastern Christian Church have been of little concern to the local populations, and quite often have merely disguised the political rivalries forming the real issues behind these divisions. Moreover, as the example of the renowned Maan and Shihab emirs shows, opportunism sanctioned conversions of convenience from one religion to another and from one church to another.

The division into structured communities must rather be seen as just one level of the general segmentation of the society. Community membership first marks individuals in their deepest natures, which explains why some people call it a primary identity in contrast to such acquired identities as professional status or class, and it thus engenders particularly firm solidarities. Furthermore, such membership structures the society and the community hierarchy around gathering places (monasteries, churches, mosques) and institutional, geographical, and even symbolic centers—the community's areas of concentration tending to form its territory. Furthermore, when the Near East and Mount Lebanon in particular fell under Ottoman dominion, the relation between the power of Istanbul and the individuals outside Islam, *the* official community of the Empire's believers, was effected through the hierarchies and within the framework of communitarian structures. Each community, identified by its religion or religious doctrine, was governed by a specific authority, was controlled by its organic institutions, and subject to an autonomous jurisdiction formed by members of the religious hierarchy, which had the state-recognized authority to apply its laws and customs and even to lay down the law in matters of personal status.[1] Hence, the communitarian identification became increasingly important in the society's organization and also tended to become congealed so that in the twentieth century all religious confessions, including the Muslim sects, formed into communities with their own doctrine, law, specific organization, and especially their political influence.

Thus today, although of all the Arab countries of the Near East, Lebanon is the most receptive to Western values and the model of the modern state, it is paradoxically the one country that has clung most tightly to the Ottoman tradition of social and political division into communities. The country now juridically lists sixteen of them, to which a seventeenth must be added: the Alawi community. The various communities are very unequal in their historical, demographic, and political importance, so that a description of them is needed before considering the economic, demographic, and political transformations under the communitarian system. Here I shall briefly mention the smaller Christian and Jewish communities before presenting the Maronite Christians, Greek Catholics, and Druzes, who formed the majority of Mount Lebanon's population during the Ottoman period. Next come the Sunnis, the Greek Orthodox, and the Shi'is, who since the creation of Greater Lebanon make up a large part of the population.

Except from a historical viewpoint, there is little to say about Lebanon's Roman Catholic, Protestant, and Jewish communities. Because most of Lebanon's Roman Catholics are Westerners or exiled Palestinians, their community is important only because it runs the schools attended by some 13 percent of the country's schoolchildren[2] and also the Jesuit Saint Joseph University in Beirut, both a pontifical and a French university and the seat of France's cultural influence in Lebanon.

It was in 1847 that the Ottoman regime first recognized the community of Lebanon's Protestants, also few in number and divided into dozens of denominations, mostly of British or American origin. They nevertheless had problems getting this right introduced in the framework of the state of Lebanon, obtaining it only in 1936, when Franco-British rivalry in the Near East had somewhat abated. Like the Roman Catholic community, the Protestant community's role in education is much more important than its size would indicate: the Syrian Protestant College in particular, which was founded in 1866, became the prestigious American University of Beirut, one of the beacons of higher learning in the Near East.

After decades of prosperity, Lebanon's Jewish community, made up partly of the native-born and partly of refugees fleeing Andalusia in the early part of the eighteenth century, experienced a decline in a few years. The Ottoman regime granted it a "constitution" only in 1911, following the example of the Christian communities. Up to the mid-twentieth century, settled in Beirut and secondarily in Sidon, their numbers swelled with émigrés from Iraq and Syria, the Jewish community prospered along with the country's economic boom. Its rights were curtailed and its security in Lebanon deteriorated following three major dates in Near Eastern political history, 1948 (the Palestinian War), 1956 (Suez and the rise of Nasserism), and 1967 (the Six Day War); as a result, its vital forces went into exile. Belonging neither to Islam nor to Christianity, the Jewish community had chosen to inscribe its history in that of a modern Lebanese state, thus reflecting the country's dynamism and weakness—and particularly its vulnerability to its surroundings.

The four Syriac-speaking (an Eastern branch of Aramaic) Christian communities have been in Lebanon only since the beginning of the twentieth century when they fled southeastern Turkey, then northern Iraq, and finally the valley of the Euphrates in northern Syria. The Syrian Orthodox Christians (or Jacobites), Syrian Catholics, Nestorians, and Chaldeans number only a few thousand, and fewer than half of them are naturalized citizens. Constantly diminishing in number, they are clustered around Beirut, its suburbs, and the city of Zahle. Their role in the country's life is marginal. The arrival of the Syriac Christians in Lebanon occasionally rekindled in the Mountain's Christians a sense of their isolation in a hostile environment, and strengthened the country's image as a mountain refuge, even suggesting to some that it would become the last Christian homeland of the Asian Near East—in Egypt, there are several million Copts—if the wave of emigration from Turkey, Iraq, and Syria dating from the turn of the century continued.

Because of their limited demographic size, these Christian minorities have been forced to merge with Lebanon's majoritarian Christian groups, and so represent only a secondary political force. It is different for the Armenians who settled in Lebanon after escaping the Turkish massacres of 1915, those who came from the province of Cilicia in 1920, and the refugees from the Sanjak of Alexandretta, a Syrian province ceded by France to Turkey in 1939. The Armenians differ from the Arab Christians of the Near East in their nationhood, ethnicity, Indo-European language, and historical origins in the ancient kingdom of Armenia on the high plateaus of the eastern part of Asia Minor. They form not just a religious community in the Lebanese population, but a veritable nation whose evolution is determined outside the country's borders.

Thus, the Lebanese state's recognition of three distinct Armenian religious communities—the orthodox Gregorians, the Catholics, and the small Gregorian Protestant community—is ultimately less important for the organization of its Armenians than the existence, since 1863, of a constitution internal to the Armenian nation that gives an important place to the laity, or than its members' adherence to three rival political groups, the Hentchak ("the bell," from the name of the party newspaper), which was pro-Soviet, the leftist Tachnag ("the federation"), and the small, conservative Ramgavar. Owing to their high levels of education and professional training, most of Lebanon's Armenians have achieved a notably high degree of economic integration as skilled workers, artisans, businessmen, and merchants. Their retention of a cultural and political particularism, however, keeps them on the margins of the country's life. Up to a certain point, insofar as the principal division of Lebanese society is that between Christians and Muslims, the Armenians remain a neutral element in the political equation.

So the exceptions to this voluntary abstention from the country's public life are all the more interesting. Thus in 1925 the Armenian militants of the Spartak Youth organization were the cofounders and first militants of the Communist Party of Syria and Lebanon: their later important position in the party is explained, first, by their working-class origins, their deprivation in the years after their arrival in Lebanon, and their high levels of intellectual training and political awareness. Second, this should be connected with the compatibility between the Orthodox mentality, traditionally independent of the hierarchy, and secularism—a compatibility favoring the community members' allegiance to parties of the modern kind. Third, it was facilitated by the permanent, steadfast ties between Lebanon's Armenian communities and the Soviet regime through Soviet Armenia: cultural exchanges between Beirut and Yerevan have constantly increased since the end of World War II, and migration back to the Armenian homeland, though modest, has remained steady. The other exception was the dramatic split that divided Lebanon's Armenians during the events of 1958. In the end, a minority of the country's Armenians adopted the Maronite confession and belong to predominantly Maronite political parties; when this group swelled the ranks of the largest of Lebanon's Christian communities, was it choosing closer integration into the country and its population or was it indicating the outer limits of its allegiance to a multiconfessional state?

The Maronite community is more important not merely because of its size but also because of its privileged ties to the West and the centuries-old role it has played in Mount Lebanon's history and economy. Though the Maronites are not the largest group of Christians in the Near East—they are outnumbered by the Egyptian Copts and the Arabic-speaking Greek Orthodox—they were by far the largest Christian community in the Lebanese emirate and later the largest Christian community in Greater Lebanon.

When we further consider that the Maronites have played a leading role in the history of the Mountain since the seventh century, this observation has an equally interesting corollary: no other religious community of the Arab

East, Christian or Muslim, has inscribed its history, as did the Maronites, exclusively on one territory—the Lebanese Mountain. All the other communities are scattered and unevenly distributed among several regions, and, later among several states formed in the Near East, so much that individuals' adherence to a religious community generally does not coincide with, and sometimes even runs counter to, their identification with a political community. The other exception in the Arab world is that of the Copts, whose history is inscribed in that of the Nile Valley and who have played a key role in the formation of a national identity coterminous with the Egyptian state. The comparison of the two communities sheds light on the tendency of certain leaders of the Maronite "nation" to confound the interests of their community with those of Lebanon as a whole.

The Maronite Christian community originated in central Syria and took refuge in the north of Mount Lebanon in two successive waves, in the seventh and ninth centuries, under circumstances that are disputed. Contemporary historians are divided about whether the Maronites left the region of present-day Qalat al-Midiq on the banks of the Orontes River to escape the Byzantines or the Muslim conquerors. Depending on their answer to this puzzle, historians describe Maronites as Easterners attached to their specific identity distinct from Western Christendom or as the frontline troops of Christendom's resistance to Islam. The fact is that the Maronites enjoyed relative tranquility for just over a century under the Omayyad Empire of Damascus (until 750). Like the other Christian communities formed under the Byzantine Empire, Islam granted them—in exchange for a stiff capitation tax—a protective contract safeguarding their lives and their possessions and respect for their religion and beliefs. Exempted from civil and military duties, the members of the community were governed by their patriarch in accordance with their own laws.

The events of the Crusades testify to the ambivalence in the Maronites' position between the Muslim political authority (the Seljuk Turks of Damascus, then the Mamluks) and Christendom in the West. Though certain tribes from the Tripolitanian coast collaborated with the Crusaders, others, on the heights of Mount Lebanon, resented the fiscal oppression exercised by the new feudal power and elected to help defeat it. The doctrinal and juridical rapprochement with the Roman Catholic Church also provoked controversies in the community until the end of the fifteenth century. At that time, however, the West and the Arab East started to form religious, cultural, commercial, and political ties, chiefly through the agency of Maronites. In the cultural domain, the Maronites benefited from the creation in 1585 of the Maronite College of Rome, a training center whose monks introduced schools and printing presses in the Mountain, which was also done by Western missionaries, particularly the Jesuits. In the economic domain, the Capitulations of 1535 granted France special privileges in the Levant, the naming of a consul in Beirut, the gradual penetration of its merchants, up to the nineteenth century when the French republic, in an attempt to weaken the Ottoman Empire in the Arab Near East, encouraged the ambitions of the Maronite community in the hope of relying on it. In Mount Lebanon, the nascent Maronite bourgeoisie were the chosen agents through whom French capital flowed for developing silk production for the mills at Lyons in France, proliferating of banks and port facilities, and building communication infrastructures.

Correlative with the development of its foreign relations, the Maronite community continued to expand its living area in the Mountain, from the first monastic settlement in the seventh century to the great peasant migration in the nineteenth. Concretely, this meant they experienced greater demographic growth than any of the other communities; this was further reinforced by the individual and collective conversions of the Shi'is who wanted to stay where they were. Further, the Maronite peasantry, most of them smallholders, exhibited greater dynamism in the occupation and exploitation of the Mountain. The chief inhabitants of Mount Lebanon proper, from around Bsharri to the hinterland of Jubayl, the Maronites became the majority in Kisrawan after the region was devastated by the Mamluks in 1302 and 1307, which provoked a massive exodus of the nonorthodox Muslim population. At the dawn of the nineteenth century, the central area of Matn, governed by the Druze emirs, was peopled by a mixture of Druzes and Maronites, with the latter in the majority. With only about 20 percent of the cultivable land in the whole Mountain, however, the central area of Kisrawan and Matn contained a third of the population.[3] Land hunger drove the Maronite peasantry farther south into the Shuf and the area of Jezzin. Thus many ingredients—modernization, the agrarian crisis, migrations—were in place to trigger political upheavals in the Mountain.

The Greek Catholic community, which is close to the Maronite community, has many associations with it in its modern Lebanese history. Born in a 1724 schism within the Orthodox Christian majority in the Near East, the Greek Catholics were recognized as a civil community by the Ottoman power only a century later. In the whole area, it is the largest of the Catholic communities, but in Lebanon itself it remains second to the first Uniate Church, that of the Maronites. It is characterized by geographical dispersion and a preference for small towns in the foothills, in symbiosis with the large rural communities; with the Maronites in their extension south of the Mountain (Jezzin); with the Druzes in the Shuf; and with the Shi'is south of Sidon. The Greek Catholics are in the majority only in Zahle, city of contact between the Mountain and the Bikaa Valley in which all the major communities are present.

In the eighteenth century, the Greek Catholics, like the Maronites, went through a wave of urbanization that made Beirut their principal place of settlement. They took up trading, serving as intermediaries for the European merchants, but that was not the community's main source of income. The religious congregations (Aleppans and Shuweiris) and the dominant families were great landowners in the suburbs north of Beirut, the foothills of the Mountain behind Sidon, the high Matn, and of course in the Bikaa plain. In addition, the community, like the Maronites, benefits from a long-standing openness to Western culture and education that gives its members access to administration, commerce, banks, and intellectual endeavors. Politically, however, notably in the upheavals of the nineteenth century, it largely shared the orientation and development of the Maronite community.

Facing the Maronite community, the first bastion of the construction of modern Lebanon, is the other bastion, the Druze community. A set of beliefs emerging at the start of the eleventh century in the Egypt of the Fatimids, which made the Caliph Hakim the embodiment of the Supreme Being, the Druze religion spread rapidly throughout the Near East among the heterodoxies of Islam, particularly, it seems, the Ismailian Shi'is. Extraordinarily esoteric and rejecting proselytism, the Druzes chose to submit for centuries to the external forms of the majority Sunni Muslims in order to avert the danger of repression by the region's masters, the Mamluks and later the Ottomans. The first and chief settlements were mountain refuges, the Jabal el-Aala between Aleppo and Antioch up to the sixteenth century, the Lebanese Shuf from which they spread to the hills of Galilee, the Wadi Taym, a deep valley in the western foothills of Mount Hermon, and finally the plain of Hauran and, in the east, the mountains later named Jabal Druze. After the Crusades, during which the Druzes of the Lebanese Mountain sided alternately with each of the opposing sides, the Christians and the Muslims, the sultan of Egypt systematically bled the region white in 1305, and for nearly two centuries the community's survivors lay low.

The glory days of the Druze emirate in Lebanon began in the sixteenth century with the Maans, and continued with the Shihabs starting in the eighteenth century. Four features have permanently marked Mount Lebanon's Druze society: its ruralism, the important role played by its army, the community's factional division, and its symbiosis with the Maronites.

Even in the nineteenth century and onward, few Druzes settled on Lebanon's plains and cities, the community remaining essentially agricultural mountain dwellers. By buying up the lands of indebted peasants, the tax collectors amassed vast domains, to the point that by the end of the eighteenth century, the community's five or six leading families possessed a tenth of the Mountain's cultivated land.[4] Their tenant farmers, although generally keeping a plot of their own, were thus doubly subject to them through taxation and landownership, which contributed, along with the initiatory system into the Druze faith, to solidify a strong social hierarchy headed by the emir.

The community as a whole is organized to deal with a constant external threat—all its members share in its defense—and the dynasties governing the Near East appreciated its unusually warlike character. These dynasties called on the Druze mountain dwellers as local auxiliary troops, thus increasing the power of the warlords, or even, like the Egyptian conqueror of the nineteenth century, extended to the community military conscription up to then reserved for orthodox Muslims. Armed force thus consolidated control of the Druze emirate on the Mountain through unending battles, notably to drive the other heterodox Muslim populations toward the south and the Bikaa.

But force was also used between rival Druze factions, which ceaselessly fought each other to extend their holdings and establish their authority; alliances were constantly made and unmade on both sides of the community's division into the Qaysis versus Yamanis. The Maans, like the Shihabs, belong to the Qaysi faction; in 1711—the date of a battle famous in Lebanese history—the Shihabs routed the Yamanis, who fled in great numbers toward the Hauran, thus ensuring the triumph of a strong and united emirate that presided over the destinies of the Lebanese Mountain until 1841. It was at exactly this period, however, that Druze supremacy began to decline in favor of the Maronite community and profound upheavals were brewing that were to traumatize the Lebanese Mountain in the mid-nineteenth century.

A Spluttering History

Relying on the many similarities between the "events" of 1841, 1845, and especially 1860 and 1861, and the "events" in wartime Lebanon today, particularly with regard to the violence exercised against the civilian population, certain analyses tend to make the division of the Lebanese populations into confessional communities the single key to the explanation of the conflicts. According to this view, religious ties play a primordial role in the formation and organization of political mobilization; organization around a power must involve the enframing religious and confessional apparatus; and the fundamental cause of the conflicts lies in the incompatibility between the confessional identities, an incompatibility that has remained unchanged for centuries.

But this rejection of history, which Ahmad Beydoun has called the "hatred of time" by relating it to hatred of the Other,[5] contradicts other analyses of the nineteenth-century conflicts and of the recent war, analyses that take into account the outstanding developments in the area and in the populations of Lebanon, particularly the impact of modernity and the opening to the West. What's more, these analyses do not consider the Lebanese Mountain an isolated microcosm with some unusual peculiarities that make it a special case; they compare its transformations to those of the surrounding Arab provinces and the whole of the Ottoman Empire at the time; along with the idea of evolution, they introduce that of relativity. Thus, when we see the birth of modern Lebanon historically and take account of its demographic, economic, political, and military changes, then the terrible attendant massacres lose their blind and fated quality; the clear-cut divisions between protagonists are shaded by many human complexities; and the description of the armed conflicts in Lebanon, those of the nineteenth century as well as today's, as a war between Muslims and Christians—"between Arabs and Christians," the press sometimes says with an inaccuracy that is also a value judgment—quite soon reveals its limits.

It is important to bring out the dominant features of the history of nineteenth-century Lebanon and to bear them in mind to understand the war now ravaging the country: the administrative and fiscal reforms that altered the agrarian structures and political hierarchies, the penetration (uneven depending on the regions and communities affected) by European capitalism, the demographic upheavals that have changed the society's internal balances, and the lusts of the foreign powers that stirred up the local conflicts, provoking the political system's destabilization.

In the first half of the nineteenth century, a series of measures taken by the authorities at Istanbul or, in the 1830s, the Egyptian conqueror Ibrahim Pasha, or even domestically by Bashir II, the "emir of the Druzes" himself, improved the system of tax collection, raised the rates, and above all initiated a new personal tax paid by all, Muslims and Christians alike. The payments constantly accruing to the higher authority at Damascus and Sidon, made heavier by the impositions of the local emir,[6] helped impoverish the "tax farmers" of the Lebanese Mountain for the benefit of the chief among them, Bashir II. The latter, who had become the Lebanese Mountain's sole representative of the pasha of Sidon, had no peer in bankrupting his rivals, enriching himself with the spoils, and building up his clientele from theirs. When in 1840 the sultan's troops and the British expedition put an end to his nearly fifty-year reign, the Mountain's traditional notables, particularly the Druze sheikhs he had exiled and dispossessed of their domains, were never to recover either their lost wealth or their lost autonomy.

The chief victims of the exorbitant tax increase, however, were the peasants, most of them tenant farmers, who took on the payment of the land tax for the notables and on whom fell the heavy burden of a series of fees and rents. The years 1820, 1841–45, and 1858–60 were marked by agrarian movements and insurrections, particularly in the central region of Kisrawan, in response to an acute social crisis. In 1860 popular agitation was to end in the abolishment of the landowners' privileges and in the division of certain domains for the benefit of the small and middle peasant holdings, which by the century's end represented nearly half the cultivated area. Demographic pressures continued to intensify the crisis, however, all the more so because for external reasons, the cost of basic foodstuffs in the 1850s was rising quickly.

The reason is that—a second characteristic of the period—the opening up of the Ottoman Empire's Arab provinces to European markets both stimulated and disrupted the local economies: for example, Mount Lebanon's marketable agricultural production suffered from the events in Europe during the British blockade of the Continent. The resumption of trade then caused a hemorrhaging of precious metals and a rise in local prices in the Ottoman Empire that affected most of the population. The entry of foreign capital—French, in the case of Mount Lebanon—into the sectors of foreign trade and communications made possible some prestigious achievements, like the carriage road from Beirut to Damascus. French investors were attracted by the possibility of obtaining high-quality silk at low prices. To meet European needs, they opened in the Mountain modern mills for spinning silk, which by mid-century became Beirut's leading export. But the appearance of wage-earning work in the mills disrupted the traditional agrarian relations: the more numerous Christian producers of cocoons took advantage of the Druzes; and the gradual diversion of the silk trade for the profit of the Beirut merchants and French industrialists ruined the traditional businesses of the Mountain and deprived the craftsmen of the cities of their raw materials. From then on, the changeover made the country more narrowly dependent on a foreign economic system and more sensitive to fluctuations in the international situation.[7]

Nevertheless, the European economies did not affect everyone adversely. Certain merchants on the coast could profit from the capitalist penetration even though the prominent families of the Mountain were indebted and the peasants more oppressed. These merchants became the indispensable agents for the European traders, buying and reselling the silk harvests and introducing new Western products into the country. Not only was this new urban bourgeoisie wealthier and better educated, it had a more dynamic conception of business and was better able to assimilate Western culture, but, through its openness, it could also make a decisive contribution to the intellectual and literary renaissance in the whole Near East; it became the champion of Arab, Syrian, and even Lebanese nationalistic ideals, thanks to the liberalization of the Ottoman Empire, and by the turn of the century became an essential actor on the political stage. Because their contacts with the West were easier and more long-standing than those of the Muslims, this new bourgeoisie was largely Christian.

This disparity between Christians and Muslims regarding Western modernity should be seen in light of the profound demographic changes in the Lebanese Mountain during the nineteenth century. When we consider the areas unified under the Emir Bashir's authority in the first half of the century, from Tripoli to Sidon and to the east, as far as the city of Zahle, we find a population of some 250,000 persons densely packed into a small area of limited cultivability. The communities were unevenly distributed: the Christians represented from 70 to 80 percent of the population, and the Druzes went through several waves of emigration—particularly in 1838 and 1853, to evade the draft—thus accentuating their demographic inferiority. On the other hand, in the Maronite-dominated areas of the north the demographic pressure was so strong that the Maronites emigrated over the years into the Shuf and south of the Mountain, where the Druze sheikhs, who needed the manpower, welcomed, protected, and assured the prosperity of new subjects. Druze seigneurs and Maronite peasantry thus lived in a remarkable economic symbiosis, symbolized at the top by the "emir of the Druzes" finding his most solid political and military support within the Maronite community. When the economic and demographic crisis led to political clashes, however, the historical, social, and even cultural unity of the Lebanese Mountain broke down.

Bashir II called on the Druze notables of the Shuf to crush the first major social *and* confessional revolt of the Maronite peasants in 1820, thus provoking the first split between the Christian peasantry and the Druze sheikhs; the latter retained control over their own peasantry, but the hierarchy based on their power as notables was weakened and replaced by communal mobilization. From then on, the social debate turned directly on the relations between communities.

In 1841, following an incident that degenerated into armed engagement, clashes between Maronites and Druzes in the Shuf went on for several months, the Druzes accusing the Maronites of profiting from the emir's confiscation of their land and thus impoverishing and weakening their community. The former "dominants"—the Druzes—suffered from the fading away of their institutions and the inequality of the outside support provided for the two groups. On the other hand, the former "minority"—the Maronites—were better united, thanks to their church's growing political role at the expense of the traditional notables. More numerous and favored by the emir, the Maronites benefited from an equality of status with the Muslims within the framework of the Ottoman Empire. In 1845 the conflicts resumed in the mixed areas of central Lebanon (Kisrawan and Matn) between the Maronites gathered around their clergy and the Druze peasants federated by their sheikhs, but the leaders of both camps secretly looked together for a way to hold onto their privileges. In 1860, after two years of particularly disastrous economic circumstances that led to a major agrarian revolt in the Kisrawan that alarmed even the Druze sheikhs of the Shuf, the conflicts flared up again in the mixed areas. This time, they produced several thousand deaths and tens of thousands of refugees; as far away as Damascus, Christians were massacred in areas they shared with Muslims; but the Druzes felt no less victimized because of the outside assistance to the Maronites, and their attacks were also acts of self-defense.

Finding a Formula

During the nineteenth century the European powers intervening in the Near East considered the Lebanese question primarily a communal one, and dealt with the different communities separately; in that way, they bore a large share of responsibility in the change of the Mountain's social and economic conflicts to intercommunal conflicts.

Several reasons explain their attitude. First, the major European powers—France, Russia, Great Britain, and Austria—were Christian, and they were confronting the Near Eastern Ottoman Empire, the leading Muslim power. Second, the Christian missionary orders were effective pioneers as the agents for infiltrating these nations' languages, ideas, and political influence, and it was they who selected and trained new local elites, the ones through whom the European governments hoped to wield their influence. Despite some quarrels between the Jesuits and the authorities in France itself, the latter consented to support them and back them financially in their evangelistic efforts in Mount Lebanon. Third, the political decision makers in the West had a partial and biased knowledge of the world in which they were intervening, through the studies of orientalists,[8] who like all nineteenth-century scholars, were steeped in Eurocentric prejudices.

The diplomatic missions, particularly the consulates in Beirut, figured prominently in the Near Eastern intrigues and manipulations. Gradually, the local clientele of each great power became clear: France, which stole the first place with the Catholics away from Italy, bet on the Maronites. Austria did the same, but with less ambitious economic designs and smaller means. Russia had openly offered its protection to the Orthodox ever since 1744. To Great Britain, long anxious to save the great Muslim unit of the Ottoman Empire from being dismantled and tempted to intrigue with the Maronites, remained the Druze community, through which it pursued its rivalry with France.

Following Bonaparte's attempt to secure an alliance with Bashir II in 1799, and then the campaign of the Egyptian governor Mehmet Ali, military interventions in a region of the Ottoman Empire could not help but shamelessly succeed one another. At Beirut in 1840, a British and Austrian fleet landed Ottoman troops and English soldiers who brought Bashir II's emirate to an end. During the summer of 1860, in reaction to the massacres by rioters in the Shuf and Damascus who benefited from the complicity of the local Turkish garrisons, France sent an expeditionary force of 7,000 men which stayed on in Lebanon for nearly a year. These diplomatic and military interventions naturally paved the way for a direct takeover by the European powers.

Nonetheless, we should not underestimate the role and initiatives of the Ottoman Empire, of which Lebanon was then a part. A history centered on Europe has long presented us with Near Eastern events in the nineteenth century as the "dismantling of the Ottoman Empire" performed by the Western powers on a passive and weak land—the "sick man" of the East. Recent advances in Ottoman studies clearly indicate the Empire's wealth of political and social life and the magnitude of the changes effected there at this period—too late, it is true. Thus, between 1839 and 1876 the Istanbul government enacted a series of *tanzimat* (reforms) directed at the empire's administrative reorganization and the central power's regaining control of the provinces. The famous Hatti-i Sharif (sultan's edict) of Gülhane in 1839 eliminating the leasing of tax collecting and proclaiming the equality of all members of Ottoman society in matters of taxation was a true revolution. The Hatti-i Hümayun of 1856, which decided that members of minorities were to have equal rights with the Muslims, was another revolution with repercussions for the Mountain as important as those of the Western interventions, for it fed the ambitions of the Christians and the anger of the Druzes.

Putting an end to the near-autonomy of the Lebanese emirate, the Sublime Porte in 1842 established a regime of territorial division and Lebanon's direct administration by two prefects *(kaymakams)* under the sitting governor in Beirut. The Christian prefect had authority over the area north of the Beirut-Damascus highway, the Druze prefect to the south. Most of the population were Christian in the region administered by the Druze prefect, the Shuf in particular—the Druze region par excellence—and so for the first time the confessional distinction between the Maronites and the Druzes officially took on a political significance. On the other hand, the presence next to each prefect of a council of representatives from each community established the *political communitarianism* that has since been a characteristic feature of the Lebanese system: the "factionalism" of the social and political functioning of the Near East—from the family unit to the regional dimension—thus congealed at the level of religious identities, often considered immutable and irreconcilable.

Under the regime of the double *kaymakamate*, the Mountain experienced one of the most violent periods in its history, for the social and political conflicts turned into clashes between communities, thus unleashing barely controllable passions. The new statute adopted by the Règlement organique in 1861 and instituted in 1864 took the same road of a communitarian political system: as in the whole empire at the time the Mountain was directly administered for the sultan by a governor assisted by an elected council representing the local populations. For Lebanon, it was stipulated that the governor be Christian (but that he not be a native of Mount Lebanon) and that the council have twelve members representing the six principal communities of the Mountain, divided equally between Christians and Muslims.

The governorate remained in effect until World War I. For nearly half a century, a unified and pacified Lebanon experienced security and prosperity that were reminiscent of the heyday of the autonomous Maan and Shihab emirates. The five great powers, France, Great Britain, Austria, Prussia, and Russia ratified the Règlement organique through an international protocol, and their consuls in Beirut controlled the governor. They imposed two clauses that were fraught with consequences for the country's future: first, its autonomy in financial matters and the maintenance of order, the seed of a future independent nation separate from the Ottoman Empire—in theory, no Turkish soldier had the right to set foot on Lebanese territory—and second, the beginnings of the institutionalization of the communitarian system, an insuperable obstacle to the adoption of democratic representation.

3

The Choice of Greater Lebanon

THE creation of the Lebanese nation in 1920 resulted from the conjunction of two antagonistic forces for once working in concert: the nascent nationalism in the Arab provinces of the Ottoman Empire and a quickly expanding French imperialism. World War I, with its secret diplomacy, successive alliances, and military campaigns, completely overturned the Eastern Mediterranean and resulted in an entirely new territorial division. But of all the Arab countries born of the dismantling of the Ottoman Empire, perhaps none had borders less natural than those of Greater Lebanon.

The Arab Renaissance

The percolating of nationalist ideas was just one of many aspects of the Nahda, a vast linguistic, cultural, religious, and scientific renaissance that spurred the intellectual elites in Egypt and in the Arab provinces of the Ottoman Empire in the latter half of the nineteenth century. The Nahda is comparable not only to the European Renaissance, but also to the eighteenth-century Enlightenment for the encyclopedic curiosity of its moving spirits, their thinking about religions, and their philosophical debates, as well as for the revolutionary upheavals that followed it. Rich merchants and prosperous mill owners in the relatively tranquil society of Beirut and the Mountain at the turn of the century gladly protected and encouraged the "new intellectuals" of the Arab renaissance. A personality like Shibli Shumayyil is a good representative of this generation: a physician and a graduate of the Protestant College of Beirut, he traveled in Europe and on his return introduced Darwinism to the East. In the last years of the century, Shumayyil published many philosophical and political articles in the Beirut press, where he appealed for "science, justice, and liberty" in the Ottoman Empire.[1] His career illustrates two features of the Nahda. First, the pioneering role in the movement played by the Christians of the Eastern Mediterranean because of their cultural advancement, long-standing educational tradition, and greater access to Western culture. Next was the central place of the press as a tool for disseminating new ideas. Whereas at midcentury the government newspapers of Istanbul and Cairo constituted the only daily press in Arabic, the Egyptian dailies proliferated, encouraging the liberalization begun by the *tanzimat*, and they were read even in India. This was of course not mass culture, but by amplifying and propagating ideas critical of the political establishment, the newspapers of Beirut and Cairo of the 1870s played a role comparable to that of the Islamic propaganda cassettes in Iran a century later.

Within the Empire then suffering the painful loss of its European provinces, there were many levels of allegiance and forms of political mobilization by individuals and groups, who were more often in league than opposed. For example, one of the most brilliant encyclopedists and popularizers of the Lebanese Mountain was Butrus al-Bustani, who of course saw himself as part of his own Maronite community. He was enthusiastic about the constitutional reforms implemented by the government of the Young Turks in 1875–76 and was delighted to see the local provincial elites granted administrative responsibilities, particularly in Mount Lebanon. Bustani's sincere allegiance to his Ottoman homeland *(watan)* was, however, not incompatible with the particular attachment he professed to his Syrian country *(bilad)*, nor with his ardor in championing and modernizing the Arabic language.

Nationalisms

Nevertheless, under Europe's influence, a new criterion was establishing itself concurrently with culture and language as the basis of political identity in the Mediterranean East: attachment to a particular territory. It should be understood that this criterion was as alien to the communitarian system—built on familial and clan solidarities—as it was to the Ottoman political system, which related the sultan to his subjects through the medium of the communitarian system, and it was hardly compatible with the vision of Islam, the region's dominant religion, which claims its jurisdiction automatically extends over the *dar al-Islam*, that is, Muslims everywhere. The notion of territory derives from Western nationalisms and was disseminated in the Arab East while France and Great Britain were setting themselves up as the two European colonial powers. Again, it was Bustani who revived the geographical term "Syria" *(Suriyya)*, which had fallen into disuse since the end of the Seleucid dynasty in 64 B.C. Like many other militant nationalists, Bustani used the terms "Syrian" and "Arab" interchangeably,[2] as though the former involved territorial connotations and the latter, cultural ones. At the turn of the century the Belgian Jesuit from Beirut Henri Lammens and the historian Georges Samné—who also wrote in French—championed the theme of the national unity and distinct character of a Greater Syria demarcated by the Taurus Mountains, the Euphrates River, the eastern desert, the Red Sea, and the Mediterranean, whose populations and cultures were distinct, they thought, from those of the Muslim Arabs, notably because of a high percentage of Christians (15 to 20 percent of the region's population at the time). Many Catholics of the East (the Maronites in particular), who wanted to indicate their difference from Rome, and the Orthodox, who wanted to be free of the Greek patriarchal authority, formed the original nucleus of the Syrian nationalist movement. Soon, reacting against Istanbul's 1909 policy of centralization and Turkification, Muslims joined in to strengthen the movement. From then on, the Ottoman power was obliged to reckon with it.

Under the regime of Sultan Abdul Hamid II, who suspended the parliament between 1877 and 1906, the common struggle of the empire's elites for liberalization blurred regional, ideological, and even religious dissimilarities. For three decades, the core of the elites' concerns was to obtain political freedom and to modernize the empire. Disparities and discords reemerged owing to the revolution of the Young Turks in 1908 whose leaders clearly displayed their ambitions for centralization and especially their ardent Turkish nationalism. Starting in 1912, movements like the Ottoman Party of Decentralization influenced Beirut through their demands for administrative and cultural autonomy for the Arab regions within the imperial framework. The Arab Congress of Paris of 1913, attended by some thirty-five political leaders, was not very bold and its final resolution did not even propose autonomy for the Mediterranean Syria from which most of them originated. Already, however, the clandestine Fatat Society, organized in 1911, was militating for the independence of the Arab Syrian region; the same year, notables from the province of Damascus made contact with Sherif Hussein of Mecca, the Hashimite emir governing the Hejaz.

What is more, encouraged by the experience of autonomous governorship since 1860, aspirations in the Lebanese Mountain were emerging for the independence of a "democratic" Lebanon separate from Syria, encompassing Beirut and the agricultural plain of the Bikaa. Independence would fully liberate the Christians from domination by the Ottoman Muslims and could favor the creation of a nation along the lines of a European model. The "Lebanese nation" that had existed from the dawn of history and was distinguished by its Christian majority and its openness to the West[3] was the most deserving of independence of the Ottoman Arab provinces. Furthermore, the Lebanese nationalists envisioned France's protecting their future nation.

For most of the movements, the line of cleavage then fell between Turks and Arabs, while the differences between the three movements—the Arab, Syrian, and Lebanese nationalisms—were not clear cut. Above all, the Syrian nationalists were proud of their Arab culture. Their leaders took part in the Arab Congress of Paris. The Lebanese nationalists considered Mount Lebanon the vanguard of a Greater Syria that should also be independent, while the Arab nationalist movement grew chiefly in the Syrian region (its other center was Egypt). Moreover, these three movements crystallized only in stages and according to a process that varied with the regions' and social groups' attachment to the Ottoman Empire. It would also be wrong to think that the different poles of belonging and political mobilization were mutually exclusive, or to interpret the birth of Near Eastern nationalism as reproducing the Western model of citizenship within the nation-state.

Once again, we need to take into account all the organizational levels in Near Eastern Arab and Mediterranean society: the family unit, the community, the region, linguistic and cultural ties, religious faith, and administrative and political organization. It is important to recall that for centuries the Ottoman system favored the coexistence and even complementarity of these various levels, so that participation in the Arab Nahda or the desire for privileged relations with France were long compatible with loyalty to the Ottoman sovereign. At the start of the twentieth century, the aspiration for modernity and an opening to the West implied the adoption of a plan for nationalism and its associated statist strategies. The birth of Turkish and Arab nationalisms—surely the term "protonationalisms" would be more apt, for these movements were loose and popular support for them was weak—and the demand for Lebanese independence unquestionably owed a great deal to European influences in the Near East: cultural and ideological influence, of course, but also direct interventions by British and French imperialisms that altered the configuration of the region. Thus the creation of the Lebanese nation illustrates the "paradox of the phenomena of dependence,"[4] according to which, in their quest for emancipation, the national strategies favored direct Western supervision.

World War I

Until October 1914, when the Ottoman Empire entered the war on the side of Germany, Mount Lebanon's governorate was politically quiescent and economically prosperous, with a stable social equilibrium. Without being truly satisfying, the regime governing the Arab areas, particularly the governorate of the Lebanese Mountain, represented an unquestionable step toward greater democracy; many people readily accommodated themselves to it. War brought this equilibrium to an end. The devaluation of the Turkish pound, the Allies' blockade by sea, the requisition of grain harvests by the imperial army that became an occupation force, not to mention a dramatic plague of locusts, caused a famine in the Lebanese Mountain in which thousands perished. The Istanbul government doubted the loyalty of its Arab subjects and suspended the Capitulary rights of foreigners; most important, in October 1915 it abolished the autonomous status of the Lebanese government and then took away the judiciary powers held by the leaders of the communities. Not only did the pasha of Damascus directly administer the Syrian region, but Turkish troops took over control of the Mountain, and conscription was more strictly applied to the Muslims of the coast. Suspected of secret dealings with a powerful enemy (France), fifty-eight militant nationalists from the interior, the Mountain, and the coast were condemned to death, and in August 1915, eleven of them were executed in Beirut, then twenty-two others in Beirut and Damascus in May of the following year; since then national memory has honored them as martyrs for independence. This time a complete break was made between the Ottoman regime and the local elites who openly sought outside support in their struggle for emancipation. Nonetheless, the militant nationalists were far from unanimous in specifying their goal. Some wished for Lebanon's independence under the protection of France. Others, however, throughout the whole of the Syrian region, struggled for the creation of an independent Arab nation.

Prepared months in advance and encouraged by the British who sought to grab the Arab provinces from the Ottoman Empire, the revolt led by the Sherif Hussein of Mecca was launched in June 1916. The Hashimite prince Faisal who conducted it from the Hejaz, together with the celebrated T. E. Lawrence with the support of a British detachment, reached Jerusalem in December 1917, at the same time as General Allenby's Army of Egypt. On October 1, 1918, Faisal victoriously entered Damascus and proclaimed an Arab government. In March 1920 he became king, but ruled only until July, when he was defeated by General Gouraud's army at Maysalun and then went into exile. The history of the Damascus government and Faisal's reign on the Syrian throne was brief, but rich in consequences for Syria, for it elevated tribal chiefs, militant nationalists, and members of the urban, religious, and commercial elites to the status of statesmen fighting for their country's independence. Because of its very slight means and its short life, the Arab government of Damascus produced few concrete achievements, but it was of incomparable symbolic importance. For decades after its fall, aspirations for an independent Arab nation centered in Damascus spurred not only the inhabitants of Syria under the French Mandate, but also some of the populations throughout the rest of geographical Greater Syria: Transjordan, Palestine, and of course Lebanon. Even after World War II and the gaining of independence by the countries of the Near East, the Arab government of Damascus is remembered as a glorious episode in the nation's history and is still hailed today both in Jordan (King Hussein is Faisal's grandnephew) and in Syria led by the Baath party, which honors General Azme and his comrades-in-arms, the unlucky heroes of Maysalun.

For eighteen months the region experienced an unusual political effervescence, stimulated by both ambitions and realism, in which the nationalists endeavored to run the new country and to ensure that all the populations of Greater Syria were represented at a congress in Damascus. The period coincided with the campaign for Arab unity that was taking place around three centers, Syria, Iraq, and the Arabian peninsula (Egypt was another world), particularly the unity of all parts of Syria freed from Ottoman domination and in which, as early as 1915, Hussein, the sherif of Mecca and Faisal's father, informed the British of his intention to create an independent kingdom. The Syrian General Congress did not, however, ignore the demands for autonomy which the delegates from Beirut and the Lebanese Mountain presented to members of the American King-Crane Commission who were making a survey on behalf of the Paris Peace Conference; in its declaration of independence of March 1920, the congress did pass a motion giving Mount Lebanon a special status.

The French Ambitions

In fact, Mount Lebanon and the coast were a part of the independent Arab nation for only seven days. Just as Faisal's troops were entering Damascus on October 1, 1918, Mount Lebanon's Turkish governor at Beirut handed over his powers to a Sunni notable who immediately proclaimed his support for the Syrian nationalists. A detachment of the Hashimite army then proceeded to the seat of Mount Lebanon's governorate, hoisted the Arab flag, convened the old council suspended by the Ottomans, and on the emir's behalf named a new Christian governor. A week later, however, General Allenby's army, flanked by a small detachment of French soldiers, arrived in Beirut. Faisal's envoys were forced to withdraw, and high-ranking French officers were appointed as military governors in Beirut, Sidon, Tyre, and shortly thereafter in Tripoli.

Confronting the nationalist movements was the powerful machinery of European colonialisms. Since 1870, the British, the French, and the Germans had fiercely competed for spheres of economic influence. Thus London was anxious to retain control of the route to India, through Egypt and possibly Mesopotamia. Under the French Third Republic, a veritable "colonial party" formed, a coalition of various interests keen to assure French sovereignty in tropical and Arab Africa as well as the Eastern Mediterranean. These ambitions were symbolized by the Congress of French Syria held in Marseilles in January 1919, shortly after French troops entered Beirut, just as the Paris Peace Conference was convening to decide the fate of the various provinces of the Ottoman Empire.

The "colonial party" comprised primarily industrialists, merchants, and bankers, all avid to make and oversee large, profitable investments facilitated by the new rights to property in the Ottoman Empire. At the outbreak of World War I, France was the source of nearly 30 percent of the capital invested in the empire;[5] and along with Turkey, the region of choice was Mediterranean Syria. French companies undertook and financed large works projects, such as the road from Beirut to Damascus (Compagnie Ottomane de la route Beyrouth-Damas), the railroad between the two cities and to Homs, and the outfitting of the port of Beirut, which then supplanted those of Sidon and Tripoli. Several European banks opened local branches.

These economic interests in the Arab East relied on French missionaries, particularly the Jesuits and the Lazarists. To disseminate the French language and culture, the missionaries favored the formation of a political clientele, especially among the Catholics, who in turn became active propagandists for direct French intervention. These priests and monks in the "colonial party" were joined by university teachers and politicians who shared their belief in France's *mission civilisatrice* and the desire for the creation of a "Greater France" on an imperial scale. The ambition of both groups lay less in economic gain than in the pursuit of national prestige. Nonetheless, this often veiled the greed of speculators, and helped ease their consciences.

It was thus the interests of the colonial powers that determined the separation of the Arab Near East from the rest of the empire and the creation of distinct nations. An illuminating example of this is the contour of the State of Lebanon's southern border with Palestine. In May 1916, while the war was still raging, the French and the British concluded an agreement dividing the Arab Near East, signed by their ambassadors Georges Picot and Mark Sykes. France got the right to extend its sphere of influence over all of Syria, the province of Mosul and Cilicia and above all, to set up a "direct or indirect administration" as it saw fit[6] along coastal Syria, west of Damascus and Homs, and north of a line running from Acre to Lake Tiberias, which didn't take into account the historic border of the Ottoman province of Beirut. The Sykes-Picot line was then the focus of acrimonious negotiations between the French and the British until the definitive setting, through a Franco-British agreement signed in March 1923, of the Lebanese-Palestinian border twelve to eighteen miles farther north, at the expense of French aims. Two elements influenced this decision: first, the British had been the main military victors over the Ottoman regime in the Middle East, while the French army had been largely deployed on its home soil. Second, were pressures from the Zionists to whom the British foreign secretary Arthur Balfour had in 1917 promised the creation of national homeland on Palestinian soil: their representative at the negotiations insisted on the indispensability of the waters of the Litani and Yarmuk rivers for the Jewish colonists' agriculture. On the other hand, the territorial divisions of the Ottoman era were not considered, the interests of the Arab populations on both sides of the new frontier were never mentioned, and their representatives (notably at the congress of Damascus) were never consulted.

The argument of the "colonial party" for the *mission civilisatrice* was vitiated by the primacy of France's interest in the richest and most developed part of Syria: the coastal area where the prewar French capital was most heavily invested and where its interests linked up with and reinforced those of one part of the Christian elites who argued for continuity with prewar Lebanon. The Maronite leaders, who called for the annexation of the coastal area and the interior plains—areas where some of them had farmland—won out over the ones who wished to limit the country to a homogeneous Mount Lebanon, a "national homeland" for the Christians of the Near East. The advocates of a Greater Lebanon invoked in particular the need for ensuring economic viability and self-sufficiency in grains in order to avoid potential pressures from Syria. Thus the interests of the "colonial party" and the Lebanese "lobby" converged to assure the creation of the state of Greater Lebanon.

The French Mandate

At the Versailles conference, where the four Great Powers debated the future of the Ottoman Arab provinces, the advocates for an independent Arab Syria were represented by Emir Faisal himself, buoyed up by British promises to his father Hussein and encouraged by the bold demands of the congress of Damascus. Mindful of the balance of power, Faisal accepted the principle of French occupation of the coastal area, on condition that it not extend to the interior plain of the Bikaa Valley. But he departed the congress in April 1919 without obtaining assurances on this matter. On the other hand, the chief representative of the Syrian Committee at Versailles, the writer Shukri Ghanim, who had not returned to Syria for thirty-five years, seized the opportunity to express his disdain for the "backward bedouins" centered in Damascus, his position favoring a French Syria, and soon even Lebanese separatism. At Beirut itself during these months, a number of meetings were held and delegations met with the French authorities in response to enthusiastic demonstrations in favor of the Arab government of Damascus. Above all, five of the seven members of the Administrative Council of Mount Lebanon (two Maronites and a Greek Orthodox, a Druze, and a Sunni) went to Paris and officially called for the creation of a Lebanese nation "in its historic frontiers," receiving the support of two successive delegations of Maronite dignitaries claiming to be "acting on behalf of the populations of the Lebanese cities and countryside" and applying determined pressure on the French delegates at the conference, to the point that on November 10, 1919 Premier Georges Clemenceau promised the Maronite Patriarch Elias Hoyek that the French government would look favorably on the creation of a Greater Lebanon, in return for local support for establishing a French mandate over the country. [7]

At the Conference of San Remo in April 1920, the Allied Powers, consistent with earlier Franco-British accords, assigned France control of "Syria and Lebanon" north of the area held by Great Britain. The Mandatory system as set forth in article 22 of the 1920 League of Nations pact theoretically corresponded to President Woodrow Wilson's humanistic, anti-imperialist vision: no question of colonization or territorial acquisitions, but rather the "rights, interests, and wishes" of the local populations, winning of their independence, and the integrity of their territory and economic development—about which a high commissioner was to make an annual report to the League. According to paragraph 4 of this article, the Mandate was particularly designed to provide assistance to "communities previously belonging to the Ottoman Empire that have attained a degree of development such that their existence as independent nations can be conditionally recognized." Thus, the Mandate would be in force "until they are capable of self-government."

History written in the West grandly ignores the amplitude of the outrage and protests aroused in the Mediterranean Arab East by the French Mandate in 1920. Numerous intellectuals and politicians in Damascus and even Beirut, such as the members of the Municipal Council, appealed to the United States whose tutelage they would have preferred to that of France, a colonial power. The Aleppan statesman Sati al-Husri's book *Yawm Maysalun* [8] relates the events of the period as experienced by the Syrian Arab nationalists; its very title underscores that a military victory by General Henri Gouraud's army had been required to impose on the country a mandatory regime whose "chief consideration" had to be, however, to "respect the wishes" of the local communities (article 22, paragraph 4).

On August 30, 1920, six weeks after French troops entered Damascus, General Gouraud, the high commissioner at Beirut, decreed the creation of Greater Lebanon, which was consistent with French economic interests and the political aspirations of a majority of the Maronites. Promulgated the next day, another decree defined the territorial extent of the new nation, which was proclaimed "independent" from Syria, an area that was to be confirmed in the constitution of 1926, and thus ruled out any debate about the question of borders. A homogeneous, predominantly Maronite Mount Lebanon and a unitary Syria were both discarded in favor of a formula for appending regions valuable to the Mountain: the coast with its ports, and the grain-producing interior plain.

Other Lebanese

To the autonomous governorate of Mount Lebanon were thus joined four eastern cantons of the Bikaa Valley belonging to the Damascus prefecture in the former Ottoman province of Damascus: Baalbek, Mu'allaqa, Rashiya, and Hasbeya; on the coast, the whole province of Beirut except for the cantons of Safita and Hosn in the prefecture of Tripoli, which thereafter became part of the "Territory of the Alawis," but without the prefectures of Acre and Nablus, which became part of Palestine.

We can see the extensive and important consequences of the change in the configuration of Smaller Lebanon to that of the State of Greater Lebanon. In particular, during the French Mandate the political and socioeconomic disparities between the various regions of the country were to play a determining role in Lebanese tensions. On the other hand, for several decades Syria's loss of its provinces was a bone of contention between it and Lebanon, which is sometimes considered one reason for Syria's later intervention in Lebanon's civil war. For the time being, the creation of Greater Lebanon sparked a radical change in the country's communal balances, which had hitherto been based on the duality between the Maronites and the Druzes; it raised the issue of participation by the Sunnis, the Greek Orthodox, and the Shi'is in the shared past of the Lebanese entity.

Of the governorate of Mount Lebanon's total population of no more than 300,000 souls, the Maronites formed more than 60 percent, the Druzes a bit less than 15 percent, and the Greek Catholics just under 10 percent. The first of the two censuses conducted by the French in 1922—which inevitably undercounted the poorly integrated populations from the recently annexed outlying areas—indicated that the country's population had doubled and that the Sunnis, the Greek Orthodox, and the Shi'is now constituted nearly half of it (see table).

Relative Size of Lebanese Communities
According to 1922 Census

Communities	Number	%
Maronites	199,182	32.7
Greek Orthodox	81,409	13.3
Greek Catholics	42,426	7
Other Christians	12,651	2.1
Sunnis	124,786	20.5
Shi'is	104,947	17.2
Druzes	43,633	7.2
Total	609,034	100

Source: Rondot, *Les institutions politiques du Liban* (Paris: Institut d'Études de l'Orient contemporain, 1947).

Of course, the addition of a large number of Sunnis not only changed the new nation's communal balances, but also signified the entry of a population without the minoritarian mind-set or devotion to the mountain refuge. Since the conquest by the Prophet Muhammad's first successors, the Sunni Muslim populations had remained in the majority in Lebanon's ports—Tripoli, Beirut, and Sidon. To a lesser extent they were spread over the countryside, mainly in the Akkar, and were even more thinly scattered in the mountains, mainly in the Shuf. In the interior, they were settled in a number of small secondary centers from Marjuyun, in the south, to Hasbeya, Rashiya, and Zahle in the Bikaa Valley, and as far as Hermil; thus the Sunni community in the new state was essentially urban, scattered on the sides of the Lebanese Mountain, and lacking territorial contiguity. Though the community included some large landowners and peasants, its members worked mainly in commerce and the crafts.

In the absence of a compact territory on which they could congregate, like the Druzes in the Shuf or the Maronites in Kisrawan, the Sunnis' other attribute (though equally true of the Shi'is) is that until the Mandate the direct source of their personal, religious, and hereditary property-owning status was the Ottoman power, without the mediation of any community representation, since the caliph-sultan was their direct religious ruler. Thus their state was the empire in which they were governed according to their own laws. Upon the collapse of this state, some Near Eastern Sunnis switched their loyalties to the new Turkish republic of Kemal Atatürk, who was considered the empire's legatee; most of them, however, supported the Arab nationalist movement and proved fervent partisans of the Hashimite monarchy in Damascus. Since the monarchy's overthrow, their expectations centered on Syria under the French Mandate, where more than two-thirds of the population were Sunni Arabs. They saw themselves as continuous with a glorious past, the history of the vast Omayyad Empire and of distant conquests. Hence the Lebanese Sunnis' inclination to look down on other communities' attachment, particularly that of the Maronites, to a mountainous enclave with barren soil, and their tendency to minimize or even deny the historical precedents used to justify Lebanese territorial nationalism. At the very most, they recognized the glorious moments of the Maan and Shihab emirs, recalling them as Arab princes who initiated Sunni dynasties. In the earliest days of the French Mandate, the freshly incorporated Sunnis' view of the new state was thus the opposite of that of the Maronites. Far from desiring Greater Lebanon, considering it their own, or putting it to advantage, they submitted to it, sometimes felt like foreigners, and wished to escape its limits.

The Greek Orthodox community shares many of the characteristics of the Sunnis. Its church, the oldest in the history of all the Christians in the Near East and of Lebanon in particular, consistently refused to assimilate with the Maronites or to forge links with the West by recognizing Roman supremacy. Hellenic, Syriac, Arab, the Christian populations whom the seventh-century Muslim conquerors called "Byzantine" *(rum)* positively welcomed the end of their region's domination by the emperors of Constantinople. Their Arabization was nearly complete by the early tenth century, and the Crusades brought them no closer to the Christians of the West. Instead, their Orthodoxy favored contacts with the Russian Orthodox Church, to the point that in the mid-nineteenth century Moscow named itself the protector of the Near Eastern Orthodox, thus finding a way through the community to exercise some political influence on the country.

The Greek Orthodox were mainly city dwellers devoted to trade. Moreover, certain Beiruti members of the community amassed great fortunes in commerce and banking, spinning mills, and especially real estate; only one rural area in Lebanon, the plain of Kura, is populated primarily by Greek Orthodox farmers, small landowners cultivating olive trees. In the cities of the Near East, the Greek Orthodox live symbiotically with the Sunnis, with whom they share the Arab identity, history, and even, since the end of the nineteenth century, nationalistic leanings. Thanks to the patronage of the community's wealthy businessmen and the influence of the Protestant College of Beirut where many of them studied, a generation of writers, pamphleteers, and journalists actively participated in the debate about reforms in the Ottoman system, particularly about the future of the Syrian region. In 1918–1920, their partiality for an independent Arab nation led, for example, the patriarch of Antioch, the head of the community, to side with King Faisal's Arab nation in Syria. Later, consequently, after the Near East was carved up into separate entities, Syria remained the nation with the greatest number of Greek Orthodox, which gave it a decisive influence over the communal authorities. In Lebanon itself, however, their situation as the oldest of the native Christians gave the Greek Orthodox a chance to act as a link between the Christian and the Muslim communities.

The demographically third largest community of the State of Greater Lebanon—and again the 1922 census ignored several areas frequented by still nomadic populations—the Shi'is could lay claim to an ancient role in the Mountain's history. Distant partisans *(shi'a)* of Ali, the Prophet Muhammad's son-in-law and successor, and faithful to the lineage of the eleven imams who succeeded him of whom the last disappeared in 873, the Shi'is have kept alive the memory of conflicts with the leaders of the Sunni empires. During the seventh century, some Shi'i tribes that probably originated in Mesopotamia fled Sunni persecution and settled in the heart of the Lebanese Mountain. In two waves, first in the fourteenth century when the Mamluks ravaged the Kisrawan region, then in the latter half of the eighteenth century when the Shi'i populations were subject to attacks by the Shihabs, they were forced to emigrate toward the Bikaa Valley and Hermil, and also to Jabal Amil. In these areas, the Ottoman power applied the same legislation as they did to the empire's Sunni Muslim majority.

When Greater Lebanon's frontiers were drawn in 1920, the Shi'is were settled in all the outlying areas of the country, on the sides of the Mountain: in the sahel between Sidon and Naqoura in the south, in the hilly region bordering Palestine, Jabal Amil and Arqoub, along the Anti-Lebanon range in the plain of the Bikaa, in Hermil, and up to Akkar in the north. They were essentially rural people, still dominated by clan chiefs like the Hamadeh family in Hermil, the Asaad family in Jabal Amil, and the Zein family in Nabatiye, whose power came from their great landed estates, the clientelization of political relations, and the hereditary transmission of religious authority. These "feudal lords" were able to come to terms with the new government of Beirut, as they had with Istanbul. Already in Jabal Amil, however, thanks to the Nahda and the dramatic events of the war, a generation of intellectuals and scholars grew conscious of their Arab identity and their ties to the surrounding regions, particularly Palestine and the interior of Syria.

World War I and the collapse of the Ottoman Empire made the creation of Greater Lebanon a relatively smooth military and diplomatic operation for the colonial powers and also the Lebanese nationalists, as indeed was the division of Syria into several communitarian states (the Druze state, the Alawi state, and the like). Difficulties of another order, however, cropped up in the development of a national economic space, the application of a constitutional and juridical system, and especially the formation of a political community—the real issues at stake in the new Lebanese state in the twentieth century.

4

The Merchant City

Dɪᴅ France's disputed and imposed decision to make Greater Lebanon independent of Syria lead to the creation of a new "national" market with a balanced infrastructure and channels for production and distribution, and thus make possible the formation of social strata on which the new nation could count? What was France's colonial plan in this regard; how did it intervene and what were its achievements? Next, to understand the Lebanese economy's very distinctive structure and identify the dominant social groups, we shall look at the major sectors of production. This view of Lebanon pertains to the nation's long formative period from 1920—when the French Mandate first went into effect—to the mid-1950s, when the fragile Lebanese prosperity took on a new dimension. While adopting an extended perspective, this view takes account of the state of the economy, particularly the worldwide economic depression from 1929 to 1935, the instituting of a war economy from 1940 to 1945, and the course set by the country's leaders once it gained independence in 1943.

Mandate as Market

The first high commissioner at Beirut, General Henri Gouraud, wrote that military control of the Levant opened the way for French capital. In reality, this control merely broadened and smoothed an already well-traveled highway. Even by the end of the Ottoman Empire, the Lebanese economy had joined the world capitalistic system through the export of silk and primary agricultural foodstuffs; local markets had been opened to products manufactured in Europe, and capital had been invested on a massive scale by the major industrial countries. The French intervention accelerated these phenomena and accentuated the imbalances among sectors of production, if only by encouraging foreign trade based on unequal exchange: thus the export/import ratio—the imports coming chiefly from France—fell from 60 percent at the end of the nineteenth century to 50 percent in 1920 to around 30 percent at the start of the 1930s.[1] In addition, French capital was preferentially invested in the most profitable sectors: banks (the Banque de Syrie et du Liban), public utilities (the Electricité de Beyrouth, the Compagnie du port, and the Société des Grands Hotels); communication networks (the Société des Chemins de Fer, Damas Hama et Prolongements), thereafter superseding the interests of the rival European countries.

The accomplishments of the French Mandate regarding infrastructure, administrative reform, and organization have been rightly hailed by historians of the period, eager to moderate the censorious uproar unleashed upon decolonization: the customs service, the chamber of commerce, the rationalization of foreign trade, especially the introduction of the metric system, the modernizing of the ports and the postal service, the creation of a telephone network, sanitary and hospital services, technical improvements in farming, and so on. One of the most outstanding accomplishments was the laying out of a road network crisscrossing the country from north to south and from the sea to the interior, with Beirut at the hub; from 300 miles in 1920, this network spanned 1,500 miles by 1943.[2] Many of the measures taken, however, had destabilizing and even counterproductive effects, such as the decline in traditional crafts. Thus, the introduction of a survey of land ownership for tax purposes to replace the Ottoman *tapu* and, in 1930, that of a new real estate code, eventually favored the registering of collective lands in Lebanon's outlying areas, particularly in the Bikaa Valley, Hermil, and Akkar, solely in the name of the head of a clan or prominent family. Rather than redistribute farm property, the effect was to concentrate it.

Another negative aspect of the French Mandate's implementation was the discrepancy between a large repressive apparatus and a fairly rudimentary civil administration—the tool for modernizing the state.[3] The Army of the Levant applied a heavy hand. Tens of thousands of soldiers were stationed in Lebanon, and their numbers mounted during the revolt of 1925 to 1927, which started in the Jebel Druze in Syria and spread to the Shuf and Jabal Amil. In 1921, the European contingent was being supplemented by locally recruited troops: gendarmes, Lebanese chasseurs, and eventually police, totaling several more tens of thousands. Far from decreasing, this number rose beyond 100,000 with the outbreak of World War II. Until independence, the exclusion of the Lebanese from positions of command and the presence of Senegalese and Madagascan units were seen as humiliating; the financial burden posed by this army's upkeep helped transform a mandate "respectful of the populations' wishes" into a colonial occupation whose end was awaited with impatience.

On the other hand, administrative services were cut to a minimum for the sake of economy, leaving most of the medical, educational, and social services to the communal organizations. In 1933, the country had just 3,600 civil servants for a population of 850,000. Five years later, only 5 percent of the secondary school pupils went to public schools.[4] One major reason for this inadequacy was the meager finances of the state itself, which were only slightly remedied by tax reform, while in Paris the members of the National Assembly regularly complained about the financial burden of the Mandate. Consistent with the recommendations of the League of Nations—and with the interests of French business—customs tariffs remained low and controls flexible. And while France's effort to equip the country remained limited, some of the Lebanese landowners, traders, and bankers with connections to French capitalism profited from closer relations with France and enjoyed an undeniable prosperity. The tradition of a liberal state with modest financial resources and power of intervention was thus inscribed in Lebanon's history during the Mandate, and from then on, this tradition carried great weight in the country's political economy.

Marginal Agriculture

Lebanon has a highly distinctive and peculiarly unbalanced economic structure that has nothing to do with natural circumstances and still less with coincidence. The production of its primary sector is unrelated to the country's potentialities and above all its needs. Nevertheless, one of the stated goals of the backers of a nation enlarged to the dimensions of Greater Lebanon—that is, annexing the coastal sahels and the interior agricultural plains—was precisely to end the Mountain's severe food shortage, and it is well known that the emirs of Mount Lebanon had always sought control of the surrounding grain-producing regions. The trauma of World War I, when the Allied blockade, requisitions by the Ottoman army, and the unbridled speculation by Beirut businessmen caused acute scarcity, intensified the sense of destitution to the point that, reacting to a dramatic rise in the price of agricultural products, rich merchants from Beirut and Tripoli began forming agricultural estates in the Bikaa Valley. Two priorities for the new nation then emerged: to meet the need for agricultural foodstuffs by enlarging the areas of production; and, because the 1920 borders of Lebanon encompassed a population two-thirds of whom lived on agricultural incomes, to improve the economic and social conditions of the rural areas.

Enlarging Lebanon's supply of cultivable land was basic: to the Mountain's nearly 200,000 acres were added a further 346,000—that is, 64 percent of the new nation's agricultural area.[5] Despite this, the country's grain supply, which was extremely inadequate in the early years of the Mandate, was still only 30 percent of what was required in 1946, and 37 percent in 1953.[6] Lebanon's agricultural yields remained poor, much inferior to those of the major agricultural countries, owing to the poor quality of technical improvements and the dearth of investments. As long as agricultural production was devoted mainly to food crops, it stimulated no investor interest or effort to modernize that could advance it beyond the dominant precapitalist mode of production.

Except for certain valleys where fruit growing was gradually replacing the waning sericulture, and especially in the coastal region where large citrus orchards were planted, unrational production and commercialization methods limited the profitabilities of agriculture. The achievements of Lebanon's primary sector remained paltry. By the end of the 1940s, agriculture, which occupied some 45 percent of the population, supplied only 15 to 20 percent of Lebanon's income. Later, its backwardness relative to other sectors of the economy only increased along with the country's dependence on imported foodstuffs.

True to their laissez-faire policy, the Mandate authorities and later the republic took only limited technical measures and did not always pay attention to any negative effects. Thus, working from studies made during the Mandate, the government succeeded in doubling the amount of irrigated land in Akkar, the Batrun plain, and especially south of the Bikaa Valley around Lake Qaraoun. With the granting of agricultural credits and a new survey of land ownership, these steps had the effect of highlighting the critical flaw in Lebanese agriculture: the deeply inegalitarian structure of rural property. The irrigation networks were laid out for the benefit first and foremost of the great local landowners, who also controlled elections. The indebted farmers did not resist the influx of urban capital lured by profits from the production and commercialization of fruits and vegetables, and in 1950, alongside a dwarf and smallholding sector (from 12 to 125 acres), the great landed estates (more than 250 acres) represented more than 10 percent of the country's cultivated land. More serious was the fact that these large agricultural estates—grain fields in Akkar, Hermil, and the Bikaa, olive groves in Jabal Amil, orchards between Sidon and Tyre—were cultivated by tenant farmers and wage earners whose disparity in income from that of the great absentee landlords was becoming more and more acute.

Thus Lebanon had, on the one hand, an antiquated and underproductive agriculture; on the other, it exhibited some of the greatest disparities in living standards in the world. The social and political consequences of the country's neglect of its primary sectors were enormous: class inequalities were accentuated by regional inequalities, mainly between the central, more urbanized section and the underdeveloped countryside on the nation's periphery. The ensuing huge rural exodus mightily disrupted ecological and cultural balances—by the early 1970s more than 60 percent of the country's population was urban—and left a serious shortage of agricultural manpower. On the other hand, the government's agricultural policy buttressed the class position of the great quasi-feudal landowners dominating the peasantry. Their wealth assured even the ones from the underdeveloped areas a central place in the Lebanese political system; as a group, they made up a fourth of the parliament after independence.[7] What's more, some of them transferred a part of their landowning capital into the burgeoning commercial and service sector, changing from traditional elites into modern ones and thus reinforcing their hegemonic position in the "power bloc."

Neglected Industry

Why wasn't it the same with owners of industrial companies? Here, too, the Mandate policy on crafts and manufacturing in Lebanon and the provinces of Syria controlled by France after 1920 represented a choice whose consequences were to be felt for a long time. Upon the creation of the state of Lebanon, the country's industries were in a growth phase, employing some 15 to 20 percent of the work force and providing higher earnings than other sectors of the economy. These industries, however, must be called traditional: the tobacco industry, food industries, tanneries, and even silk mills were merely huge unmechanized workshops using unskilled labor. One might as well say, wrote the rapporteur of a French investigative team in 1919, that industry as such did not exist in Syria or Lebanon.[8] This assessment went further: not only was Lebanon (like Syria) not industrialized, but its shortage of raw materials and its low level of human skills were a handicap, as spelled out in the French report of 1929 to the League of Nations: "One should not overestimate prospects for the creation of modern industry in the nations under the French Mandate. While a fair amount of inexpensive manpower exists in Syria and Lebanon, these countries do not offer the conditions necessary for large-scale industrial development."[9] The logic of the Mandate's functionaries and the French entrepreneurs in this new territory of Lebanon was in fact that of a trading economy: privileged capital investments in the immediately profitable sectors, and the opening up of the local market to French-manufactured products from whose influx local production was minimally protected.[10]

Lebanese crafts, which the French observer regarded with some deri-
sion, remained very much alive. Despite problems in commercialization, they
continued long after independence and in 1971 still provided a third of the
country's total production and employed close to 40 percent of its industrial
wage earners.[11] Lebanon's industrial sector exibited a dualistic structure,[12]
for several thousand small workshops with fewer than five employees each
coexisted with a modest number of large enterprises that tended to become
concentrated: the Asseily textile mills, the Ghandour food products facto-
ries, and the Chekka cement works represented examples of successful capitalism in the final decade of the Mandate.

In 1949, despite its structural flaws, industry supported about 10 percent of the population, and its share (14 percent) in the national income was
close to that of agriculture.[13] Although limited by the modest size of the
national market, it compared favorably in quality to the industries of Palestine and Egypt. Two factors contributed to this relative success. First, the
infusion of capital repatriated by Lebanese emigrants during the Depression.
Nearly a fourth of the population of Mount Lebanon had emigrated during
World War I, and the process continued apace under the Mandate: between
1921 and 1938 nearly 80,000 people left the country.[14] Money from the
emigrés was invested mainly in the modern industrial sector, of which some
of them had gained experience in America or Africa and which in 1929 com-
menced vigorous growth, particularly in the food and textile industries and
also construction materials. For example, the Arida brothers' cotton-spin-
ning mills in Tripoli just before the war supplied 12 percent of Syrian and
Lebanese consumption. [15]

Later, owing to the British and Free French forces' conquest of the Levant in 1941, the war gave a new boost to modern industry. Not only did the
Allies place orders with local producers, but the domestic demand could no
longer be met by the now-scarce imports from Europe. In certain sectors,
domestic production succeeded for a few years in supplanting those imports.
Although several firms reaped substantial profits, they neglected to bother
about the investment and rationalization that would have enabled them to
meet the onslaught of the "liberal" businessmen when the country gained its
independence.

When the French troops pulled out in 1946, Lebanon found itself at an
economic crossroads: Should it take advantage of the war's boost to its own
industrial and even agricultural production, or exploit further its Mandate-
assigned role of entrepôt and middleman? Relatedly, should the country retain its financial and commercial ties to France, or choose, in concert with
Syria, to set up an autonomous and coherent economic sphere?

Nineteen forty-seven saw a lively debate between the advocates of economic liberalism, a free market, and Lebanon's isolation from the other Near

Eastern countries versus the partisans of state intervention, protectionism, and Arab solidarity.[16] The former, dominated by the great merchants and Christian bankers of Beirut, were called the New Phoenicians, in allusion to the prosperous city-states of antiquity, because they extolled the laissez-faire capitalist. They argued that Lebanese industry was incapable of turning out products in sufficient numbers to meet domestic demand or, above all, of guaranteeing their quality and profitability. So it would be better to import, favoring commerce and services. Their opponents comprised industrialists, Arab nationalists, and reform-minded technocrats. To protect the recent and insecure progress of industry, they called for customs barriers, import quotas, and state aid.

Three issues fueled the debate: monetary problems, foreign trade, and Syrian-Lebanese economic unity. In 1948, Lebanon and France signed an agreement connecting the former with the "franc zone," unlike Syria which chose monetary independence. Later, to cope with inflation, Lebanon preferred encouraging imports rather than resorting to devaluation: between 1949 and 1952 most customs restrictions were lifted and industry's requests for credits denied. Finally, the stakes were sizable in the negotiations with Syria about the customs union, the chief element in the economic and financial "common interests" established by the Mandate: because of the creation of Israel and the ensuing war, Lebanon had just lost the Palestinian market, and because it depended on imports from Syria for its grains and meat, a break with Damascus would be all the more calamitous. The advocates of a liberal economy, however, were fearful of Syria's economic nationalism and the *dirigisme* of its new military government in power since 1949; some of them even feared an alliance between the two countries' employer classes and between their workers' organizations, which would lead to the two countries' political unification and attenuate Lebanon's ties with the West. That is why, following Beirut's refusal to comply with Damascus's urgent request to coordinate the two nations' political economies, the customs union broke up in March 1950 and trade was halted for several months. The most acutely disturbed sector in Lebanon was of course industry, for 60 percent of its production went to its neighbor,[17] and it imported raw materials like cotton from Syria as well.

The battle between the free-marketeers and the *dirigistes* thus culminated in the victory of the former. The government's decision struck a hard blow at Lebanon's industries, which were already impaired by the unequal nature of their employment structure,[18] which suffered from huge disparities in qualifications and salaries between a minority of workers and skilled craftsmen on the one hand, and the mass of unskilled labor on the other. In the year following the break with Syria, the total value of textile imports rose to two and a half times what it had been during the war, and 56 percent of all

Lebanon's imports came from the United States and the industrialized countries of Europe. These imported goods—cheaper, higher-quality, and more appealing to the Westernized elites—wrecked the prospects for industrial growth. On the other hand, they brought in a fortune for the merchants.

The industrial sector's relative decline during the early years of independence noticeably affected the Lebanese social structure and hence the class system and general orientation of the state. It slowed down the formation of a working class already hampered by the conflicting interests of, and cultural differences between, the craftsmen and the workers in large industry. The craftsmen remained tied to their village community of origin, very often bound by a personal relationship to their employer, and were strangers to proletarian ideology. For their part, the workers in large industry, who succeeded in establishing the first Federation of Unions in 1945[19] and obtained the promulgation of a Work Code in 1946, were weakened by the unemployment resulting from the industrial recession, as well as by the managerial repression and the encouragement of reformist or corporatist unions by politicians close to the authorities like Henri Pharaon. On the other hand, this decline deprived the secondary-sector entrepreneurs of getting a hearing by the government. Certainly, there were great successes, like that of Emile Bustani who managed to get elected deputy, as did his daughter after him. The heads of industry in the parliament, however, were much less numerous or influential than the merchants: four as against eighteen in 1964, and only three as against nineteen in 1968.[20] While the industrialists included a high proportion of Muslims, the great majority of the merchants were Christians.

The Triumph of the Merchants

In the end, Lebanese prosperity depended mainly on the service industries, whose importance is shown in just two numbers: by the mid-1950s it supported half the country's population and supplied nearly two-thirds of its income. The country's singular economic structure fitted the role that the industrial West, France in particular, assigned it in 1860: a channel of penetration, a relay station between France and the Arab interior. Ensuring the circulation of people, commodities, and capital between these two poles, Lebanese tradesmen and intermediaries built up the occupations connected with this circulation and, in the process, deducted their share of the profits.[21] The development of the service sector in the Lebanese economy was originally the product of a deliberate Mandatory policy from 1925. France became Lebanon's primary supplier of foreign goods, while Lebanon's exports to France covered only a fourth of the cost of its imports. France held on to this position until the start of World War II during which it was reduced to third place, which it occupied from then on, below Great Britain and the United States. In exchange for preference for French agricultural and industrial products, the high commissioner reserved the Syrian market for Beirut merchants: between 1925 and 1939, more than two-thirds of the imports of the areas under the French Mandate passed through the port of Beirut. Also during these years, France made public investments, subventions, and loans to encourage tourism, while French capital was involved in the building of the Kirkuk-Tripoli oil pipeline, completed in 1934, and in the development of the banking sector.

This "tertiarization" was clearly desired, however, by the francophile, mainly Christian, prominent bourgeoisie who had supported the creation of Greater Lebanon and the French presence there. Their commercial and financial interests were closely tied to those of the French capitalists operating in their country. Their cultural and political leanings impelled them to wish for the country's Westernization and isolation from the Arab region. Starting in 1919, the best-known of them wrote articles in *La Revue phénicienne*, where they argued about the vital nature of imports and Beirut's trading role in the Levant and expressed their ambition to make the country "the Switzerland of the Near East."[22] In 1921, the same group founded the Progressive Party whose motto was: "For Lebanon, with France."

We find the same ideological stream among the New Phoenicians during the early years of independence. They were ardent defenders of the liberalism surrounding Gabriel Menassa, members of the Lebanese coterie that adopted—and adapted—the theoretician Michel Chiha's theses favoring the "merchant republic." These bankers, traders, and intellectuals haunted the corridors of power to which they were drawn by multiple family ties. Thus, it is unsurprising that in the decade 1944–54 the government further underscored the primacy of the service industries by committing some 60 percent of its expenditures to the development of infrastructures, the coastal highway, the Khaldeh airport, cold rooms for the port of Beirut, and a telephone network—all of which benefited commerce and services.[23] When, in accordance with Point Four of the Truman program of 1949, the United States granted Lebanon economic aid partly earmarked for irrigation and hydroelectric production on the Litani River, this benefited Beirut's middlemen and large firms overseeing the project, but did little for the peasants of the Bikaa.

The adoption of liberal measures and the creation of a climate favorable to a fast return on private capital invested in the service sector played a decisive role in Beirut's transformation into the principal port and center of commerce, finance, tourism, education, and medicine for the whole Near East. The Lebanese capital's growth and enrichment indicated the success of the service sector, but mainly underscored the deeply unequal treatment of the nation's commercial center compared with its outlying agrarian, artisanal, and even industrial locales such as Tripoli. Beirut's relative overdevelopment and its financial and commercial hegemony over the Mountain justified the antagonism between it and the "Lebanese desert," to use a once-familiar French expression. In the nineteenth century, Beirut, Tripoli, Damascus, and Haifa were all commercial centers of Ottoman Syria, and interlinked by currents of brisk trade. Once the Mandate went into effect, Beirut was privileged; the modernization of its port, which was favored over Tripoli and Latakia, produced a threefold increase in its traffic. In 1948, the creation of Israel suspended the role of Haifa as a port supplying the Arab hinterland; despite the determined efforts of Turkey, Syria, and Jordan to promote Alexandretta, Latakia, and Aqaba, respectively, the value of Beirut's reexports to the interior underwent a fivefold increase in the first five years of independence. The city's population, which had doubled between the censuses of 1922 and 1932,[24] continued its rapid growth with the creation of a new commercial center—bordered by the avenues Foch, Allenby, and Weygand—and next the urbanization of the new district of Hamra around the American University and that of Ras Beirut, so that exorbitant real estate profits were added to commercial and financial profits. As Beirut's bustle indicated, the economic motor of the country was not production but distribution, circulation, and even speculation.

After World War II, international trade soared; by the early 1950s, it supplied close to 30 percent of the country's income. The merchant bourgeoisie freed itself from supervision by the large French companies to which it had been closely tied, repurchased the stocks of concessionary companies that managed transportation, energy, and so forth, and "Lebanized" the companies' Franco-Lebanese capital. These moves were accompanied by a new economic concentration securing the monopoly of some Beirut commercial firms now in a position to discourage local industrial production. The two pillars of their foreign-oriented operations were the importing of manufactured goods and their reexport to the Arab region.

Onto this commercial sector were grafted service activities that played a greater role in the country's economy, supplying 40 percent of its income and contributing to a positive balance of trade that otherwise would have been severely in deficit. At the heart of the financial boom were the network of modern telecommunications and the gold market: in 1951, 30 percent of the world's private transactions in the precious metal went through Beirut.[25] The influx of deposits and the creation of new institutions were encouraged by the system of secret banking and financial liberalism and also by the increasing political and military tensions in the neighboring countries, particularly in Egypt, in Syria—where one military coup followed another—and above all in Palestine, from which hundreds of thousands of Arabs fled in 1948–49. Most Western companies operating in the Middle East counted on

Lebanon's political stability; for them, Beirut was a stronghold of technical skills and modern services. Real estate and tourism were booming. The pipelines of the Iraq Petroleum Company (1934) and Tapline (1950), and the refineries in Tripoli and Zahrani brought in substantial royalties. And contraband, especially locally produced hashish, was a not-inconsiderable source of profit.

The paradox of the merchant economy as shaped by the new legislation, the development of infrastructures, and Western investments during the Mandate, and then reinforced by an official policy of laissez-faire and the influx of Arab capital after independence, was its extreme fragility. Lebanon's prosperity depended on the development of nonproductive sectors; it exhibited a growing imbalance between the service sector and an industry marked by high unemployment as well as a stagnant agriculture. The country's dependence on the West for imports and on the Arab countries for capital formation made it vulnerable to external pressures and interventions. Finally, the leaders' choice at independence for excessive deregulation and laissez-faire deterred the formation of an articulated national economic space.

This profound structural imbalance also marked Lebanese society: in a country that at independence was still largely rural, the great majority of families lived in poverty, usually without the benefits of modern progress or access to education and technical training. As a result, great numbers of them were induced to leave the countryside and come swell the poorer urban areas now teeming with unskilled and subproletarian irregular laborers. Given the small size of Lebanon's secondary sector, only a tiny minority managed to find wage-earning work in industry. The privileged position of a head of industry remained marginal. Small employers and craftsmen were in relative decline, confined to the most traditional and often peripheral sectors of production. On the other hand, the salaried urban strata of employees in the service sector—commerce, banks, the civil service, and the like—continued to increase and to diversify. Between 1930 and 1950, alongside the self-employed merchants, white-collar employees in the leading firms, in particular those dealing with foreign countries, even represented a petite bourgeoisie in the first stages of expansion.

At the top of the pyramid, next to the land-owning aristocrats, the dominant strata were increasingly made up of traders and bankers with ties to world capitalism. Up to 1939, upper-bourgeois businessmen were barely represented in the parliament, but soon after they made up some 25 percent of its deputies.[26] Quite logically, these merchant elites aimed to make quick profits, without weighty infrastructure or long-term prospects; their ethic was deeply individualistic—in a pinch, familial and clannish—unfamiliar with collective development and national interest; their methods were those of pliability, personal contacts, and a minimum of regulatory constraints. In wielding the power they collectively dominated, the traditional landed elites and the new merchant elites, whose interests were closely intertwined, were to transpose their vision of social and economic relations to the political level and hence to condemn the Lebanese government to helplessness.

5

Patrons and Clients

In the early 1980s, French television presented a documentary by the Syrian filmmaker Omar Amiralay on the ravages of the war in Beirut,[1] an original study of the western part of the city; most people interviewed for the cameras complained at length about the reign of the "boutiques." A "boutique" is a headquarters maintained by a head of a gang who, whatever his announced political program, pays a group of armed men to impose his law and run rackets in an area covering a few blocks. To open a "boutique" all one needs is a gang leader, a slogan, and often subsidies from abroad, and then one can control the life of a neighborhood. Whether ironic or disillusioned, the comments were unanimous in stressing what an obstacle the "boutiques" were to the city's political debate, mobilization by political parties, the free play of democracy, and, in the end, the return of peace.

Pursuing the commercial metaphor, one could say that, even during the Mandate and even more so after independence, social and political relations in Lebanon were essentially those of clientelism, and that "bosses" or patrons dominated the whole of public life, from the village to the capital and the whole national territory. Not only do they play the lead on their particular stage, sometimes for several decades, but because they possess a critical mass of economic wealth and symbolic powers, they are the indispensable key to the system and the most effective of political agents. So Lebanon's political institutions and their operations need to be seen in light of the relations between patrons and clients.

How is that? Lebanese culture is characterized by enduring primary— familial and religious—identities, strong village solidarities, and predominantly local attachments and personal loyalties. The primordial bonds that play a role in all societies, even those that claim to abjure them, are essential and eminently functional in Lebanon. They have long helped preserve a naturalness in social relations, and have to some extent enabled the country to confront the demands for modernization, openness, change, and the quieting of tensions without dehumanizing the social fabric. Furthermore, Lebanon's political history is largely one of primary communities seeking protection, security, and the redistribution of benefits. To the patron who assures them of these things, clients in turn promise fidelity and loyalty, thus assuring him a large measure of political autonomy and perhaps a way to extend his influence[2] and thereby strengthen the clientelist relation.

As it reflects the mosaic-like, fragmented structure of Lebanese society, political clientelism is a heritage of the mediating role of the Middle Eastern tax collectors and warlords up to the mid-nineteenth century. The French Mandate of 1920 replaced the Ottoman power, as represented by the pashas of Damascus or Sidon; after 1943, the Mandate was replaced by the Republic of Lebanon as the center of political power. But the Lebanese patron has always been the pivotal intermediary between the center and the periphery. The disappearance of political "feudalism" did not at all weaken clientelism, which simply evolved and grew stronger by extending and diversifying its instruments, modalities, and areas of intervention. The feudal patron, the great and often absentee landowner, was joined by the urban patron with access to the bureaucratic and judiciary system and hence the means to mobilize a proletarian clientele; the businessman-patron who dominated the upwardly mobile salaried strata; the political patron who manipulated slogans and built his power on a party; the patriarchal patron who handed down his authority over a local community to his sons. The creation of benevolent societies, political parties, and support for unions opened up additional spheres of activity for the patrons. Among themselves, the patrons not only formed a network of economic exchanges, matrimonial relations, and financial support, but also sometimes engaged in bloody rivalries to stay in power. The use of local agents and henchmen as well as the employment of private militias to achieve one's own justice and to control an area were in a manner of speaking institutionalized.

Though the clientelist system ensured Lebanon's rather supple and effective social and economic relations, which were otherwise impeded by weak professionalization and underutilized individual abilities, it also had some extremely negative consequences. Because of its principle of granting power in return for favors, it fostered corruption and favoritism; it systematically imposed reliance on a nondisinterested intermediary and paralyzed political development by giving precedence to individual and local interests over the general interest and implementation of a national policy.

Reflecting both a social culture and a balance of power, the new Lebanese nation's institutions, which were developed at the Mandate's start and amended several times before and after independence, bore the mark of this clientelist system, beginning with the republic's 1926 constitution produced by the Representative Council of Greater Lebanon headed by the banker and journalist Michel Chiha. While taking their inspiration from the Belgian model and the French model of parliamentary democracy in the Third Republic, the drafters sought to make provision for the specific features and needs of Lebanese society, as shown by the call for public consultation.

True, the consultation was limited, very often not going beyond the circle of urban elites. What's more, many of the Orthodox Christians were reluctant and few Muslims took part, for they were hostile to a nation dominated by France in 1925, during which the Jebel Druze revolt extended from Syria to the areas recently annexed into Lebanon: the Bikaa, Jabal Amil, and even the Shuf. In fact, the high commissioner in Beirut kept the upper hand in the constitutional project. He imposed articles that explicitly referred to the Mandate and that were expunged only between 1943 and 1947, after independence. Moreover, judging that under his tutelage the Lebanese had to undergo an "apprenticeship in democracy," the high commissioner reserved the power to suspend the constitution, which he did on two occasions: between 1932 and 1937, to exclude a Muslim, Sheikh Muhammad al-Jisr, from presidential candidacy, and between 1939 and 1943, because of the state of war.

The officials of the French Mandate turned the clientelist system to good account. While allowing Lebanese officials few important responsibilities, the French gave the local politicians some experience of a constitutional regime, but one limited to a familiarization with parliamentary, ministerial, electoral, and bureaucratic procedures. In the new mythology, the patrons claimed to be indispensable middlemen between the Mandatory power and the local populations. Their clients trusted only them and only they could muster the clients at the request of the French authorities. On the other hand, it was only through them that it was possible to reach the Mandatory power, which was often resented as alien and even hostile. The French authorities excelled at the art of manipulating rivalries and alliances: between 1926 and 1941 the governmental coalitions were dominated by the tandem of Emile Eddé and Bishara al-Khuri, two Maronite patrons who each fought to control their community. We find the same tug of war among the Shi'is of the south, where the opposition between factions loyal to the Khalil and Zein families, on the one hand, and to the Asaad family on the other, reflected the split between collaborators with the Mandate and its opponents.

The Electoral Law

The tool par excellence for institutionalizing Lebanon's political clientelism was the electoral law of 1926. Seats in parliament were astutely distributed according to a twofold proportionality, communal and regional.

Each community controlled a number of deputies proportional to its relative demographic size.[3] Until 1953 the electoral districts were the five great "governorates" and from then on the twenty-six cantons. Deputies were elected every four years in a single round of voting by a single electoral body made up of all the voters from each district. Ten of the constituencies each had a homogeneous population, but the sixteen others were composites and candidates depended on votes from outside their own community. For example, in Beirut II (the Ain Mreissé and Basta districts), four Sunnis and a Greek Orthodox were required to be elected and several lists of at most five candidates were presented from which the voters, whatever their community, chose a combination of four plus one.

The advantage of the single electoral body in each constituency was to make the deputy elected not only from his own community, but also from other communities to which he must be acceptable, for article 27 of the constitution stipulates that "each member of the Chamber represents the whole nation." The purpose of this novel system was to obtain cooperation between factions and to calm, at least formally, tensions between the communities. In principle it also made competing candidacies possible within the same community as well as a variety of choices and prospects for change: in the general elections of 1960, for example, the voters of Beirut I (Ashrafiye) could choose between the two leading lights of the Maronite community: Pierre Eddé—banker and prime mover of the National Bloc, and opponent of the regime of acting president Fuad Shihab—and the Kataeb party's founder Pierre Gemayel, who was then allied with this regime.

The electoral system had other, less fortunate effects, however. First, it institutionalized the communal distribution of power. In normal times, this distribution could be thought to guarantee a maximally harmonious representation for each community. In a crisis, however, it became the focal point for all antagonisms and demands.[4] On the other hand, the law helped enhance the power of the patrons and perpetuated domination by the traditional elites, for each patron acted like a feudal lord over his electoral territory, where he encountered virtually no opposition. He chose members for his list according to the electoral or financial benefits they could bring in, and he laid down the official line of the electoral program. Far from reflecting any cooperation between the elites, the system of pluricommunal lists represented their clientelist power locally. This was the case, for example, with the "Bloc of Independents" led from 1925 to the war by the candidates of the Asaad family in South Lebanon. A rich and powerful leader—he was regularly the president of the parliament—was the chief architect for the election of the members of his list, colorless individuals who supported him unconditionally and delivered bundles of votes in return for their deputy's seats. Rarely could a candidate run for office outside this system of patronage and intense factionalism: more rarely yet could he then manage to get elected.

The campaign and the election were of course the high points of the system. Lebanese law stipulates that everyone votes at his birthplace, so for many the election is an occasion for a return to their village, often financed by the patron-candidate and seen to through his services: the taxi is therefore an electoral agent of the highest importance. Formerly, the candidate would have made a tour of the local personages, particularly the clerics, promising his constituency public funds for roads, telephones, running water, and the like, and even disgorging largess in exchange for pledges of votes. In some years, the cost of a single vote was close to a month's wage for an unskilled laborer, and the patron's liberality during the campaign was eagerly awaited while "outsiders" who lacked financial backing stood little chance of edging their way into the system. At their boss's side, a squad of henchmen saw to it that the operation went properly, intimidated bothersome rivals, prodded the populations to vote "the right way," and made sure the vote count turned out favorably. With machinery like this, the per capita cost of a campaign and an electoral operation was one of the world's highest, eight times that of West Germany and twice that of the United States, where candidates dispose of huge sums.[5] From the first general elections held under the French Mandate to the last ones before the war in 1972, the endemic corruption and fraud in parliamentary institutions discredited them in public opinion. The electoral results were rarely surprising, for they always reinstated a high proportion of the members from the prominent families or their satellites, tending to make the parliament a closed club, a microcosm of families, clans representing local or communal interests, and private economic interests that wrongly claimed popular representativeness.

The Parliamentary Club

The exclusive and congealed composition of the Lebanese parliament is revealed by several objective criteria. That of age, first of all, for the proportion of deputies over the age of fifty constantly increased while that of those under forty regularly declined, two findings that should be seen in light of the simultaneous rejuvenation of the country's population.[6] When young deputies were elected, they were necessarily, with the exception of the Greek Orthodox *and* Nasserist Najah Wakim who was elected in Beirut in 1972, sons of prominent families who inherited the family seat: Kamel al-Asaad, elected at twenty-four, Kamal Jumblat at twenty-six, Amin Gemayel at twenty-eight, and Tony Frangieh at thirty.

In other respects, while the parliament seemed to have a high rate of turnover,[7] a look at the social origins and especially the family and financial ties of the deputies-elect shows that they were either clients of a patron firmly established in his deputy's seat or members of his family. The kinship network eventually proved the most efficient conduit to parliamentary representation and especially its longevity: from 1920 to 1972, 965 deputy's seats were occupied by fewer than 250 families. Twenty-six families alone uninterruptedly monopolized 35 percent of these seats for over fifty years, and a look at the facts shows a constant and marked increase in this "dynastic" pattern in the workings of the parliament.[8] For example, from Qabalan Frangieh, deputy from Zghorta in 1929 to his great-grandson Suleiman Jr., elected in 1992 (he had already held a ministerial post), the heritage was transmitted by Hamid Frangieh, the negotiator of the financial accords with France in 1943, by Suleiman Frangieh, patron of the northern Maronite Mountain and president of the republic from 1970 to 1976, and by the latter's son, Tony, assassinated in 1978.

Certainly, the recruitment of the parliamentary elites changed over time, mainly because the landed aristocracy gradually capitulated to businessmen and representatives of finance and large firms. We also see a constant rise in the educational level of the deputies, and in particular the presence of a substantial number of lawyers—who could also be property owners or businessmen or their clients—for, since the last decades of the Ottoman Empire, education opened the way to the civil service and governmental posts. On the other hand, a growing number of deputies, nearly a quarter of those elected in 1972, claimed allegiance to a political party.

Parties Old and New

But what kind of political parties? The Lebanese organizations with this name in fact belong to various groupings with different relations to the exercise of political power. It should first be noted that, according to a still-living Ottoman tradition, no party can enter official political life without the authorization of the government, which can, as it did in 1949, declare opponents of the system illegal. We can roughly distinguish two different kinds of political parties: those that are actually personal coteries functioning through patronage relations, and those with a platform and an apparatus; the latter kind have rarely been legalized, let alone gained access to the parliament. In addition, we should set aside two parties located at the intersection of the two categories.

Before the constitution went into effect and the parliament first convened in the mid-1920s, Lebanon had no political parties. At that time, two coalitions formed in the Chamber that were to dominate Lebanese politics for the duration of the Mandate; Emile Eddé's National Bloc and Bishara al-Khuri's party, which was later to become the Destour, the party of the constitution. The split between the two groups originated in their different assessments of Lebanon's relations with France, which for Eddé were indissoluble, or with its Arab neighbors, which for Khuri were essential. The National Bloc and the Destour were officially registered as political parties in 1946. Both were actually Christian—to be more exact, Maronite—factions that rallied segments of the community in certain areas, chiefly Beirut and Mount Lebanon. They had neither members nor a platform, strictly speaking, and were active mainly at election time, drawing up and promoting lists to assure their candidates the vote of the local clienteles.

At about the same time, there formed parties with programs opposed to the traditional system of domination; some of them even broke with the clannish and communal mode of recruiting activists. The chief ones were first the Syrian Social Nationalist Party (SSNP), formed in 1932 and better known as the Parti Populaire Syrien, which more or less explicitly sought Lebanon's union with Syria, Jordan, and Palestine in an authoritarian corporatist state. The SSNP worked out a secular doctrine, hostile both to the powerful Maronite Church and to the Muslim clergy, who were accused of buttressing Islam's role in the Lebanese political system. Though it recruited militants of various origins, its ideological orientation more closely approximated the Orthodox Christian political culture; moreover, it was primarily rooted in the Kura and the high Matn, homelands of the community.

Later, in 1930, came the Communist Party, which remained underground until independence when it separated from the Syrian branch, though it remained illegal until 1948. Most of its earliest recruits were urban laborers—stevedores, textile workers, transport employees—among whom it organized opposition to the savage laissez-faire policy of the independence leaders.

Then came various pan-Arab groups: the National Action League (1932), which until independence called for reunification with Syria; the Najjadeh [Rescuers] Party (1936), which in the name of Arab unity opposed the powerful patron Saeb Salam's leadership of the Sunnis of Beirut; the Arab socialist Baath [Resurrection] Party (1947), the Lebanese branch of a Syrian-born party; the Movement of Arab Nationalists centered on the struggle for the liberation of Palestine; and finally, several organizations, such as the Liberation Party, inspired by the Islamic movement of the Muslim Brotherhood, which were neither legalized nor considered full-fledged political parties.

All these parties with platforms, each with a few thousand members, were excluded from the government. There was virtually no way for an outsider to open up the system of electoral lists sponsored by the traditional notables; the SSNP had one elected deputy in 1957, the Najjadeh one in

1960, the Baath one in 1972; the Communist Party, which regularly sponsored several candidates, had none. Barred from joining the club constituted
by the Lebanese parliament, these parties were often active on the fringes of
legality, sometimes even clandestinely; some relied on a paramilitary organization, and formed ties to political forces (a government or a party) outside
Lebanon. Some were tempted to use nondemocratic methods to seize power,
witness the SSNP's two failed coups in 1949 and 1961. This process of exclusion also strengthened the opposition parties: though they were illegal,
their activities appeared increasingly legitimate in the eyes of their members
and sympathizers.

At the center of the political spectrum, two parties pulled off the impossible feat of being both the electoral organization of a traditional clientele
and a party of the modern kind: the Kataeb and the Progressive Socialist
Party (PSP). In 1936, Pierre Gemayel and a group of Maronites founded the
Kataeb or Lebanese Phalange, which backed a conservative program ("God,
fatherland, family") for the defense of Lebanon's independence and the preservation of the intercommunal balance, but also for social development. The
party was legalized upon independence and got its first deputy elected in
1951; it then had some half-dozen members in each successive legislature.
Like that of the other traditional parties, its success hinged on the quasi-
automatic vote of its Christian, mostly Maronite, clientele in sharply defined
electoral districts: of its members, 50 percent were from Matn and Kisrawan,
and 20 percent from Beirut. But to win out over its rivals and become the
accredited representative of the Maronite middle class, the Kataeb Party was
also a party of the modern kind; it began life as a sporting and cultural
organization modeled on the fascist movements in central Europe. Of all the
parties in Lebanon, the Kataeb was the most highly organized and authoritarian, though it had declared itself favorable to a Western-style democracy.
Finally, though it has been part of the political establishment, the party was
also revolutionary in that, from its creation, it assigned a central role to its
armed organization; a heavy investment in training and equipping militants
enabled it to intervene effectively in times of political crisis.

The Lebanese system's other Janus-like party is the Progressive Socialist
Party (1949), which regularly sent two or three deputies to every parliament,
thanks to the votes of the Druze faction from the Shuf loyal to the Jumblat
family. It is thus a traditional clientelist party and its success was largely due
to the charisma of its founder, Kamal Jumblat. The party's modern side is a
progressivist political program opposed to the privileges of the traditional
notables, which wins support for it outside its own communal stronghold,
among Christians and Sunnis.

Despite the existence of these traditional, modern, or mixed parties, it
cannot be said that Lebanon's politics has been worked out on the basis of

Communities in Lebanon (1975)

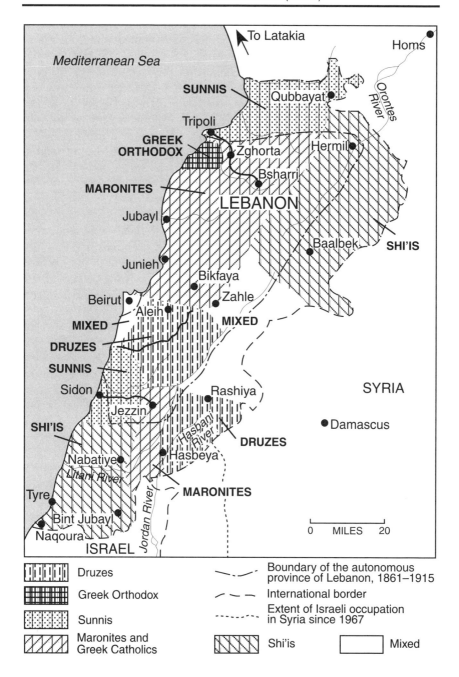

To Latakia
Homs
Mediterranean Sea
SUNNIS
Qubbayat
Orontes River
Tripoli
GREEK ORTHODOX
Zghorta
Hermil
Bsharri
MARONITES
LEBANON
Jubayl
Baalbek
SHI'IS
Junieh
Bikfaya
Beirut
Zahle
Aleih
MIXED
MIXED
DRUZES
SUNNIS
Sidon
Rashiya
SYRIA
Jezzin
•Damascus
SHI'IS
Nabatiye
Hasbani River
Hasbeya
DRUZES
Tyre
Litani River
Jordan River
MARONITES
Bint Jubayl
0   MILES   20
Naqoura
ISRAEL

Druzes		Boundary of the autonomous province of Lebanon, 1861–1915
Greek Orthodox		International border
Sunnis		Extent of Israeli occupation in Syria since 1967
Maronites and Greek Catholics	Shi'is	Mixed

political groups organized to compete for control of government. One eminent figure at the time of independence, Prime Minister Riyad al-Sulh, publicly deplored this just after the elections of 1947, the most corrupt in the country's history. Not coincidentally, he was assassinated some years later by members of the SSNP seeking vengeance for their repression after their unsucessful coup in 1949 and in particular for the arrest and execution of their leader Antun Saadeh. The electoral system tended to preclude any real and legal political participation by large segments of the urban middle classes from which the prohibited modern parties recruited their members and supporters. It also excluded the lower classes from the political arena, for clans and patrons stood in the way between the electors and their deputy, who in any case was more concerned with consolidating his position than with the collective interest.

In the final analysis, the law and constitutional practice confined the parliament to a game of buildups, alliances, and breakups of coteries formed to maximize benefits with no particular concern for ideological or communal divergences. Elected from lists representing compromises, the deputies cultivated positions of compromise; they systematically avoided controversial subjects touching on Lebanon's fundamental directions: the economic system, the communal system, or foreign policy. Only once in the parliament's history, in 1930, did they agree to censure a government, and the president kept a tight rein on their legislative initiatives. Moreover, it is significant that the lack of elections from 1972 to 1992, owing to the war and general disagreement about the demographic facts on which to base the communal balance in the government of the country, has neither paralyzed nor transformed parliamentary activity. Diminishing in number (they were only seventy-two in 1990) as well as aging, the deputies have convened, debated, and bargained. Above all, they continue to fill their main function: they elect the president of the republic, the summit of the clientelist hierarchy.

The Patron-President

The practice established at the country's independence gave the president considerable powers and freedom to maneuver. He not only was the chief executive, named the government and senior civil servants, and commanded the army and security services, but could also decree urgent legislation that hadn't been voted by the parliament, and veto laws adopted by that body. Elected for six years, he was not accountable to the parliament and so had the time and tools needed to build a powerful political machine.

Basically, this "machine" is electoral. A presidential candidate sought a majority in the chamber—two-thirds on the first ballot, a plurality on the second—to assure his election. In addition, he verified that the leading electors have voted as they promised, by a check of the voting, which had in principle been carried out by secret ballot. For even before being elected, he had begun distributing positions of power, particularly ministerial seats, among his supporters.

Second, the president exercised his patronage in forming the government. He held office for six years whereas, since 1926, ministries have lasted an average of eighteen months. On being nominated, a minister must quickly garner benefits for his familial, village, and communal clientele, on the one hand, and secure his participation in the next government, on the other. The record on this score belongs to the emir Majid Arslan, a member of the Druze faction from Shuf, a colorless political personality but needed to maintain the communal balance in the various governments: he was involved in nearly all the ministries from 1930 until his death in 1984.

A ministerial post under the Sunni prime minister, whose room for maneuvering depended chiefly on his relations with the Maronite president who appointed him, involved a masterpiece of balancing confessions, regions, and factions, with the result that ministerial life turned into a game of musical chairs, as described by Michael Hudson:

> To fill the vacancies created by Frangieh and Salem, it was necessary to find a Maronite notable from Mount Lebanon and a Greek Catholic, preferably from the Bikaa. The two prominent candidates were Philippe Taqla (Greek Catholic) and Yussef Istaphan (Maronite). Taqla, however, would not join a cabinet unless his Destour colleague, Majid Arslan (Druze), was also made a minister; but Sami Sulh could not include Amir Majid without displacing the incumbent Druze, Dr. Jamil Talhouk. Such a move would upset the Druze followers of Kamal Jumblat. Kamal Jumblat, meanwhile, was on the verge of throwing his support to the Karami-Pharaon Independents. Furthermore, because Gabriel Murr, the Greek Orthodox Public Works Minister, was also in sympathy with the Jumblat group, to replace Talhouk would be to risk Murr's resignation. . . . [9]

This quick glimpse at the ministerial game yields only a faint idea of its extreme sophistication and the Lebanese politicians' exceptional skill in maneuvering between the state apparatus and their community of origin. For example, all during 1960, Pierre Gemayel, leader of the Kataeb, and Kamal Jumblat, head of the Progressive Socialist Party, were involved in a constant dispute in their respective dailies, *Al-'Amal* and *Al-Anba*, while they were both ministers in the same government. In the long run, however, this subtle game is fatal, for it centers on personal quarrels and conflicts of personal ambitions, with such goals as nominating a high civil servant or awarding the right to hold a public market, while the serious problems—the social inequalities and attendant military tensions—continue to intensify.

Apart from the parliament and the ministries, the president can build up a third category of clientele through his near-monopoly over the country's vital resources, particularly security and employment. Because of presidential favors, the civil service, which was minimal at the time of independence, swelled so rapidly that by 1964 it had to be reorganized and many posts eliminated. The president surrounded himself with a veritable court of favor-currying relatives, counselors, and intermediaries, some more powerful than the ministers themselves.

Bishara al-Khuri's term of office as the independent Lebanese republic's first president from 1943 to 1952 illustrates the bent toward nepotism typical of every chief executive. Khuri was a gifted politician, raised to the highest office in 1943, shortly after the last general elections held under French supervision. Not the least of his achievements was getting the chamber to vote the constitutional amendment abolishing the Mandate in November. In retaliation, he was imprisoned at the fortress of Rashayya along with his prime minister and several members of the government. The public demonstrations for his liberation marked the official date of Lebanon's independence on 22 November 1943. Later, Khuri, together with Riyad al-Sulh, crafted the consensus known as the National Pact determining the country's basic directions.

Bishara al-Khuri inherited an underdeveloped administration, army, and infrastructure and had to work with inexperienced ministers. The frailty of this political setup enabled him to wield and extend his personal influence, meddle in all decisions, and get around ministerial networks and the civil service with the help of a personal team headed by his brother Salim, an important businessman. By falsifying the election results of 1947 and handing out large emoluments, he assured himself of the chamber's devotion. In May of the following year it passed a constitutional law exceptionally empowering him to run for a second term. The death knell to his ambitions, however, was sounded by the defeat of the Arab countries, including Lebanon, in the Palestinian war of 1948–49, Riyad al-Sulh's assassination in Amman in 1951, and the rise of popular discontent during this inflationary period. The deputies whom he had installed and who had granted him a second mandate were seduced by the siren songs of the opposing coalition, the National Socialist Front, led by Kamal Jumblat, and a number of other potential presidential candidates—Camille Chamoun, Suleiman Frangieh, and the Eddé brothers—who called for a "purification" and a revision of the electoral law. Because the patronage system was based on the expectation of future benefits, deputies and ministers forsook the president in 1952, and

Khuri was forced to resign owing to a climate of general strike and the military command's refusal to intervene on his behalf.

Nevertheless, corruption and nepotism continued to prevail under the presidency of Bishara al-Khuri's "overthrower" Camille Chamoun (1952–1958). Pierre Gemayel, one of the winners of the legislative elections of 1960, said for example that the elected deputies then represented less than 10 percent of the electorate. Certainly, the crisis that marked the end of Chamoun's presidency in 1958 had other causes than just the excesses of clientelism. Far from abating, however, clientelism persisted as a prominent feature of the Lebanese system and even made a return in force with Suleiman Frangieh's elevation to the presidency in 1970. The head of a Zghorta clan, he was famous for unhesitatingly gunning down a local rival faction in a church in May 1957. The parliament momentarily suspended the process of electing him when his armed men burst into the chamber, but on the second ballot 100 votes were totted up for 99 voters!

In Lebanese society the marked corruption resulting from political clientelism provoked contempt for the law, bringing both elected political representatives and the civil service into disrepute and slowing down the development of civic awareness. On the other hand, the patrons and their mediator, the president, were incapable of adopting a political line, and even less of sticking to it, for fear of disrupting the delicate balance of mutual benefits between coalitions. In fact, from independence on, the government allowed clientelist criteria to override bureaucratic criteria, and its business amounted to deciding "who gets what, when, and how."[10] The government had only one strategy for coping with the international situation, the imbalances in growth and the opening up of the social system: immobilism. Since the mid-1950s, for example, politicians, technocrats, financiers, and the Lebanese press lengthily held forth on the plan to irrigate South Lebanon with the millions of cubic meters of water from the Litani River that were lost each year to the sea. In reality, the complex debates about the "600-meter mark" and the "800-meter mark" as the proper height for placing a dam were a cover-up for the huge private interests at stake and the competition between the landowners and the heads of public works firms; the president carefully avoided coming out in favor of either and even less of the local peasantry. The controversy raged on and the politicians assumed control of the technocrats' and magistrates' sphere of jurisdiction, but eventually no decision was made. Under these circumstances, the government, identified with the group that monopolized its benefits, did not respond in any way to the populations' expectations; it was often unjust and, above all, dramatically absent. To the French sociologist and future hostage Michel Seurat who questioned him in 1983 about the reasons and meaning of his permanent insubordination,[11] Khalil Akkawi, gang leader in the Tebbaneh neighborhood of Tripoli, spontaneously answered, *"Yaret fi dawla"* ["If only there were a state"].

6

A "National" Pact

THE decree creating Greater Lebanon in September 1920 was by itself insufficient to establish the reality of a state whose origins were contested, whose borders had been carved out of the flesh of the Arab provinces of the Ottoman Empire, and whose pluralistic political culture was nourished simultaneously by universal religions and by local loyalties. While the French Mandate had no difficulty imposing its authority, the new nation clearly did not represent all the people, but was created at the request of and for the benefit of certain categories of the population and was more or less rejected by others. To establish its legitimacy, in Max Weber's sense of the term, and to enable its leaders to deal with internal conflicts, the new state had to create institutions suited to the segmented character of its society, institutions for building a national identity or at least grounding a bond of citizenship between the state and all the country's populations equally.

The institutions of the Lebanese republic were set up in two phases: first, in 1926 the constitution officially adopted a communitarian political system, thus legitimating the French authorities' maintainenance of unequal relations with the various Lebanese populations, Christian and Muslim. Yet tensions smoldered under the Mandate and in the 1930s flared into open dispute over Lebanon's existence; for a while, Greater Lebanon even appeared threatened with dismantling. Then, however, the struggle for independence provided the basis for a consensus among the Lebanese about the sources of their nation's legitimacy. The National Pact of 1943, the country's second fundamental institution, was the fruit of a compromise between the country's elites. Because of its originality and its exceptional success in the Near East, the pact is considered even more basic to the Lebanese political system than the constitution. It was a precarious and dangerously static pact, however, as the crisis of 1958 was to reveal.

Political communitarianism as inscribed in the institutions and implemented in governmental practice means that the communities making up the
country are the basic elements for popular representation and the distribution of power. In Lebanon these are the *religious* communities—the Kurdish
population, for example, is officially categorized as Sunni Muslim; the Armenians are classified according to the church and rite they belong to; on the
other hand, large groups of refugees from Iraq and whole families from areas bordering Syria remain stateless. Theoretically, ethnic distinctions are
not involved, which is why the communitarian system in Lebanon is called
"confessionalism." Of course, when the Lebanese drafters and the French
lawyers assisting them inscribed the communitarian system in the constitution of 1926, they were simply taking over the system instituted by the
Règlement organique of 1861 by which the major European powers had
already imposed a communitarian settlement of the Lebanese question. Up
to a point, the drafters were also conforming to the first article of the Mandate of the League of Nations that directed the tutelary power to respect the
principle of "local autonomies." Moreover, several of the successor states of
the Ottoman Empire preserved the communitarian regime in their civil codes.
In Lebanon, article 9 of the constitution stipulates that "[the nation] guarantees to all groups, whatever rite they belong to, respect for them as individuals and for their religious interests."

The novelty, however, lay in getting the Muslims, both Sunnis and Shi'is,
as well as the Druzes to adopt the communitarian system to which they had
not been subject in the Ottoman Empire. The 1926 constitution, and especially the Mandate policy, aimed to make these three religious groups into
communities on a par with the others. The Muslims living on the coast, cut
off from their religious and political ties with the Arabs of the interior, of
Syria, and Palestine, found it hard to resist this standardization, all the more
so as they felt the need, like the Christians, for their spokesmen to deal with
the governmental authorities. Nonetheless, for a long time they rejected the
plan, and their reluctance was finally overcome only after independence,
when each of the major communities was granted its own legal status: the
Sunnis in 1955, the Druzes in 1962, and the Shi'is in 1967.

As an integral part of the civil organization of Lebanese society,
communitarianism also controlled its politics: article 24 of the constitution
and the electoral law decree the balance of communal representation in the
parliament, while article 95 states: "As a provisional measure . . . the communities shall be equitably represented in the public service and in the composition of the ministry." This legislation, which has never been revised,
thereafter formed the legal basis for treating Lebanese society as a collection
of communal groups. As the jurist Edmond Rabbath noted, it "has within it
the power to expand until it overruns the whole machinery of the state which
then becomes wholly communitarian in character."[1]

The Communities under the Mandate

Clearly, the changeover from Ottoman domination to French tutelage benefited the Catholic populations, particularly those of the Maronite Mountain. They had a feeling of security and confidence in the "mother country" that, combined with their intellectual and professional advancement, encouraged the flowering of their spirit of enterprise. Paradoxically, while their Westernized elites were basically attached to Mount Lebanon, they had come to identify with Western Christendom. On the whole, they ignored or rejected the consequences of including Beirut and Tripoli in their new state.[2] They more or less consciously maintained the gulf separating them from the rest of the country and the other Lebanese populations. At this time, in his *La Montagne inspirée* the famous Maronite poet Charles Corm wrote two lines that are eminently representative of an outlook both naive and arrogant:

> *Mon frère musulman, comprenez ma franchise;*
> *Je suis le vrai Liban, sincère et pratiquant.*

> My dear Muslim brother, appreciate my candor;
> I am the true Lebanon, practicing and sincere.

In 1929, the same spirit moved the then prime minister Emile Eddé to propose, along with a number of measures for reducing the nation's expenses to cope with the economic crisis, closing some of the public schools, which were attended almost exclusively by Muslim pupils.

The Mandatory authorities encouraged and exploited this loyalty and this split. They privileged their Catholic interlocutors, if only because the latter often spoke more fluent French and made up a majority of the employees in the high commissioner's administration in Beirut. The Catholic monasteries and schools flourished. In the special troops (*Troupes spéciales*), most of the recruits were Maronites, Greek Catholics, and Roman Catholics.

Some qualifications need to be made about this dichotomous image of the privileged Christians (largely Maronites) versus the excluded Muslims (mainly Sunnis) under the Mandate. At the time, most of the peasants from the Christian Mountain were exploited and relatively impoverished, much as they had been under the Ottomans. On the other hand, with a show of dynamism the great Beirut traders from all the communities used their position as intermediaries between the French entrepreneurs and the consumers of the Mountain and the interior to make huge profits. In addition, the high commissioner endeavored with some success to gain the confidence of the members of the Muslim elites, particularly among the Shi'is and the Druzes, for the purpose of securing their collaboration and undermining the Arab nationalist movement in Damascus. Realizing that the age of British protection was long gone, the Jumblats of the Shuf played the French card as early as 1920. Members of the great Shi'i families in the south like the Zeins and the Osseirans entered parliament in 1920 and 1922, respectively. But this represented a collaboration between "patrons" replacing collaboration with Istanbul during the empire, and not comparable to the popular movement that inclined the Maronite community toward France.

The unequal distribution of responsibilities and political posts among communities—the reality of power remained in the hands of the high commissioner—was justified by the results of the 1932 census, the only official census in the republic's whole history, for since then the authorities have never taken the risk of facing up to a change in the demographic balance (see table 2).[3] This census counted a few more Christians than Muslims. It placed the number of the Maronites well ahead of all the other communities and so was said to justify conferring the country's presidency, with its extensive executive and legislative powers and its role as supreme arbiter between the patrons, on a Maronite. Though the first president, Charles Dabbas (1926–1934), was Greek Orthodox, all his successors up to the country's independence—Habib Pasha al-Saad (1934–1936), Emile Eddé (1936–1939), Alfred Naccache (1941–1943), and Bishara al-Khuri (1943–1952)—were Maronites, with the exception of the brief interludes of the Protestant Ayyub Thabit and the Greek Orthodox Petro Trad for a few months in 1943. In any case, all were Christians.

Relative Size of Lebanese Communities According to 1932 Census

Communities	Number	%
Maronites	227,800	28.7
Greek Orthodox	77,312	9.7
Greek Catholics	46,709	5.9
Other Christians	44,925	5.7
Sunnis	178,130	22.4
Shi'is	155,035	19.6
Druzes	53,334	6.7
Others	10,181	1.3
Total	793,426	100

Sunni Frustration

Even at the time, the Muslims disputed the accuracy of the census, insisting they were a demographic majority in Lebanon. Their criticism was not, however, just a matter of numbers. It reflected their general hostility toward the state of Greater Lebanon, the regime of political communitarianism, and the domination of the French Mandate, none of which had they asked for or had a chance to object to. They were damaged economically: for a major city with a Sunni majority like the port of Tripoli, drawing a frontier between Lebanon and Syria that made Tripoli part of Lebanon meant the beginning of an inexorable decline, since the traders of Homs, Hama, and Damascus thereafter preferred the better-equipped ports of Beirut and, after 1950, Latakia. For Sidon and its environs, the break-off in trade with Palestine and the suspension of transit through Haifa caused economic dislocations that led to the marginalization and underdevelopment of South Lebanon. The Muslims' frustration also had an equally important cultural and political dimension, fueled by two rejections: that of the domination by Christians compared with a nostalgia for their erstwhile inclusion in the Ottoman Empire, a Muslim power; and that of the division of the Arab nation that had just experienced a united thrill during the revolt of 1916 and the independent government of Damascus.

Under the French Mandate, which ruled that political representation in Lebanon function via communal organization, the Sunnis gradually became one minority among others. Their most typical reaction was to boycott the official institutions. Thus, the community's prominent families—the Salams of Beirut, the Karamehs of Tripoli, or the Sulhs of Sidon—were rarely represented in parliament and even more rarely in the government. Another of their reactions was to attack the Maronite privileges: in January 1932 the participants in the Muslim Congress of Beirut announced that they represented the demographic majority in the country and also paid three-quarters of its taxes. The congress decided on the candidacy of Sheikh Muhammad al-Jisr for president, with the support of many of the Greek Orthodox and even Maronites like Emile Eddé. Tipped off by the Maronite patriarchate, the French high commissioner reacted to this bold move by suspending the constitution for five years.

Paris's policy intensified the friction between the communities regarding the country's future. The treaty of independence signed in November 1936 by the government of the Popular Front reflected the attachment of the Christian majority to Lebanon's separation from Syria and also to French guarantees concerning the status of the nation and respect for its borders. It provided for the stationing of French troops in the country for twenty-five years, while a parallel treaty signed by Syria in September made no mention of

Damascus's demands about certain provinces in Lebanon. Certainly, the Beirut parliament, representing all the communities, unanimously adopted the 1936 treaty. Remaining disengaged from the official institutions, however, the Muslim leaders gathered at the "Congress of the Sahel" demanded a return to a formula of Lebanese autonomy within the framework of an independent Syrian state, and they had the support of popular demonstrations and long strikes.

Toward Independence

Paradoxically, it was the colonial power that helped bring the two antagonistic courses together: for the time being, the obstructionism of the "colonial party" in the French parliament forestalled discussion of the Lebanese and Syrian treaties; later, the establishing of a direct military administration owing to the war silenced all political demands. The prevarications of the leaders of the Free French, after General Charles de Gaulle promised independence in 1941, and the intrigues of the British mission led by General Edward L. Spears, made the Maronite leaders realize that the benefits of French protection were limited, all the more so as a superpower, the United States, was looming on the horizon. The heads of the community had acquired self-confidence; they wanted to control the machinery of government themselves. For their part, the partisans of Syrian Arab unity realized that the war offered them a unique opportunity to have done with the Mandate.

The struggle for independence—which only marginally involved armed conflict—thus became a watchword for most of the Lebanese, who helped the republic overcome the centrifugal tendencies and secure its base of legitimacy. Briefly in 1943, exemplary coordination took place between the two rival political forces, the pro-Lebanon Kataeb Party dominated by the Maronites, and the pro-Arab Najjadeh Party dominated by the Sunnis, and the two parties' joint demonstrations impelled the conservative leaders to forge ahead. This mobilization for independence illustrated the ascendancy of the Lebanese cities, particularly Beirut, which assumed a hegemonic role in the country's life, while the Mountain, as it had since the turn of the century, continued to lose population. Lebanon reasoned less in terms of communities and more in terms of the relations between Christians and Muslims. In the capital's new districts with mixed living conditions, a modern upper bourgeoisie sprang up and broke free of the clan and religious hierarchies of the rural world and, without being wholly secular, perhaps saw themselves as citizens of Lebanon, with all confessions intermingled. At the society's other extreme,[4] rapid growth encouraged the development of a mixed proletariat in the eastern and southern industrial suburbs, evolving a class identity and mobilization.

The Pact

At the government's apex, the new independent Lebanon was symbolized by a close and dynamic collaboration between the Maronite president Bishara al-Khuri and the Sunni prime minister Riyad al-Sulh. This made it possible to harmonize the two conflicting visions of the country and to develop a common policy. Drawn up in lengthy talks between the two men and discussed in al-Khuri's speech upon his election on September 21, 1943, and in al-Sulh's ministerial declaration on October 7, the tacit but formal agreement between Christians and Muslims about the principles that were to govern their political association was named the "National Pact."[5]

The first section of the National Pact deals with the independence of Lebanon, a sovereign state among all states, Western and Arab. A conditional independence, as it were: in return for the Muslims' recognition of the distinct nature of their country, marked by its communitarian system and historic ties with the West, the National Pact upheld the principle that the Christians would renounce any protective links to the European powers; it affirmed the Arab character of the country and its membership in the Arab world, called for cooperation with the Arab nations and even "entering the Arab family" once these countries recognized its independence and territorial integrity and showed respect for its "governmental regime."

The adoption of the National Pact by the Lebanese leaders—Christian and Muslim—should be viewed in its regional and international context at the end of World War II. At the time tensions between the West and the Arab world were far from intractable. The balance of power was profoundly unequal. Even as the Arab nations attained independence, the West exercised economic, political, cultural, and above all military domination of the Middle East. The British sponsored the inter-Arab dialogue prior to the March 1945 signing of the Arab League Pact, and Lebanon ran no risk in joining the League along with Egypt, Saudi Arabia, Iraq, Syria, and Transjordan. Until the disastrous Palestinian war of 1948, which Professor Hisham Sharabi dates as concluding the "liberal era" in the Middle East, the elites of these Arab countries not only cooperated with each other, but even shared likeminded views and goals. Their moderate and liberal parties included Nahhas Pasha's Wafd Party in Cairo, the National Bloc led by Shukri al-Quwwatli, Jamil Mardam and Faris al-Khuri (a Christian) in Damascus, and the Destour party of Bishara al-Khuri. Certainly, the independent nations of Syria and Lebanon still did not exchange ambassadors, but both signed the Arab League

Pact which implied mutual recognition of and respect for each other's territorial integrity, and they engaged in trade and many official visits on a reciprocal basis. The 1950 rupture between their "common interests" (essentially customs administration)—when Lebanon chose liberalism and mercantilism while Syria preferred *dirigisme* and industrialization—though it harmed both partners, gave further proof of their mutual independence. Thus, all in all, Lebanon's choice of two memberships, Western and Arab, and its claim to two identities, Christian and Muslim, did not seem to generate insurmountable contradictions.

The other section of the National Pact diptych concerned Lebanon's internal balance. Basing themselves on article 95 of the constitution and reaffirming the provisional nature of the arrangement, the Lebanese leaders agreed on the division of powers based on political communitarianism, particularly the distribution of the chief political and administrative responsibilities, among the six largest communities: Maronite, Greek Orthodox, Greek Catholic, Sunni, Shi'i, and Druze. At the suggestion of General Spears, the British delegate in Beirut, the number of parliamentary seats proportionally assigned according to data from the 1932 census was to be a multiple of eleven: for each six Christian deputies, the chamber would include five Muslim and Druze deputies. In the government and the civil service, the ratio accepted was 50:50, but according to a hierarchy in which the Maronites still held to the top: the presidency and command of the army. The office of prime minister went to the Sunnis, the presidency of the parliament to the Shi'is, and the vice-presidency to the Greek Orthodox. Certain posts, such as minister of defense, were generally reserved for a Druze, or minister of foreign affairs for a Christian. Thus, on the pretext of securing an "equitable" distribution of power and its perquisites, the criterion of communitarianism took precedence over that of competence at every level of the political hierarchy: the administration, the judicial apparatus, the municipal councils, the army, and even the banking sector.

The National Pact's implications were plainly equivocal, whether in its distribution of offices or in its decisions about foreign policy. On the one hand, Lebanon's political functioning seemed to require acceptance of its principles, but on the other hand, the organization it lay down was to prove ineffective and even counterproductive in the face of the new issues the country now had to confront. At the moment of independence, the National Pact formula was considered "organic" because, following a century of communitarian political experience, it closely fitted the Lebanese social structure and collective mentality. This was, for example, the conviction of Michel Chiha, father of the constitution:

Confessionalism in Lebanon . . . is the guarantee of equitable political
and social representation for the associated confessional minorities. . . .
These minorities take the confessional label because Lebanon has
always been a refuge for freedom of conscience. . . . The confessional
basis of the Lebanese balance is not arbitrary. It does not result from
prejudice, but from the need to recognize distinctive characteristics
that differ as widely as those between political parties. With time,
these differences may diminish and slowly disappear. Presently,
Lebanon's reason for being lies precisely in its distinctive confessional
balance and this is first revealed at the level of legislative power.[6]

An important term in Chiha's discussion is "minority." For the basic
idea in the political communitarianism set up according to a ratio of 6:5 in
the parliament and 50:50 in the government and civil service is that Lebanon
is a collection of minorities where none must take advantage of its numerical
superiority—and even less of a majority—to change the balances adopted.
With the system of quotas, each of the six major communities consequently
possesses an implicit veto power in case of dissension, and *that* constitutes
its guarantee within the state. The balance was maintained through the systematic banishment of political debate about all issues dividing Lebanese
society and through the continual negotiation of compromises between the
political patrons whose prosperity of course depended on the regime's stability. In this sense, the intercommunal consensus formed the very basis of legitimacy for the independent Lebanese state and, of all the Near Eastern
Arab nations, its political system was the one that most closely approached a
liberal democracy.

It only *approached* one, however, for the chief defect in the National
Pact is that it represented a compromise among elites whose goal was to
secure the benefits they could get from their position of power. So it is wrong
to talk of a Lebanese "democracy by consensus" comparable to the Dutch
and Swiss systems, for the Lebanese populations were clearly not consulted
and the system that was adopted had the effect of keeping them in the communal framework under the thumb of the traditional notables, heads of families, landowners, and clerical authorities. A consensus comprehending only
elites eventually polarizes the society and "may become a source of corruption, provincialism, conservatism, and immobility." [7] Furthermore, it slows
down class mobilization and forms a barrier to the individual's loyalty to the
state. So it would be more precise to speak of a "communitarian" pact than
a "national" pact, and more reasonable to seek the chief source of the consensus system's lurchings and dramatic failure in the difference between the
two options, communitarian and national. Furthermore, this was not a pact
between all the communities, but essentially between the two most powerful

ones, the Maronites and the Sunnis, who together dominated the political scene and whom the system thus assured of the lion's share: 30 percent and 20 percent of the deputies, respectively, and the two leading roles. No provision was made for adapting this distribution to changes in the country's demography. Moreover, the definitive reversal of the demographic balance in favor of Muslims that occurred after conclusion of a pact making the Christians ascendant over them reveals the subordinate role of the democratic principle.[8] Rather than expressing a popular consensus, the National Pact of 1943 was, as Michel Chiha wrote, a system of guarantees to minorities.

The 1958 Troubles

In the search for a middle way between two contradictory visions of the country's foreign alliances and between the competing ambitions of several domestic communities, the National Pact offered only limited means for responding to a request by various social groups to participate, for integrating new elites into the government, and for dealing with the spread of class or nationalistic ideologies and pressures from the international system. The events of 1958 well illustrate the role of clientele relations and the effects of political communitarianism in the formulation, intensification, and resolution of dissension in Lebanon. Beset by a pressing demand for modernization and also by regional tensions, the president made decisions to which he was entitled by his inprinciple broad powers. But the steps he took threatened the static balance set forth by the National Pact, whose principles were soon swept away by a grave political crisis.

Domestically, however, the disparity between the demands of the progressivists and the reforms Camille Chamoun proposed after his 1952 election did not presage any very serious clashes—in any case, nothing that threatened to bring on a civil war. Mustering urban militants separated from their traditional leaders, the parties of the left—Arab nationalists, Baathists, the Najjadah, the Communist Party, and the PSP—demanded greater social justice, particularly on behalf of the outlying areas with a Muslim majority. Their platform called for the creation of a central bank, an office for development, and a social security system. The reforms undertaken by President Chamoun, however, amounted to mere change rather than genuine progress. Certainly, freedom of the press was regained and the judicial system improved. Nevertheless, the measures adopted served mainly to reinforce the personal power of the president. The nationalization of certain public services helped him to widen his circle of clientele in the government bureaucracy while the new electoral law of 1953 reduced the number of deputies from seventy-seven to forty-four, threatening to diminish the power of the traditional patrons: the Hamadehs, the Asaads, the Salams, the Karamehs, the Jumblats, the Frangiehs, and the Khuris. Many of those patrons who had ensured Chamoun's victory in 1952 lost in the general elections of 1957, which had been cunningly manipulated by the partisans of the president who relied on the organized forces of his allies, the Kataeb and the SSNP. Opposition then formed between a president—who had managed to get a "matchless chamber" elected, did not deny that he wanted a second term, and had a stranglehold on the resources of the legal system—and, facing him, the conservative patrons who joined the reformers to demand Chamoun's departure from office at the end of his term together with the rebalancing of the executive branch in favor of the prime minister and Muslims in general. Up to that point, the crisis of 1958 closely resembled the one of 1952 in which President al-Khuri was pitted against the National Socialist Front; it could surely have been similarly resolved if regional and international events had not intervened to bring about an overload and breakdown in the operation of the Lebanese system.

Beginning in the mid-1950s, the unusually tense situation in the Middle East affected the very principles of the National Pact. The United States inaugurated a dynamic policy supplanting the declining colonial powers of France and Great Britain. The Cold War took on a new dimension in the Middle East when, in 1951, Washington presented the Arab nations with a plan for a common defense against the Soviets. The cornerstone of American policy in Southwest Asia was the 1955 Baghdad Pact between Turkey and Iraq. On the Arab side too, however, the situation had changed since the struggle for independence in the 1930s and the time of liberal democracies of the 1940s. The collective defeat in the Palestinian war sounded the death knell for several parliamentary regimes and set the stage for a string of military coups, beginning with those in Syria in 1949. The coming to power of the "free officers" of Cairo in 1952 ushered in an era of militant Arab nationalism, led by Gamal Abdel Nasser, that was sparked by the appeals of the 1955 Conference of the Non-Aligned Nations in Bandung, Indonesia. The Arab nations calling themselves progressive rallied to support Egypt, and their concrete response to the signing of the Baghdad Pact was to establish a common command over the armies of Egypt, Syria, and Saudi Arabia. The following year, the Franco-Israeli-British attack on Egypt at Suez generated a wave of popular outrage and a number of breaks in diplomatic relations with London and Paris. Between Western liberalism and Arab progressivism, between imperialism and revolution, the Arab East was henceforth divided into two camps: on the one side, Jordan and Iraq; on the other, Syria and Egypt. Lebanon had to choose.

Choosing, however, meant disturbing the neutralist equilibrium of the National Pact. Shortly after the signing of the Baghdad Pact, President

Chamoun made a friendly visit to Turkey; following Suez, he refused to break with France and Great Britain. In March 1957, he backed the Eisenhower Doctrine for coordinating the pro-Western forces in the Middle East against the "Red peril." The denunciation of this foreign policy of alignment gave the traditional patrons and progressivist leaders a chance to take concerted action against the chief executive. The power of conviction of Nasser's words, broadcast from Cairo by the "Voice of the Arabs," galvanized the Sunni populations in particular.[9] In February 1958, Egypt and Syria's unification into the United Arab Republic (UAR) rekindled the pan-Arab enthusiasms of the 1930s in Lebanon, all the more as the Syrian leaders multiplied their appeals for unity, and similarly Nasser his diatribes against President Chamoun. The UAR roused the fears of the advocates of Lebanese independence. Thenceforth, discord concerning foreign policy was to be added to internal dissensions. One part of Lebanon, dominated by the Muslims, was opposed to the government. Another part, predominantly Christian, supported it. Certainly, many Christians, in particular Paul Méouchi, the Maronite patriarch himself, went over to the opposition—some for ideological reasons, others to bring down a rival. Few Muslims, however, sided with the government, all the more so as it would have been costly for the Sunni patrons not to share the popular enthusiasm for Nasserism.

The revolution of 1958 produced some 2,000 to 4,000 victims, and did considerable harm to Lebanon's merchant economy. It seems benign, however, compared to the famine of 1915 or the ravages of the war to come. Nevertheless, it warrants special attention because of its character as a portent for the liberal and communitarian Lebanon, and because the protagonists of the war in the 1970s were tempted to repeat some of its strategies out of a conviction that the same causes will produce the same effects: the assassination of a journalist close to the opposition in May 1958; a general strike by the Sunnis of the large cities, notably Tripoli; altercations with the police; a military insurrection against the center of power, particularly the presidential palace of Bayt al-Din in the Shuf; the mustering of "peripheral" Lebanon—Tripoli and Akkar, Hermil, the Bikaa—and the Shuf, against the "central" Lebanon of the Mountain, Kisrawan, Matn, and again the Shuf, while the still unorganized Palestinians remained on the sidelines; a division between primarily Christian East Beirut and primarily Muslim West Beirut; confrontations between armed groups, particularly between the SSNP defender of Lebanese independence and the pan-Arabist PSP, while the army held back from intervening for fear of its own breakup; official accusations of "massive interference" on the part of Syria, and the sending in June of 135 observers from the United Nations Observation Group in Lebanon, who proved unable to confirm or disconfirm the infiltration of weapons and combatants from the Syrian half of the UAR; a presidential appeal for U.S. military intervention, complied with on July 14 because of the Iraqi revolution's overthrow of the Hashimite monarchy, a worrisome event for the West; 15,000 U.S. marines backed up by the 40,000 men of the American Sixth Fleet patrolling Beirut while British parachutists landed in Amman, Jordan; American pressures to extract a promise from Camille Chamoun to leave office in September and to support the election of General Fuad Shihab to the presidency; Shihab's naming in September of Rashid Karameh, patron of Tripoli and head of the opposition, as prime minister in order to guarantee both an opening to Nasserism and a domestic rebalancing in favor of the Muslims; the "counterrevolution" of September-October, led by the Kataeb in accordance with communal alignments, Christians against Muslims, in a short, but bloody incident; and communitarian compromise with the formation on October 14 of a ministerial cabinet of four members, two Sunnis including Rashid Karameh, and two Maronites, Pierre Gemayel and Raymond Eddé, under the slogan "Neither conquerors nor conquered."

The ideas inspired by the 1958 crisis, especially those concerning the National Pact, were contradictory. Although the Lebanese concluded the turmoil with relief and the intention to turn the page as quickly as possible, their assessments of the events were profoundly divergent. Some were convinced their country's independence and liberal orientation had been preserved and, thanks to American intervention, an imminent takeover by Nasser avoided. Others were delighted to see an end put to Chamoun's corrupt regime and its abuses, and the beginnings of a more just social policy and a reintegration of their country in a now mobilized Middle East. For most, it seemed absolutely necessary to preserve the balance intended in the National Pact, and that this process of regulating tensions guaranteed the survival and coexistence of all. The following decade—or near-decade (1958–67)—confirmed the instrumental nature of the National Pact during a time in which Lebanon enjoyed security and prosperity. While preserving its relations with the West, the country opened up further to the Arab world to which it presented itself as a land of asylum and dialogue where it was happy to play the mediator, with the hypocrisy of an ultra-laissez-faire political system that was more hospitable to great fortunes than to the poor, and to Christians more than Muslims. Domestically, stricter application of the 50:50 relation made possible the promotion of groups and individuals hitherto considered outside the system. The public freedoms and individual security Lebanon's residents enjoyed were rare advantages in the Near East.

Nonetheless, it cannot be overlooked that, through its very principle, the National Pact helped fuel the crisis of 1958. First, the pact defined a Lebanese foreign policy shot through with contradictions that were bound to blow up when it had to confront the dynamics of international relations in the 1950s. Chamoun betrayed the National Pact by attempting to assimilate Lebanon to the Western camp; the leaders of the opposition did likewise by playing the Nasserism card to muster their clients in the competition for power. Was it thinkable, however, that both should refrain from taking any political position and stick with immobilism?

Thereafter, the Pact imposed the communitarian division and, more broadly, the dichotomy between Christians and Muslims as a paradigm and a framework for mobilization in Lebanese political life. The Lebanese mobilized at the start of the 1958 crisis on the basis of social and political demands, defending or attacking a foreign policy. But political communitarianism soon dictated their alignments according to clan, religious, and regional solidarities that were unrelated to the political positions on either side. From then on, the only accusation needed against an adversary, one that was enough to fuel a confrontation, was that of being different.

Finally, in the resolution of the 1958 crisis, the return to the principles of the National Pact meant giving up most of the demands that had caused the revolution, putting on ice many reforms then envisaged, and returning to an ambiguous foreign policy. It was as if the political elites, strengthened in their recovered consensus, believed even more in the regime's immutable stability—and this in a Near East that was to undergo dramatic upheavals.

The Palestinian Factor

COULD Lebanon hope to remain sheltered from the crises and wars that plagued its part of the world? Could the comparison with Switzerland, so dear to the New Phoenicians viewing their country as a tourist paradise and banking refuge, also be valid politically? Even today, despairing of a rebirth for the whole and independent Lebanon of the National Pact, certain exiled Lebanese embrace the idea of making it the Middle East's first politically neutral country. Then Beirut—for this view focuses on the capital, relegating the rest of the country to the rank of dependent areas—could effectively devote itself to economic, financial, technological, and human-resources trade between the developing Arab world and the industrialized Western countries, and play its role as a mediating peacemaker to the full.

Political and military events in the Middle East since World War II have made this utopian plan completely unrealistic: the birth of Israel in 1948 was not accounted for in this Lebanese formula, nor was the gradual escalation of the Arab-Israeli conflict over the Palestinians' demand for nationhood. On Lebanon's very borders, Israel represents a challenge to the merchant and communitarian state: the same scant territory on the edge of the Mediterranean, the same meager natural resources, even a privileged relation to the Western economies and political regimes, but a radical disconnection from its Arab neighbors. The Zionist leaders' decision to make their state a Jewish state whose Arab populations—Muslims, Druzes, and Christians—do not enjoy the same rights as the Jewish citizens was in its very principle opposed to the Lebanese scheme of coexistence and equilibrium. The Lebanese system is unstable, marked by impasses in functioning, open friction, and an edgy conservatism. The Israeli system is efficient, admirably democratic, and exceptionally dynamic, at least when considered from the viewpoint of its Jewish populations. But seen in the context of the underdevelopment of the whole Near East, and taking into account the rights and aspirations of all its inhabitants, Jews and Arabs alike, without counting the hundreds of thousands of people who fled upon the creation of the State of Israel, the comparison between Lebanon's imperfect pluralistic choice and Israel's exclusive and operative choice makes the wisdom of the latter questionable. Can either the Lebanese preference for democracy "by consensus" among elites or Israel's preference for a democracy by exclusion serve as a standard for criticizing the authoritarian regimes of the Middle East? Can either of these claim to be a model for the region's political evolution? And though the adventure of Lebanese democracy has failed amidst the strains of a long, cruel war, does this represent the triumph of the Israeli "model"?

Not only does Lebanon compete with Israel in its relations with the West and in the political management of its society, but the fundamental opposition between the Arab and Jewish nationalisms, and the Arab assessment of Zionist colonization as a tool of Western imperialism, involve a political stance in the Arab-Israeli conflict. The ideal neutrality that would ensure its security and prosperity is dead. When on November 29, 1947, the United Nations resolved to partition Palestine under the British Mandate into two states, one Arab and one Jewish, Lebanon sided with its allies in the Arab League in opposition to the proposed dismemberment, and it took part in the attack against the Zionist forces shortly after the State of Israel was proclaimed in May 1948. After breaking through the border in June, the two Lebanese battalions retreated, and for a few months the Israeli armed forces occupied several villages in the south. The armistice signed with Israel on March 1, 1949, parallel to the agreements with the other belligerents, Syria in particular, made express provision for the return to the international border of 1920 between Lebanon and Palestine, under the control of United Nations observers for the surveillance of the truce, and of a Mixed Armistice Commission headquartered in Naqoura on the border between the two nations.

Thereafter, the fifty-mile border between Lebanon and Israel, which gradually rises from west to east up to the foothills of Mount Hermon, was closed to the circulation of goods and people. For more than twenty years it remained calm but completely sealed, reflecting relations between Lebanon and Israel: there was no recognition or relations of any kind, but there were no hostilities either. During this period, Beirut's official attitude clearly differed from the Arab community's increasingly militant positions, particularly those of Israel's two great neighbors, Syria and Egypt, during the Suez crisis and the Franco-Israeli-British aggression against Egypt in 1956 and then again in 1963 following Israel's unilateral decision to divert part of the Jordan River for its own use. For Beirut, it was as though the partition of 1947 and the war of 1948–49 had permanently settled the Palestine question. With the return to its international borders of 1920, Lebanon went back to its affairs and commercial activities, which in their way served the Arab community.

Still, Lebanon did not escape one dimension of Arab solidarity, and this belied its claim to isolation: the Palestinian presence in the country. During the summer of 1948, some 140,000 Palestinians were driven out of Galilee and crossed the border into Lebanon. Of all the Arab nations neighboring Israel, Lebanon was second only to Jordan in admitting Palestinians. Most of the refugees were peasants who brought nothing with them, thinking they would be able to regain their lands once hostilities ceased. The United Nations Relief and Work Agency, assistance arm of the UN, took responsibility for half of them, assigning them to fifteen camps on the edges of Beirut, Tripoli, and Sidon, and in the south, near Tyre and Nabatiye. The Israeli authorities' refusal to allow them back in the country, however, transformed them into de facto permanent residents of Lebanon, where they took full part in the country's social and economic life. Furthermore, on their arrival the Lebanese authorities "communalized" the Palestinian refugees by preferentially settling Christian families in two camps in the capital's northern suburbs of Dbayyeh and Jisr al-Basha, and the army's security forces, the Deuxième Bureau, assumed strict control over the new immigrants.

It would be incorrect to see the influx of Palestinian refugees into Lebanon after 1948 as an additional and costly burden on the Lebanese economic system. The arrival of a cheap and relatively skilled labor force lacking both political rights and the right to unionize was a godsend for many of the agricultural landowners, who offered them seasonal jobs, and also for the entrepreneurs and industrialists, so that certain service sectors like hotels and air transport welcomed them in large numbers. Moreover, in Beirut, which had just been freed from competition with Haifa, the local bourgeoisie had no cause to resent an urban bourgeoisie that settled there with its capital, its know-how, and its spirit of enterprise and gave new dynamism to the Lebanese economy. The beacon of success of the Palestinian diaspora in Lebanon was Yusuf Baydas, leader of the Intra group, which in a few short years became the country's leading bank, only to be brought down by a clever operation by a coalition of its Lebanese competitors in October 1966. Generally, whereas the government authorities rather favored granting Lebanese nationality to the Palestinian Christians, who made up some 10 percent of the refugee total—the problem of the numerical deficit of Christians in relation to Muslims was already critical—the Intra affair showed the mistrust and even hostility provoked by the Palestinians' settling in Lebanon, even though they were fellow Arabs and of the same religious confessions.

1967: A Defeat for Lebanon

The Palestinians upset the delicate balance of the Lebanese consensus primarily because of the climate of the inter-Arab cold war hovering over the Middle East since the 1950s. The focus of the grievances was the conflict with Israel over the lost homeland of 1948, the object of a dangerous escalation among the leaders of the major Arab nations in the region. Of the three countries most involved, Jordan—which had annexed the Arab part of Palestine partitioned in 1947, or at least what remained of it—was content with the status quo with Israel. The announced goal of the leaders of Egypt and Syria was to liberate occupied Palestine, but these countries lacked both the economic infrastructure and the military might to enable them to do battle. They knew this, but they also knew that popular support for their fragile regimes largely depended on their adherence to the unitarian, progressivist, and liberating message that served to legitimate them. An initial wave of Nasserist enthusiasm swept over Lebanon in 1958. Starting in 1964, however, the rivalry between Egyptian Gamal Abdel Nasser, General Abdul Karim Kassem in Iraq, and the Baathists in power in Syria (the United Arab Republic combining Egypt and Syria had broken up in 1961) led directly to war, which the Israeli military command had expected and well prepared for. The first infiltrations by the Palestinian fedayeen through Jordanian territory with Syria's support provoked Israeli reprisals and a cycle of border clashes that grew increasingly fierce throughout 1966. On behalf of Arab solidarity, Egypt goaded its allies into acts of provocation. Nevertheless, the justified anxiety then felt by many Lebanese lessened neither their economic prosperity nor the casualness of their political leaders.

At first sight, the dramatic Arab defeat of 1967 scarcely touched Lebanon. The government took some passive defense measures, provided its war-making allies with technical and medical assistance, and passively observed Israeli fighters flying over its territory. Popular reactions were fairly moderate, even though they reflected the internal antagonisms in Lebanese society: the Maronite Mountain of Kisrawan saw general rejoicing at the announcement of the dazzling Zahal victory over the Arab nationalist and revolutionary forces; in the Muslim areas of Beirut, Westerners were subjected to abuse while the United States hastily evacuated its citizens to Cyprus and Athens; the resignation announcement by Nasser, the great leader and the great loser of the June war, prompted emotional demonstrations in his support, echoing those in Cairo. But crisis quickly resumed. Of the four Arab countries bordering Israel, only Lebanese territory was spared invasion: Egypt had lost the Sinai and Gaza; Jordan, Jerusalem and the West Bank; Syria, the Golan Heights. Israel immediately announced that it would not hand back these provinces, except for the eastern part of Jerusalem, unless a peace treaty was

signed, thus forcing the Arab leaders and their ruined credibility into a political impasse. In this sense, the 1967 defeat was not just a bitter military
fiasco, but also one for the Arab progressivists in the face of the conservative
pro-Western nations, chief among them the monarchy of Saudi Arabia.[1] The
period of the war crisis was followed by a more realistic climate of political
openness and free enterprise hailed by the gratified Lebanese elites. The pan-
Arabist utopia was superseded by the special interests of each state—Syrian,
Egyptian, Jordanian, and even specifically Palestinian interests—to the point
that Lebanon was less isolated in its demand for the "right to be different."
Regionally, the war weakened the fragile national economies that were thenceforth unable to overcome their dependence on financial aid from powers like
the Soviet Union, Saudi Arabia, and the United States. On the other hand,
Lebanon, not content simply to recycle this money, which mostly passed
through its banks, seized the chance to give a fresh boost to its industrial
production.

Nevertheless, the war that it did not take part in, and the defeat that was
not actually its own, had more dramatic consequences for Lebanon than for
any other Arab country. In 1970 it became, and until 1982 would remain the
chosen terrain for the Palestinians' struggle to recover their lost homeland.
Indeed, freed from the tutelage of the Arab nations, the Palestinians took
their future into their own hands. The number of resistance fighters grew
from several hundred before the June 1967 war to several thousand in the
three years that followed. The Palestine Liberation Organization (PLO), created in 1964 under the patronage of the Arab League, then dominated by
Nasser, was joined by al-Fatah in 1968 under the leadership of Yasir Arafat,
who worked to ensure its autonomy, got the new National Charter adopted,
and developed a new strategy for the struggle.[2] The classic tactics of conven-
tional warfare between regular armies, which failed utterly in June 1967,
were replaced by the use of guerrilla operations and attacks from bases located in areas bordering Israel—no longer Egypt, which was too far from the
front, but Syria, which controlled the Sa'iqa [thunder] movement connected
with its Baathist government, and particularly Jordan, half of whose population were refugees from 1948 and 1967.

Despite its even tighter military control over the refugees than the
Hashimite kingdom's, Lebanon too became a base of action for the resistance. According to the PLO's Research Center, more than 240,000 Palestinians were living in Lebanon in 1970, and in the next two years were joined
by more than 100,000 others from Jordan. The camps, where a third of the
refugees were still living, brought in arsenals, and the militias trained their
commandos; a year after the Israeli victory, ammunitions and militants began to flow from Jordan to southern Lebanon, passing through Syria and
then the western slope of Mount Hermon north of Rashiya and Hasbeya as

far as Kfar Shuba and Khiam in the Arqoub, from which the fedayeen overlooked the Israeli kibbutzim in the Hula basin. West of the border area, the
three camps at Tyre and the two camps at Sidon—small apartment houses
and permanent barracks—sheltered more than half the Palestinian population of the country's camps, breeding grounds for the resistance, which also
set up permanent bases in the central region, at Ainata and Aita al-Cha'b.
Isolated villages of the Jabal Amil and the Arqoub, hitherto indifferent to
regional tensions and ignorant of governmental affairs in Beirut, which was
only a few dozen miles and five hours' travel away, saw commando groups
take up positions on their edges and sometimes in their centers, and from
there launch armed operations while calling on the inhabitants to mobilize.
Late in 1968, several incidents occurred daily between Lebanon's Palestinian
resistance and the Israeli army, most often exchanges of fire across the border and, more rarely, commando raids and acts of sabotage in Israel.

In the "Black September" of 1970, the PLO, which had rejected the UN
Security Council's resolution 242 of November 1967 because it did not recognize the Palestinians' right to nationhood but considered them refugees,
criticized both President Nasser and King Hussein of Jordan for accepting
American secretary of state William Rogers's plan for settling the conflict
with Israel. The PLO came into open conflict with Hussein's regime. Led by
its extremist wing—the Democratic Front for the Liberation of Palestine
(DFLP) and the Popular Front for the Liberation of Palestine (PFLP)—the
PLO clashed with the Jordanian army in a battle that decimated its fighters.
As a very grave result, the PLO lost its chief base of intervention: starting in
June 1971, Jordan prohibited Palestinian political organizations and combatants from circulating within its borders. Thereafter, Beirut and Lebanon
became the chief center of the Palestinian resistance.

The large Lebanese cities housed the administrative and cooperative institutions, orphanages, hospitals, research centers, press centers, an information agency, and the like, for the social, cultural, and educational structuring
of Palestinian society, which became an important goal of the new generation of the exiled people's elites. Most of the Palestinian political and military organizations, particularly those belonging to the PLO, were headquartered in Beirut or along its southern edges. They employed several thousand
management-level workers in dynamic companies, that fit well into the Lebanese system and were financially strong thanks to contributions from the
Palestinian diaspora and annual subsidies from the Arab states. Even more
important, the resistance in Lebanon numbered several tens of thousands of
combatants, more men than in the Lebanese army. Buoyed up by a wave of
militancy in Palestinian society, but also in the neighboring Arab regions and
especially Lebanon, the resistance grew in numbers and visibility: armed men
in combat uniform, their officers' jeeps being driven in the heart of the city,

troops and ammunition transports, support rallies, and scenes of military training became familiar to a civilian population that nonchalantly thought it justifiable to profit from the spectacular dynamism of the country's economic and cultural life. Seen from Beirut, the south, where the Israeli-Palestinian clashes occurred, was far away, economically insignificant, and sociologically backward. Lebanon didn't yet know that it was at war—a foreign war and yet very close by, for the Palestinians made up nearly 15 percent of its population—that its largest armed force was the resistance, and, above all, that Israel had identified it as the leading source of danger.

A Latent War

The Israeli government considered Lebanon responsible for the Palestinian resistance operations on two counts. First, were the border incidents and the incursions of the fedayeen, which the Lebanese army should have interdicted out of respect for the 1949 armistice, stipulating that "no element of the land, naval, or air forces, military or paramilitary, of any of the parties, including irregular forces, must commit any act of war or hostility of any kind." Then came Palestinian commando raids against Israeli interests and citizens throughout the world, since these commandos belonged to groups based in Beirut where they got their training and orders, and from where they went off to carry out their terrorist operations. This explains why the Israelis directed their army's reprisals against the Lebanese quite as much as against the Palestinians: thus, in June 1968, the village of Meiss al-Jabal was the target of a mortar attack in response to Palestinian gunfire across the border. On December 28, in reprisal for an attack in Athens two months earlier by the PFLP, who had transited through camps in Lebanon, the Israeli air force blew up thirteen planes of Lebanon's national Middle East Airlines at the Beirut airport. Bolstered by international opinion, notably by the strong protests of French president Charles de Gaulle, the Lebanese government felt it was the victim of a great injustice. Between June 1968 and June 1974, the Lebanese army counted more than 30,000 Israeli violations of their national territory, including Israeli "policing" operations, control measures taken with impunity using patrols and fixed observation points, blows at the civilian population in the camps or at resistance leaders in the cities, and attacks aimed at Lebanon itself: its border area, Beirut, and further north. This figure, which is substantial but abstract, says little about the daily insecurity of the southern villagers during this period, the destruction of houses, the costly and dangerous presence of Palestinian combatants, the human losses, the obstacles to travel and farming, and the inevitable exodus toward Sidon and Beirut that accentuated the poverty of the Arqoub and Jabal Amil. In February 1972 and again in September, in retaliation for the massacre of its athletes at the Olympic Games in Munich, the Israeli army invaded the south, penetrating as far as several points along the Litani River for the purpose of neutralizing the fedayeen and their Lebanese sympathizers; on each occasion, the Israelis left more than 100 dead and destroyed more than 150 houses.

The primary goal of Israeli operations in Beirut and against other Lebanese targets was to get the government to order its army to intervene and to put a halt to the Palestinian operations. The escalation of reprisals had been wholly effective in the case of Jordan, which had violently liquidated the Palestinian armed forces on its territory in September 1970. In Lebanon it had a strong psychological impact: not only were the Israeli raids devastating the country's economic potential and producing in the population mixed feelings of solidarity with and bitterness toward the Palestinians, but they also were endangering the country's political equilibrium by upsetting the consensus about national defense. Above all, the escalation produced a reaction in the army. The 1968 operation at the airport in Khalde had been an early blow. In April 1973, the presence in Beirut during the night of several Israeli commandos who assassinated several leaders of al-Fatah in their homes "caused widespread stupefaction. Lebanon thus was not only a weak, but also a defenseless country whose army had not made a move."[3] Faced with these bold attacks, anxiety vied with anger both at the resistance, whose provocations endangered the country's security, and at the army that had once again disclosed its passivity regarding Israel. Lebanon was abruptly confronted with questions it had dodged since gaining its independence: questions about its defense policy, its Arab policy, and its policy toward the Palestinians.

On the first question, a national slogan proved to be hollow. "Lebanon's strength lies in its weakness" poorly masked the critical shortcomings of the Lebanese army: not so much its numerical insignificance—around 15,000 men and no national conscription—and its outmoded equipment—the purchases of materiel from abroad were more often a matter of earning a commission for the intermediaries than of national defense—as its strongly communitarian structure; its increasing politicization was perhaps not unrelated to the fact that its commander-in-chief, Fuad Shihab, became president in 1958. The troops came from poverty-stricken areas with rampant unemployment, like the large Maronite market town of Qubbayat in Akkar, and especially from the Bikaa and the Shi'ite south: in 1970, 62 percent of the army's privates were Muslims. At the top of the hierarchy, the majority of the command was Druze (because of their military tradition) and Maronite, and had close ties to the country's president; its positions on alliances and defense were pro-Western; it was increasingly tempted to take actions without giving an account to a troubled political power.

Regarding Lebanon's solidarity with the Arabs and its policy toward the Palestinians, voices were raised pointing out that the army's immobility in the south was foolish, that Lebanon was no longer safe from Israeli designs (the 1919 debate over the waters of the Litani River had not been forgotten), and that wisdom dictated the coordination of its defense policy with that of its Arab neighbors and especially the Palestinian resistance. On the other hand, some Lebanese had heard the Israeli message loud and clear: promptly stamp out the presence of the Palestinian army, chief cause of the Israeli attacks on the country. Very understandably, disagreement about the mounting dangers followed the main cleavage between the predominantly Maronite Christian Lebanists and the mostly Muslim Arabists; the Maronite leaders engaged in a bid to encourage the army to confront the fedayeen; on the other side, the Muslim leaders, although normally allied with them in the same traditional political class, denounced the president's Palestinian policy as repressive. The disagreement, however, was also marked by a new split, one between conservatives and progressives.

The initial clashes between the Palestinian resistance and the Lebanese army attempting to impose its authority over it occurred in 1966. Later, the rise in power of the PLO and the Israeli raid of 1968 caused a hardening of the army and a series of engagements in April 1969 in Beirut, the south, and the Bikaa. President Charles Helou (elected in 1964) and Prime Minister Rashid Karameh came into direct public opposition; the president insisted on Lebanese sovereignty, while the prime minister declared it indissolubly linked to the fedayeen's freedom of action. The resumption of clashes between the army and the resistance, which in October took the form of a pitched battle in the south, provoked the Baathist leaders in Damascus to react against Lebanon, accusing it of betraying the fighters for a holy Arab cause. The border was blockaded and units of the Sa'iqa entered the country. On the other hand, the Saudi leaders almost openly encouraged the Lebanese president to stand firm against the Palestinian movement threatening international order and spreading dangerous revolutionary propaganda. Egyptian president Nasser, aware of the menace to the Lebanese and the Palestinians from both Israel and Syria, tendered his services as mediator. To assuage public opinion at home, preserve their future, and pursue on Lebanese territory the fratricidal rivalries that for years had absorbed their energy, the Arab nations of the area were quite prepared to burden the Beirut government with the Palestinian question that they themselves wished to be free of. The two great powers, the United States and the Soviet Union, were indifferent to Lebanon's fate, one through an excess of confidence, the other by ideological choice. Moreover, the merchants and bankers in Lebanon on business, the tourists on vacation, and the diplomats and officers using it as an observation post on the Arab and Iranian world generally had nothing to say about the worrisome developments in the country.

The Cairo Accord, signed on November 13, 1969, between the commander in chief of the Lebanese army, General Emile Bustani—the political leaders deliberately kept in the background—and Yasir Arafat himself, faithfully reflected the complex relations between the Lebanese government and the PLO: it was secret, vague, contradictory, open to endless revisions, and subject to daily violations. Its text,[4] moreover, appeared to be the juxtaposition of the claims of each of the two signatories: on the one hand, it gave "authorization to the Palestinians residing in Lebanon to take part in the Palestinian revolution through armed struggle" and acknowledged that this "Palestinian armed struggle is an action that serves Lebanon's interests, for it serves the interests of the Palestinian revolution and all Arabs"; but on the other hand, it gave notice that "the Lebanese authorities, civilian and military, will continue to exercise their full rights and responsibilities in all areas of Lebanon under all circumstances." Concretely, the annexes to the agreement confirmed the extraterritoriality of the refugee camps under the control of Palestinian military police and the authorization of armed fedayeen to move to and from the southern combat zones, particularly the Arqoub, where the Lebanese army was even directed to supply them with provisions and medical assistance.

The PLO's situation in Lebanon was not very different from that of the liberation movements based in the frontline nations of southern Africa: under retaliatory fire from the Union of South Africa, Angola and Mozambique were caught between their solidarity and their desire to put a brake on the commando activities operating out of their territory. In Lebanon, the differences—both ideological (revolution versus status quo) and strategic (war versus coexistence with Israel)—between the armed Palestinian movement and the leaders of the government were even deeper than any of the protagonists dared make public. Certain radical Palestinian organizations like the PFLP (founded in 1967) and the DFLP (founded in 1969) had the stated goal of "confronting reactionary Arab regimes"; they made no distinction between the liberation of Palestine and the Arab revolution; they fraternized with the Lebanese left and even gave it new impetus. Even when they had a purely national Palestinian orientation, like al-Fatah, and meant to respect the host country, these organizations, because of their situation as the dominant force and their need to pursue their anti-Israel goal, could not avoid coming into conflict with Lebanese interests and needs.

Starting with the Cairo Accord, the member groups of the PLO went on to interpret broadly, or simply to ignore, the limits imposed on them by this agreement, thus causing the escalation of reprisals and, beginning in 1974, even provoking "preventive" Israeli operations against Lebanon. Negotiations, clarifications, and promises to evacuate sensitive frontier zones, or to have the combatants unarmed when they moved about outside the camps, remained fruitless, so that the civilian population ended up bitterly resenting the presence of the fedayeen.

At the beginning of May 1973, the Lebanese army, humiliated by its failure to reestablish state authority in the south and tested by several clashes with the resistance forces, tried to take over the camps on the edges of Beirut. The Lebanist parties, particularly the Kataeb and Camille Chamoun's National Liberal Party, urged the army to do battle, while the Israeli leaders publicly exhorted it to follow Jordan's example of 1970–71. The siege, however, which was supported by aerial bombing, soon sparked a popular uprising by the supporters of resistance and Arab unity, who showed their distrust of and even hostility toward the army. Tripoli and Sidon rebelled and the residents of the Muslim areas of Beirut took to the streets. The clashes produced more than 100 Lebanese and Palestinian deaths, and ended in the prime minister's resignation while the president announced that he would not let "the resistance behave like an occupation army." The protocol of the Hotel Melkart on May 17 opened the way for a fragile truce, but also kept the regular army out of a crisis that would later intensify. An army that avoided confrontation with Israel but attacked Palestinians was already an object of protest. Because the army also proved unable to defend the integrity of Lebanon's borders, it lost its legitimacy as a national defense force. When its leaders decided once again to have it intervene, it could only splinter into opposing factions. And when in the northern suburbs of Beirut in July 1974 the first serious skirmish occurred between the Palestinian fedayeen and the forces of the Kataeb Party, the war in Lebanon became a war between militias.

The successive episodes of clashes and negotiations between the Lebanese army and the Palestinian resistance forces took place under the gaze and with the mediation and even intervention of the Arab players. Kuwait, Boumedienne's Algeria—then at the height of its diplomatic activities—and the Arab League in the person of its secretary-general Mahmud Riyad were the chief negotiators of compromise solutions that did nothing to settle the basic problem of the Palestinians' loss of their national territory. Egypt, of course, but especially Syria took a close interest in the Palestinians' liberation struggle, which was connected with their own efforts to regain the provinces they had lost in 1967. Cairo and Damascus supported the fedayeen's actions based in Lebanon—particularly those based in Lebanon—and pressured Beirut to grant the fighters facilities and extraterritoriality. The Syrian government, while refusing to intervene on the side of the Palestinians in Jordan in September 1970, sent units of the Sa'iqa and the Palestine Liberation Army (PLA) to Lebanon to fight beside the PLO in 1969 and again in May 1973.

Nineteen seventy-three was the year of the October War, which was launched in a context of a rationalization of political life and a cooling off of ideological fever and, above all, of a retreat from the pan-Arab aspirations in favor of national mobilizations. The Arab regimes of the Middle East adopted a new strategy concerning Israel, whose two main features were to work together with the United States from the Rogers Plan of 1970 onward, and to be limited in its goals. The following year, this strategy was accepted by the PLO, which had reverted to a primarily Palestinian plan. In July 1974, supported by broad international recognition, notably at the United Nations, the PLO endorsed the principle of an independent Palestinian state limited to the West Bank and Gaza, and prepared to take part in the international negotiations in Geneva. For the Lebanese state, the process meant the end of a condition of latent war, the abrogation of the privileges granted to the resistance by the Cairo Accord, and the possibility of a full reestablishment of its sovereignty, even if several hundreds of thousands of Palestinians chose to remain on its territory, from then on as resident aliens. On behalf of the entire Arab community, Lebanese president Suleiman Frangieh went to the UN General Assembly to defend the national rights of the Palestinians: Who more than Lebanon could wish for an end to the injustice done to the Palestinians?

Nevertheless, this return to the state order in the Near East was not to take place in Lebanon as in the other Arab countries. Israel's intransigence excluded the PLO from multilateral negotiations in Geneva, while certain resistance movements like the PFLP rejected the compromise solution adopted by the Palestine National Council in 1974. The sequence of Lebanese-Palestinian-Israeli incidents of violence accelerated enormously. The Palestinian powder keg, skillfully confined to Lebanese territory by neighboring regimes determined to maintain order in their own lands, added fire and blood to a Lebanese society already inflamed by its domestic divisions.

8

A Society in Crisis

For some people, the matter appeared self-evident. The resistance organizations were pursuing their struggle on Lebanon's home territory, and the neighboring Arab countries were in turn brandishing threats and interventions, while the Israeli army was escalating its retaliatory operations in contempt of national sovereignty. Lebanon succumbed to a state of war, the victim of a conspiracy; if the country had not been deliberately saddled with the Palestine issue by regimes only too happy to be relieved of it, and perhaps even pleased to see the ruin of Lebanon's prosperity and political equilibrium, it would have had enough resources to deal with the changes within its society. Many of the Lebanese "isolationists" naturally bought this assumption: they wanted Lebanon to break off relations with its Arab neighbors, bring the Palestinians to heel, and make peace with Israel. But this hypothesis was also invoked in various political circles in the country since all saw the Israeli aggressions, invasions, destructions, and occupations as a direct result of the Palestinians' presence in Lebanon. It may even have tempted the political leaders in Damascus who were trying to "settle" the Lebanese and Palestinian questions separately and successively so as to untangle the Lebanese knot and have a "Syrian" peace prevail over their neighbor.

Lebanon's geostrategic position as a small country interposed between Syria and Israel, its twofold Western and Arab membership confirmed by the National Pact, and its merchant role meant, however, that the goals of unyoking the Lebanese from the Palestinian problem and of insulating Lebanon from the regional tensions of the Near East were largely illusory. A Lebanon that was cut off from its Near and Middle Eastern Arab neighbors would simply no longer be Lebanon. Nevertheless, there is a Lebanese distinctiveness in the face of the Israeli-Arab conflict and the Palestinian question. The other Arab countries of the area had also been ensnared in the war; they too had to cope with the presence of hundreds of thousands of Palestinian refugees and the organization of armed struggle based on their territory. Egypt, Syria, and Jordan, however, were sufficiently well organized to prevent the Palestinian problem from destabilizing them, though possibly at the cost of terrible confrontations. Lebanon, on the other hand, was already a divided state, and since the end of the 1960s had been weakened by its own economic, cultural, and political tensions. By casting Lebanon into the heart of the Arab-Israeli conflict, the Palestinian question played a catalytic role in an international crisis that was *also* a serious domestic crisis.

Shihabism

Nevertheless, the years following the revolution and counterrevolution of 1958 witnessed an attempt by the country's leaders to correct the excesses that had touched off the explosion. Shihabism—so named after its initiator, President Fuad Shihab (1958–1964)—spread, continued, and eventually ran out of steam under his disciple and successor as president, Charles Helou (1964–1970). Shihab's proposed reforms were intended to improve the country's economic functioning and to increase the social protection of its inhabitants. To put these measures to work, Shihab recruited a team of intellectuals and young technocrats who were drawn to modernity and who wished to impose some order on the rabid competition of Lebanese capitalism: their watchword was rationality. To circumvent ministerial convolutions and overcome parliamentary immobilism, Shihabism relied on new institutions: the Bureau of Planning, Bureau of Statistics, Office of Social Development, Water Services of Beirut, and even a Center for Scientific Research, which formed a sort of shadow ministry, all devoted to the president.

Just after the "events" of 1958, a survey by a team from a French organization, the Institute for Research and Training for Development[1] (IRFED), brought home to Lebanon's leaders the extent of the inequalities in their country, which were among the world's largest: 4 percent of the "very rich" tied up 33 percent of the personal income in the country while half the population partook of only 18 percent. The menu of Lebanon's "needs" brought out the dramatic shortages in roads, electricity, potable water, schools, and hospital facilities in areas at some distance from the capital where families were particularly destitute: in southern Lebanon, the most notably underdeveloped region, the average income was a fifth of what it was in Beirut.[2] Because these were very largely Muslim areas, the government's economic measures and social policy represented a partial response to the demands for sharing and participation by the insurgents of 1958. The virtue of Shihabism was to get the state to attack inequalities, and it made extraordinary progress in many areas, particularly in building up the country's infrastructure. With the support of the Kataeb Party, resolute partisans of modernization and favoring a social policy, Shihab set up a social security system, one of his regime's most noteworthy accomplishments.

Politically, Shihabism represented a strict application of the principles of the National Pact, with which the regimes of Bishara al-Khuri and Camille Chamoun had taken a few liberties. After 1958, Lebanon resumed its dialogue with Nasser's Egypt, to the satisfaction of the country's Sunni Muslims. Above all, Shihab imposed parity between Christians and Muslims in the civil service; in the early 1960s a new generation of Sunni and, to a lesser extent, Shi'i technocrats entered the state bureaucracy, enlarging and enriching the Beirut leaders' vision of the country. Nevertheless, though Shihab's plan was to give back to each community its just share, he did not foresee any challenge to the traditional division of political power, which would have been an affront to the patrons of the system. Those important Christian and Muslim electors, Pierre Gemayel and his Kataeb, Camille Chamoun and his National Liberal Party, and Raymond Eddé, head of the National Bloc, together with leaders such as Saeb Salam, Kamel al-Asaad, and Kamal Jumblat, sometimes supported and sometimes just tolerated Shihab's moderate economic and social reforms. When, however, they felt their "democracy" was threatened with military and bureaucratic domination—when the Deuxième Bureau, completely devoted to Shihab, began to intervene drastically in elections—they agreed in September 1970 to make Suleiman Frangieh, that prototype of the traditional Maronite patron, the next president.

Shihabism was thus an unfinished endeavor with some wayward effects: with the arrival of electricity and mechanization, the roads were used more for urban commerce and rural exodus than they were for upgrading the back country. More serious was the fact that the economic and social measures were taken without crucial political changes, the need for which had been made clear by the crisis of 1958. Certainly, the pronounced increase in the government's budget, the creation by presidential decree of a Council of the Civil Service, the strengthening of presidential powers, and even the hypertrophy of the Deuxième Bureau marked a gain in the Lebanese state's autonomy from the dominant strata made up of the patrons and their elected representatives in the parliament. In the long run, however, like the revolutions discussed by Marx in his *Eighteenth Brumaire*, which strengthened the regime that they wanted to unseat, Shihab's policy of modernizing Lebanon's infrastructure facilitated the domination of the state by the merchant and financial oligarchy that he had hoped to check.

The Lebanese Miracle

The remarkable dynamism of Lebanese merchants, bankers, and entrepreneurs[3] enabled them to profit from the achievements of Shihabism. The opening to the underdeveloped outlying areas smoothed the way for the arrival of capitalism, with its vehicles, machines, and also its agendas and mode of functioning. Enriched by exports to the Arab world, the big traders of Beirut, Tripoli, and Zahle bought back unused or underexploited land from the absentee landlords. With mechanization and a monopoly on water for irrigation, they could replace food crops with fruits (particularly citrus), sugar beets, and battery poultry-raising. These new agricultural businessmen controlled the imports of fertilizers and farming equipment as well as the banks and lending institutions, organized the distribution networks, and doubled and sometimes even tripled the price of foodstuffs from producer to consumer.[4]

The Lebanese capitalists did not give up their preference for the logic of trade and exchange rather than production. It was the sugar importers, for example, who controlled the cultivation of sugar beets and made sure it was of limited extent. The partially state-owned national tobacco company made larger and quicker profits taxing imported cigarettes than they did granting new licenses to tobacco growers in the south. Overall, the primary sector continued to decline, providing a mere 9 percent of the country's gross national product in 1974. Lebanon's food dependence, especially in grains, rose to nearly 75 percent of its needs; even during these years of prosperity, the Lebanese were reduced to consuming milk and *lebne*, traditional white cheese reconstituted from casks of powder imported from Europe.

The economy was set up in a triangular mode of operation that yielded sensational profits—for the traders. Foodstuffs and manufactured products came from Western Europe, which supplied more than two-thirds of the country's imports. Some of these were destined for domestic consumption and some for resale on the Arab markets, sometimes after a local rebate: nearly 60 percent of Lebanese exports were bound for the Persian Gulf countries and the Near East. The growing profits from oil had indeed made the Arab countries producers, but also nonproducers who lived indirectly from this income, consumers with seemingly unlimited purchasing power. To make this merchant economy work, Arab and even European cash poured into Beirut.

After the period of crisis following the Arab defeat of 1967 and the closing of several banks after the Intra group went under, the volume of the deposits bounded back, encouraged by some free-enterprise legislation, especially that establishing banking secrecy in 1956; in twenty years, deposits increased by a factor of 40. Nevertheless, Lebanese banks represented only

15 percent of the country's financial institutions,[5] thus making its most dynamic and profitable sector more dependent on the outside. The money from petrodollars (the Lebanese income from the Persian Gulf, Arab investments in Lebanon, and payment for local services in Beirut) reproduced the traffic of commodities in reverse; this money passed through Beirut banks to pay for goods from the West or for investment in the industrialized countries, so that the Lebanese state found itself in the paradoxical position of lacking the money to finance its own social projects while its banking sector made international loans to large French firms like Renault.[6] As for money invested in the country, the state chose the commercial sector (which received twice as many credits as industry and agriculture combined) and tourism (another way to exploit wealth from the Persian Gulf) or even real estate (which yielded quick and easy profits since in the early 1970s the cost of land in the center of the large cities doubled annually). Lebanon's prosperity can be seen in its rate of growth and the rise in the average standard of living, much higher than that of its Arab neighbors, at least in the service sector (accounting for 50 percent of the country's working population and 70 percent of its GNP), and comparable to Europe's. This translated into luxury buildings (in the business districts, the downtown, and Hamra), new consumption habits regarding luxury products, and the development of leisure centers, beaches, ski resorts, and casinos to meet the demands of the higher social strata.

Industry underwent some relative development—in 1974, it still accounted for only 17 percent of the GNP—in the framework of a division of work imposed by capital, which limited Lebanon's industrial capacity to light manufacturing and the food and textile industries, or to construction materials, notably cement. It was content with modest investments and employed unskilled labor. A few of the large firms made spectacular profits while many projects, though government supported, were thwarted by monopolistic importers, for example in the pharmaceutical industry. In 1975, on the eve of the war, even though the secondary sector was booming, the Lebanese strategy for financial and commercial capital made possible only a limited future, and the imbalance between the country's monetary and its economic dimensions was a source of fragility.

The imbalance in Lebanon's economic growth affected its social structure. Owing to the lack of a governmental policy for redistributing wealth or protecting wage earners, prosperity not only didn't reduce the inequities denounced by the report of the IRFED, but increased them. The great fortunes now came less and less from real estate and more and more from monopoly and international associations, with capital from the oil-rich kingdoms of the Gulf, a strategy that allowed the elites to expand: Shi'is and Maronites, frequently enriched by money from emigrants, soon found a place among the country's privileged set next to the Sunnis and the Greek Orthodox. For capital's part, the Lebanese economy functioned effectively within the pluricommunal framework extolled by the promoters of the National Pact: the oligarchy that dominated the state and the directions they imposed on it belonged to Christendom and Islam, which were closely associated. Money had no odor when it came to setting up a cement plant, importing electronic equipment, or having shared interests. As an American economist showed, the Lebanese banking system was to replace even the political system as a guarantee of balance and cooperation among communal elites when the war divided the country.[7]

At the society's other extreme, families were driven from the land by mechanization, debt, and the constant insecurity of the border areas. By the eve of the war, half of Lebanon's population was urban; in the disadvantaged and threatened southern region, 65 percent of the families were forced to emigrate northward. The former tenant farmers lived off agricultural or industrial wages, seasonal work (especially construction), and the myriad minor services produced by urban life in the East: doorkeepers and porters, errand boys and street vendors. For a thousand new jobs in industry, there were five times more workers leaving the countryside and moving into the shantytowns and hastily thrown up apartment buildings on the edges of the cities into which were packed families of the unemployed and Palestine refugees. The "Qarantina," for example, at the northern entrance to Beirut, bordering the highway used by skiers and swimmers each weekend, sheltered several thousand Shi'i, Palestinian, and Armenian families who had no running water or electricity and whose many children were fed on bread moistened with a little oil. The presence of the Palestinians, and especially that of the 400,000 to 500,000 Syrian temporary or resident workers, supplied entrepreneurs with a reserve of cheap labor, inadequately protected and regularly replaced: in 1970, at the height of the Lebanese economic "miracle," 10 percent of the work force was unemployed and on the eve of the war, 15 percent. Here again, the communitarian cleavages were often circumvented but this time by poverty and proletarization: in the industrial area on Beirut's eastern edges, where more than 40 percent of the workers were Christian, the mixed habitat grew rapidly with the arrival of new migrants.

Accelerated by the influx of money, inflation officially rose to an annual 11 percent; according to the federation of Lebanese unions, the General Council of Labor (GCL), it was more than 20 percent. Besides the most disadvantaged categories, inflation affected urban middle-level wage earners whose incomes couldn't keep up with the rise in prices, particularly rents. The country's educational effort was rendered futile by a costly exodus of technicians, teachers, doctors, and also less educated workers—more than 150,000 persons,[8] representing 16 percent of Lebanon's work force, left temporarily for the Persian Gulf or permanently for North and South America.

Affected by the economic transformation and staggered by accelerated ur-banization, the two most rural communities, Shi'is and Maronites, paid a particularly high price for the Lebanese "miracle."

In the decade preceding the war, social protest against the deterioration in economic conditions was extremely disorganized, both weak and violent. When the GCL denounced the state's neglect and demanded an increase in salaries, a reduction in the price of basic foodstuffs, the organization of the market, and the amendment of article 50 of the Work Code permitting the arbitrary dismissal of workers, the representatives of the patrons, business-men, and industrialists replied categorically that these demands represented a threat to free enterprise and the country's prosperity. The moderate mobi-lization by the GCL in 1972 was overpowered by wildcat strikes among the best organized, the workers in the food industry on the southern edge of Beirut and the elementary-school teachers in 1972, and among the most de-prived, the workers in the tobacco fields in the south in 1973, which were accompanied by popular marches and student demonstrations, particularly at the Lebanese University and the American University of Beirut. The inter-vention by the police—the Internal Security Forces—the incidents, and even the death of two demonstrators in November 1972 thenceforth formed part of a direly eroded social landscape, a propitious setting for consciousness raising and political struggle.

Callings to Account

The 1967 defeat was a frightful shock for the Arab countries and brought about changes of regime in Syria and Iraq, putting an end to Nasser's glory. Later, its consequences altered the strategies of the new regimes: henceforth, the Syrian and Egyptian leaders warned, it was imperative to silence domes-tic criticism and devote their countries' vital forces unanimously and prima-rily to regaining the lost occupied territories. In Lebanon itself, this defeat occasioned profound disarray and, in the years that followed, fueled philo-sophical, cultural, and political thinking of exceptional depth. "The out-come of the Six Day War," wrote an American professor of Lebanese origin, "was a textbook case of a revolutionary situation, with all its standard in-gredients: military defeat, internal exhaustion, the disaffection of intellectu-als, a generation gap that was rapidly turning into an abyss, scathing cri-tiques of the most sacred facets of a culture's life."[9]

Of course, Beirut was the ideal setting for this turmoil. Only Cairo ri-valed the Lebanese capital in the scope of its university life, quality of its publications, and number of publishers. Furthermore, Lebanon had one in-disputable superiority over Egypt: liberalism, long enjoying the status of a doctrine, encouraged the settling of Arab artists, intellectuals, and politicians driven out of their own countries or fleeing intolerance. The twofold orientation of the National Pact made dialogue possible between Arab and Western thinkers. Prosperity and security, even though precarious and unequal, encouraged reflection and creativity. A symbol of the burgeoning diversity of cultural and intellectual life was the existence, in this small country of fewer than 3 million inhabitants, of five universities of different leanings and status: the thriving American University of Beirut, the French Jesuit Saint Joseph University, the fast-growing Lebanese University, the Arab University created by the Arab nationalists in 1960, and the University of the Holy Ghost of the Maronite monks in Kaslik.

Heightening Beirut's intellectual effervescence in the later 1960s were two revolutionary movements that influenced ideological debate and unsettled political life. In that city, where the most arrant luxury rubbed shoulders with the suffering Third World, the student revolutions of 1968, the war in Vietnam, the writings of Frantz Fanon, Che Guevara, and Régis Debray were enthusiastically discussed. Strikes, solidarity marches, and student sit-ins punctuated the social conflicts and workers' demonstrations, and responded to Israeli attacks and to clashes between the Lebanese army and the Palestinian combatants. The radical ideology of resistance movements, like the PFLP, which linked the goal of liberating Palestine to a process of revolutionary change in the whole Near East and which after 1973 rejected American secretary of state Henry Kissinger's proposals for a negotiated settlement of the Arab-Israeli conflict, intensified the attacks on the Arab regimes and the Lebanese political system in particular.

The criticism of Beirut's thinkers was directed first at the failure of the nationalist regimes, chief among them Nasser's Egypt and Syria's Baathists, which were denounced by the intellectual Sadeq al-'Azm.[10] As al-'Azm bitterly and lucidly pointed out, after 1967 the Arab East was suffering not only from a severe military defeat but also from a grave cultural and moral crisis. It was all of Arab society that had to change, not just its leaders, echoed the nationalist Constantine Zurayk,[11] while the independent Marxist Elias Morqos, master thinker for the young generation of leftists, exposed the contradictions and weaknesses of Arab socialism. In parallel and within the same protest movement, the mobilization of Arab nationalism gave way, on the one hand, to support of and allegiance to the Palestinian cause, unifier of all protests, and on the other hand, to the development of Islamist groups within the Muslim Brotherhood's sphere of influence, like the Islamic Unification Movement of Tripoli.

The scathing analysis didn't spare Lebanon's domestic situation, which was caught between economic imbalances, social frustrations, and the growing affronts to its independence and security. The analysis addressed chiefly the communitarian system which constituted, wrote the sociologist Nassif Nassar, a veritable set of shackles marked by the esprit de corps of bedouin society, to the detriment of individual freedom and social justice.[12] The underground journal *Lubnan al-Ishtiraki (Socialist Lebanon)* published Marxist analyses of the Lebanese economic and social system, which remain a model of the genre. To get beyond the blockages apparently caused by the consensus among the patrons of the communities, secularism now appeared a necessary precondition for national modernization, the democratization of political life, and the guarantee of individual freedoms. Ever more numerous were protests against communitarian rulings imposed even on the most personal choices, for example, matrimony, for only religious marriage exists in Lebanon according to the laws of each rite. The communitarian question, along with the attitude toward the Palestinian resistance and decisions regarding economic policy, was the touchstone of the political cleavages in Lebanon at the start of the war of 1975.

Mobilizations: Reforming . . .

Concerning the Palestinian struggle in Lebanon, the economic regime, and the communitarian system, there were of course as many opinions as there were Lebanese. Schematically, the Lebanese were divided into three large groups with differing assessments of their government's political orientation and management.

Most Lebanese tended to favor reforms: first, the revising though not the abandonment of communitarianism, and second, the reform of leadership practices within the communitarian setting. Since the end of Shihabism, the state apparatus, the administration, and the parliamentary deputies were the prey of unbridled clientelism, which made even the most minor political decision subject to private economic interests. Elected in 1970, the "patron of patrons," Suleiman Frangieh, handed out emoluments to the relatives and allies who had ensured his victory, and appointed to key posts men whose only qualification was being Maronite like himself and loyal to the "communitarian democracy" guaranteeing their privileges. In the early 1970s, more than half the directorships of the principal ministries were, contrary to custom, assigned to Maronites. Their stranglehold on the state nettled the Greek Orthodox, who were unhappy at being dominated by these ambitious and exclusive mountaineers. To the Muslims, particularly the Sunnis, it was unbearable. The Sunnis had at a pinch accepted a Greater Lebanon separated from Syria when the National Pact of 1943 had promised power-sharing in the state and the opening of Lebanon to its Arab neighbors. Since the end of the 1960s, however, the executive branch had scoffed at these principles: Frangieh in particular thrust aside the two leading lights of Sunnism (Rashid Karameh of Tripoli and Saeb Salam of Beirut), preferring younger prime ministers who lacked a clientelist base and so could be easily manipulated, thus tipping the balance of power toward his own community. The main Sunni demand was summarized in the formula *musharaka* (participation) while the underlying debate on the relations between Islam and political power remained submerged just beneath the surface.[13] During the siege of the camps in Beirut in May 1973, the Sunnis' broad support for the Palestinian resistance in its conflict with the Lebanese army, for example, grew as much out of a desire to weaken an opposing power as it did from Arab and Islamic solidarity. The Sunnis already knew, however, that because of their dispersion in the cities, the plurality of their leadership, and the fact that they belonged to a political space extending beyond the borders of Lebanon, they lacked the militant and military cohesiveness to get their demands respected, with a few exceptions like Ibrahim Qulaylat's *Murabitun* (the Combatants) or Kamal Shatila's Union of Nasserist Workers.

Though *musharaka* was less popular among the Shi'is, their protest against the regional, economic, and political imbalances marking communitarian Lebanon was sharper yet. Not only was the primarily Shi'i south the most unsettled by the presence of the Palestinian guerrillas and the most affected by the Israeli reprisals, but demographic surveys in the early 1970s[14] revealed that—despite the existence of some great land-based fortunes and the upward social mobility of a minority whose well-heeled emigrants were able to settle in the cites and gain access to education—the criteria of income, professional status of heads of families, and level of education put the whole Shi'i community at the bottom of the Lebanese social pyramid. These surveys also confirmed a clear trend apparent already in the 1932 census and still ignored in public discourse: the birthrate among the Lebanese Shi'is was on the average more than eight children for every married woman, 58 percent higher than the average number of births in Christian families, and so considerably shifted the Lebanese demographic balance in favor of the Muslims in general and particularly the Shi'is, who had become the largest community.[15]

How is it that the Shi'is would not feel the urgency of the "participation" demanded by the Sunnis? The Shihabist authorities helped them acquire a jurisdiction distinct from that of the other Muslims, and also an elected communal organization, the Higher Shi'i Council, established in 1967. Under the presidency of an Iran-educated clergyman, Sayyid Musa Sadr, the council contested the authority of the traditional patrons who had sacrificed the collective advancement of the Shi'is for the personal benefits from their alliance with the other leaders of the country. The new Shi'i elites—clergy, lawyers, minor military functionaries and civil servants, professional people—

envisaged a revision of the National Pact of 1943, which had granted their community only secondary positions, like the presidency of the parliament, nineteen out of ninety-nine deputies, and, until 1974, no high post in the civil service. Their strength came from the financial aid proffered by bourgeois emigrants, and above all their capacity for mobilizing the masses. The underprivileged of the community—tobacco growers under pressure from the nationalized tobacco company, victims of Israeli reprisals, and the subproletariat of the Beirut shantytowns—were armed by Musa Sadr's Amal movement; they took part in demonstrations in Tyre, Sidon, and Baalbek, which united tens of thousands of enthusiasts whom Imam Sadr reminded of the events marking Shi'i history to draw lessons for the present day. Even though the movement's themes were largely derived from the religious world of Shi'ism,[16] Amal's demands centered on reforming the Lebanese system and modernizing the consensus state. Its chief goal in demanding better defense of the south and an end to discrimination and economic injustices was to obtain a rebalancing of responsibilities and power in favor of the Shi'i community.

The need for reform was felt by men of highly diverse political outlooks, who deplored the communitarian balance system's blocking the search for a solution to Lebanon's social and regional problems. Before angrily resigning as prime minister in 1975, Rashid al-Sulh delivered a strong indictment of the obstructionist forces that were stifling Lebanon and had thwarted its plans for reform; a speech whose violence created a scandal at the time, but which sounded like a last appeal to reason before the battle: "Within the framework of the evolution of Lebanon and its relations with its Arab neighbors, the political privileges forming the basis of the Lebanese political system were transformed into an obstacle precluding any progress and threatening to provoke a regression and to blow up what the architects of independence put together." Liberal Maronites like Raymond Eddé, head of the National Bloc, members of the Orthodox Youth Movement, spiritual leaders like the Greek Catholic bishop Gregory Haddad, tried to strike up a new dialogue among the Lebanese. During Lent of the year preceding the war, Musa Sadr came to the Catholic cathedral of Beirut to give a well-attended lecture on sacrifice and charity. These goodwill gestures, however, could not bridge the gulf dividing Lebanon.

. . . Revolutionizing . . .

The abandonment of the Shihabist program and the growing tensions with the Palestinian resistance upset the balances, compromises, and traditional accommodations among the Lebanese. The communal and local mediators who made the system work saw their role undermined and contested.

On the other hand, since the end of the 1960s, the hitherto marginal radical political parties with ideological platforms were gaining in numbers and perceptible influence. The ambitions of a younger and better-educated generation, the frustrations aggravated by the growth of unequal prosperity, the conflict with the elders of each community unwilling to share their power, and the influence of the Palestinian resistance organizations led numerous adherents to parties of the left.

The Communist Party held its second congress in 1968 and its third in 1972. It reorganized, solidified its position in the forefront of social struggles by overwhelming the reformist GCL, mobilized among the students, organized agricultural workers in the south into strikes and protest demonstrations against the National Tobacco Company, and fought beside the Palestinian resistance in the border villages. Its political stand in favor of the PLO broke with the USSR's policy, which had been cautious up to 1973. It was winning a growing audience through its radical criticism of the Lebanese bourgeoisie, the National Pact, and the compromise strategy of the Arab regimes after 1973, as did its rival, the Organization of Communist Action in Lebanon, created in 1970. In the years preceding the war the Lebanese Communist Party, originally mainly Christian, particularly Greek Orthodox, had more than 10,000 members, of whom more than half were new Shi'i members and close to 15 percent Sunni and Druze. Full of this new momentum, it led a coalition of the nationalist (i.e., Arabist) and progressivist parties whose other pillar was not a party, but a man, Kamal Jumblat.

Hereditary chief of one of the Druze clans, Jumblat belonged in principle to the "club" of deputies and potential ministers. But this remarkably complex intellectual added to his historical legitimacy reformative ambitions concretized in the creation of the Progressive Socialist Party (PSP). An assailant of his own political class, Jumblat nevertheless assured the election of Suleiman Frangieh to the presidency in 1970, shortly after obtaining, as minister of the interior, the legalization of several radical parties, the Communist Party, the Baathist parties (both the pro-Syrian and the pro-Iraqi), and the SSNP. In both the parliament and the government, he delivered blistering criticisms of clientelism and political communitarianism, and demanded a distributive policy and a commitment of the Lebanese army to fight alongside the PLO. Because his supporters were divided between members of the Jumblat clan and genuine militant socialists, their political stances were sometimes unclear. But in the Progressive Front, which on the eve of the war became the Lebanese National Movement (LNM), some fifteen groupings of unequal size agreed, to varying degrees, on a program of radical changes for Lebanon: the Communist Party, of course, the Organization of Communist Action, the Greater Syrian nationalists of the SSNP who in the early 1960s had swapped their corporatist program for more progressivist options, the

Baathists who met the crisis of confidence in Arab nationalism after the 1967 defeat by forming a more socialistic plan, and the Murabitun who aimed to mobilize the Sunni lower classes, as well as nearly a dozen other groups.

The unifying theme of the National Movement was support for the Palestinian resistance, accompanied by violent criticism of the army and the executive branch, and a demand for strict respect for the Cairo Accord of 1969. The LNM was a founding member of the Arab Front for Participation in the Resistance (1972), a coalition of a dozen parties and progressive organizations. The LNM also had a program for Lebanon, synthesized and finalized in August 1975, during an early lull in the war.[17] The program called for reorganizing the army to return to the job of defending the national frontiers, restructuring the civil service to weed out corruption and nepotism, and above all eliminating "political confessionalism," that is, the communitarian distribution of power. The adoption of proportional parliamentary representation on a national scale, without regard to the candidates' communal membership, would be a step toward the complete secularization of Lebanese society, guaranteeing true democracy.

It should be understood that the positions of the LNM were primarily militant, for Lebanon was on the verge of warfare. The urgency of an explosive situation masked the basic problems, like that of the articulation between the nature of the state and the Islamic view of the world, between the cultural references of Christianity and the relation of individuals to the authorities, and even the problem of the mode of functioning of Lebanese society in particular and of Mediterranean Arab society in general. Priority was given to the armed struggle and revolutionary change: popular memory went back to 1840, 1861, and 1958. Each of the LNM's member groups prepared for the struggle in its own way and with its own means. This went from the defense of the Druze areas for the members of Jumblats' organized and seasoned PSP, to some hundreds of volunteers from the Marxist parties who were trained in both handling weapons and dialectical debate, and to the urban *jama'at* (bands) of minor Sunni neighborhood bosses. The Palestinian organizations often organized, equipped, and trained nascent Lebanese militias: that of the Shi'i Amal movement, for example, or the Nasserite militia of Sidon. At any rate, there was no lack of weapons, for families traditionally possessed them; other, more modern ones, among them the grimly famous Russian-made Kalashnikov assault rifles, flooded in thanks to subsidies from Iraq which had assumed leadership of the Arab radicals of the Rejection Front rallied against negotiations under the aegis of the Americans, and subsidies from Libya as well, which supported the Sunni militias. Syria was more selective: at the start of the war, it did not control even the "Syrian nationalist" SSNP; on the other hand, it did sponsor several Palestinian organizations, particularly the Sa'iqa. All in all, "progressives" of the

LNM and "Islamist" partisans of the traditional Muslim leaders represented several thousands of combatants. Almost as many as those opposing them.

. . . or Preserving?

Opposing them were those who were anxious about the rising power of the Palestinian resistance in Lebanon. Not only did the resistance invite Israeli reprisals and function too much like a "state within a state," but, more subtly, it led to increased interventions by the Arab nations in Lebanon's domestic affairs and, above all, introduced into the delicate communitarian balance a powerful political and military force, identified by the Christians as both Sunni and favorable to the radicals. Once again, nervous minorities shattered the vision of a Lebanon fully attached to the Arab Middle East with not only its wealth, like that of the Gulf states, but also its problems, like the Arab-Israeli conflict.

Opposing them were also those who, even when they weren't the beneficiaries of uncontrolled growth, remained steadfast champions of free enterprise, individualism, and antistatism; who, even when they were packed into the impoverished neighborhoods of the eastern suburbs, from Dekwaneh to Furn al-Shabbak and Ain al-Rummaneh, distrusted class solidarity and preferred the redistributive guarantee of communal solidarity; who by taking part in the vast wave of urbanization, education, and "tertiarization" pulled themselves up to the level of a petty bourgeoisie.

Opposing them, finally, were those who clung to legal guarantees and the political supremacy afforded them by communitarianism, who preferred to perpetuate a segmented system that helped maximize their advantages rather than to construct a Western-style democracy, who flourished in this twofold communitarian dynamics—security and progress domestically, rejection and competition in foreign relations—and who swore that to meddle with the traditional balances of Lebanon would be to court its destruction.

One of the cruxes of the Lebanese conflict lies in the makeup of a group of Christian leaders who were very solidly united in their social and political conservatism and their hostility to Palestinian foreigners, in the face of a heterogeneous coalition of "reformists," of Muslims and of "progressives" of various stripes and from various communities. Conservatism was entrenched almost exclusively on the Christian side because the traditional Muslim patrons were losing ground—owing to the decline of pan-Arabism, conflicts arising from solidarity with the Palestinians, and the breakup of their traditional clientele. And conservatism was voiced mainly by Maronites because the Catholic and Orthodox Christian minorities had been relegated by the French Mandate to a role secondary to the Maronite nucleus and had been raised in an urban tradition of coexistence and cooperation with the Muslims. Because the Maronite community had experienced several decades of demographic and economic dislocations, its historical patrons gradually gave way to the Kataeb Party, the only "modern political instrument that could take direct action in behalf of the system," and confront "post-1958 pressures, . . . especially from Nasserite, pan-Arabist, Baathist, and Palestinian guerilla forces."[18] The growth of the Kataeb is such that in 1970, 82 percent of the 70,000 members of the party were Maronites (14 percent were from other Christian confessions) and 70 percent were natives of Beirut and Mount Lebanon. In addition, the Kataeb were linked to other Maronites: Camille Chamoun's NLP, Suleiman Frangieh's Zghorta party, and Charbel Kassis's Organization of Maronite Monks, in an organization that was to become the Lebanese Front.

After the defeat of 1967, the evolution of the Kataeb reflected the tensions in the relations between the Arab states and the radicalization of Lebanese political life. While the party had been opening to intercommunal cooperation during the reign of Shihabism, it now presented itself as *the* protector of Lebanon and nationalism. In the general elections of 1972, it unconditionally defended the private sector, opposed the demands of the Muslims, and declared itself against any amendment of the constitution. Constantly denouncing the resistance organizations' nonobservance of the Cairo Accord, it considered that it alone was entitled to make up for the weakness of a state and an army paralyzed by the Muslim leaders' compromises in the face of the Palestinian danger. Its military branches—the Kataeb Security Service, the "phalanges," and armed partisans—took precedence over its civilian sections. At the start of the war, the Kataeb mustered some 15,000 combatants. Intensive training was organized in the Mountain, with retired officers in liaison with the LNP and extremist groups like the Guardians of the Cedar, the *Tanzim* (the Organization), the Kisrawan Front, the Zghorta Army of Liberation, with the collaboration of the Maronite monks, defenders of "Lebanonness" but mainly of the status quo. Here too, weapons flooded in, chiefly from Israel.

Starting in 1970, the Kataeb clashed with Palestinian militias in numerous skirmishes. At the beginning of 1975, a memorandum from Pierre Gemayel, the party chief, demanded that the president pull the fedayeen out of the south and subject them to Lebanese authority. The purpose of this ultimatum was to provoke the army into siding with the conservative militias in the coming major confrontation with the "Palestinians and the leftists."

9

War Violent and Rampant (1975–1981)

I⟁ has become customary to date the war's start from the bloody clash between the Kataeb and the Palestinian fedayeen at Ain al-Rummaneh in April 1975. This choice has the virtue of coherence for the uninformed observer: while in 1970 a disciplined Jordanian national army had fought the Palestinian resistance that was upsetting the kingdom's balance, in 1975, in a similar confrontation, the militarily inexperienced and politically paralyzed Lebanese national army was replaced by the Kataeb. In reality, however, the Lebanese war was the product of antagonisms on several levels, involving many players and cut across by complex strategies. Most of the ingredients had already figured in a crisis three months before, when the army stepped in against a protest demonstration by Palestinian militants in the Sunni city of Sidon, and the next day Christians from Beirut, spurred by the conservative parties, took to the streets to proclaim their support for the military command.

It is true that this was the war that dared not speak its name. People spoke of "the crisis" or "events," and they recoiled from "civil war," for every combatant was convinced he was defending "his" Lebanon from an outside threat, since the enemy was mentioned only obliquely, the goals presented with all kinds of detours, and explanations reduced to the claim of a "plot." The gunmen poised for ambush were anonymous, murderers remained undiscovered, and kidnapping victims disappeared for good. The extreme confusion encouraged by the political leaders and the press, which spoke of "armed elements," quoting "officials" and vaguely mentioning "locations in the south (or north, or the Bikaa)" intentionally fueled distrust, fear, and hostility. In this, the war merely exacerbated the old practice of doublespeak—what was said inside the group was one thing, and what outsiders were given to understand quite another[1]—and the systematic encoding of official speech, probably inherited from a long history of foreign domination.

A shifting front line, a nebulous relation between the goals of the different parties and the strategies adopted: A fire breaks out here, smolders there, rekindles elsewhere, and the civilians are unable to put it out or even shield themselves from it. On the evening of the demonstrations in Sidon and Beirut, on the day after the engagement at Ain al-Rummaneh, militiamen loomed up from all sides, in the capital and in isolated villages, and guns bombarded targets identified in advance. Zahle fought against the surrounding villages, Tripoli faced militiamen from Zghorta, Damur was encircled, the approaches to the Palestinian refugee camps were blazing infernos. During the fall of 1975, in several weeks of extremely violent fighting, Beirut's port and its financial, touristic, and commercial center were destroyed. Was this because it was on the front line between two opposed camps continually machine-gunning each other? Week after week, the Murabitun and the Palestinian combatants forced the Kataeb and their allies to withdraw to the place des Canons, the heart of old Beirut, and the Damascus road. Or was it through a calculated desire to destroy the very sites of the merchant city's prosperity, the space common to all, carried out in concert by the opposing militias?[2]

The war was all the more difficult to puzzle out because the Lebanese state was powerless to contain and arbitrate the conflicts, and even less able to define national goals. The state had always been weak, dominated by economic and communitarian regional coalitions and influenced by foreign powers. Suleiman Frangieh's rise to the presidency in 1970 signaled a return of the reign of the patrons. Public service was a matter of indifference to the defenders of clan interests. Even the Kataeb, which had long advocated a strengthening of the state, developed a strategy for systematically undermining it. Increasingly, the clamorous disagreements between the president and his prime minister reflected a disintegration of the consensus between the elites. From then on, it was not the president, his ministers, and the political leaders who managed a state, but the "warlords" who fought and tore each other apart. In May 1975, after Rashid al-Sulh's resignation, Frangieh made his cabinet, consisting almost entirely of moderate military men, responsible for bringing about the return of peace. The Sunni leaders unanimously condemned this choice. The confrontations mounted and the president saw himself saddled with Rashid Karameh as prime minister. In November, Karameh, as defense minister, ordered the commander in chief of the army to seize a load of arms that had entered through the port of Junieh; the Kataeb all the more easily forestalled this military intervention as Camille Chamoun, minister of the interior, disapproved of the prime minister. In March 1976, while

Suleiman Frangieh was besieged in the presidential palace in Baabda and threatened by his opponents' armed forces, sixty-eight of the ninety-nine deputies voted for him to resign. He refused to comply and took refuge at Kfur in Kisrawan with his Christian allies, resolved to carry out his mandate to term in September. Communal strategies and individual ambitions had swept away the compromises of the National Pact.

As predicted, the army was unable to withstand the collapse of the state. As long as a facade of consensus had been preserved, the army could at least refrain from taking sides and by default be generally thought of as an instrument of national unity. But when in 1973 the executive branch ordered it to intervene against the Palestinian camps on Beirut's outskirts and against the demonstrators in Sidon in 1975, some of the officers and troops rebelled. When in January 1976 its leaders decided to send it against the besiegers of Damur, who were Palestinian and Druze radicals, the army splintered into partisan factions: the Lebanese Arab Army (LAA), with headquarters in the Bikaa, controlled the barracks of the south and the Akkar; Major Saad Haddad led the Army of Free Lebanon around Marjuyun. Some brigades followed President Frangieh in his retreat to Kisrawan. During the general confrontation of the spring of 1976, some units even fought each other, some fighting along with the Lebanese Front, others with the National Movement.

"Christian Conservatives" and "Islamic Progressives"

The "little wars" setting Lebanon ablaze often represented a chance for local gangs to settle scores with old rivals or enlarge their fiefdoms. Every neighborhood and village had its militia, with evocative names taken from pre-Islamic mythology, the history of the Arab conquerors, or American television. Some young gang leaders, suddenly reinforced by an influx of weapons or made famous by an unexpected victory, presented themselves as the future leaders of a storm-tossed Lebanon: Faruq al-Muqaddam, the "hero" of fights around the fortress of Tripoli in 1975; Ibrahim Qulaylat, whose Murabitun conquered the grand hotels of Beirut in 1975; and later Elias Hobeika, who led the Lebanese Forces' assault on the Palestinian refugee camps of Sabra and Shatila in 1982. Nevertheless, despite their dispersion and the extreme confusion in their goals, the opposing groups followed two main cleavages: that between conservatives and progressives, on the one hand, and that between Christians and Muslims on the other.

From the street to the leading patrons, the war began through the revolt of all those who rejected the old order. The member groups of the progressive National Movement (LNM) were at the head of the opposition to the establishment, but the LNM also mobilized the Arab nationalist parties, the

Baath parties, and the Murabitun, all of which wanted Lebanon to make a decisive commitment to the cause of Palestinian resistance. Associated with them were the Sunni elites who considered themselves weakened by the National Pact's reservation of prerogatives for the Christians in general and the Maronites in particular: former prime ministers like Rashid Karameh and Saeb Salam, leaders of Dar al-Fatwa, the judicial authority of the community, or the Grand Mufti of the Republic, who early in 1976 convened a "Palestino-Islamic" summit at his home in Aramun. Along with the Shi'i clan heads and the communitarian Amal movement, each of these patrons had a clientele ready to send armed men into battle. In addition, this opposition camp had reserves of more than 10,000 combatants from the Palestinian resistance, whose leaders were still divided about which side to join in the new war: the radicals of the Rejection Front (the PFLP and the pro-Iraq Arab Liberation Front) and especially the left wing of al-Fatah were resolutely committed to the side of the Lebanese leftists. The moderates gathered around Yasir Arafat tried to stay out of the conflict; Arafat met with Frangieh and then Chamoun twice over in the fall of 1975, after battles around camps on the northern outskirts of Beirut; he affirmed a wish to confine himself to defending Palestinian security and autonomy, to a strict application of the Cairo Accord. As for the Sa'iqa movement and units of the Syrian-controlled Palestine Liberation Army, Syria was not afraid to fan the conflict but refused to side with the National Movement. Altogether, then, this camp represented a heterogeneous coalition with three focuses—leftist, Muslim, and Palestinian—that sometimes was given the name "Islamic progressive" and sometimes "Palestinian progressive."

Although the Muslims constituted the great majority of the opposition coalition, it also included some Christians, particularly from the prosecular movements in the LNM like the Communist Party and the SSNP. On the side of the conservatives, Muslims were a very small minority. Though inclined to preserve the traditional system, the Muslim patrons were forced by tactical reasons to echo the frustration of their clientele and to break off alliances with their Christian partners. The leaders forming a bloc around the presidency for the preservation of the traditional order were almost exclusively Christians, and perpetuated the confusion between the defense of the privileges of the patrons—Maronites, Greek Catholics, or other Catholic confessions—and the advancement of the collective interests of their own communities. Furthermore, the partisans and clients of the Kataeb, Chamoun's National Liberal Party (NLP), and Frangieh presented themselves more as Christians than conservatives and displayed solidarity with their leaders in the face of enemies labeled "Islamic Palestinian radicals."

Political unification went hand in glove with a desire for communal homogenization, with dramatic consequences for the population and the very identity of the Lebanese state. From the earliest days of the war, when the internal and regional stakes were still uncertain, the attackers made combatants and even civilians from other communities their target, fabricating a clearly identifiable enemy. In Beirut, where the dense intermingling of the population at the workplace and in the new residential areas had become natural, militiamen arrested, kidnapped, and murdered members of other communities or Palestinian refugees after checking their sectarian affiliation on their identity cards. On the memorable "Black Saturday" of December 1975, members of the Kataeb killed several dozen anonymous Muslim passersby.

As the war grew on many fronts, security was increasingly sought within the family and the community: hostilities prompted a reversion to ancient solidarities that linked individual survival to fusion with the group of origin. Often, mobilization of the combatants obeyed the most immediate imperatives: the defense of close relatives or fellow villagers was more urgent than the struggle for some distant or abstract cause; communal solidarity won out over class solidarity and ideological choices. In areas with relatively homogeneous populations, patrons were transformed into warlords and exploited the strange mixture of community unity and compliance with their leadership. The majority of the Druzes in the Shuf, for example, belonged to Kamal Jumblat's Progressive Socialist Party and hence rallied to the LNM. In the central areas of Lebanon with a heavily Maronite majority—the Kisrawan and the Northern Matn, East Beirut and its suburbs—the internal solidarity of the Christian communities enabled the Kataeb, the NLP, and Frangieh's partisans to impose a double exclusion: of the leftists *and* the Muslims.

The growing convergence of the "Christian" and "conservative" categories, far closer than that of "Muslim" and "radical," was the result of crude policies of force. In 1975–76, when combat was raging, the formerly communist families of Bikfaya were made an offer to stay in this small town, fiefdom of the Gemayels; their security was guaranteed on condition that they renounce membership in the Communist Party. If they refused, they would be exiled across the political and communitarian border that the war was in the process of drawing. In the leftist parties, this ultimatum provoked such a copious hemorrhaging of the Christian militants that the Communist Party of Lebanon, for example, whose leadership remained, however, primarily Christian, appeared as the ally of the Muslims, and was sometimes denounced as the defender of Shi'i *communitarian* interests. Another example is that of Kura, at the juncture of the Sunni area of Tripoli and the Maronite Mountain, whose population is mostly Greek Orthodox: there the exclusive domination of the SSNP staved off penetration by the Kataeb and Frangieh's partisans.

To the victims, who in a few months numbered several hundred, the violence gripping Lebanon seemed blind and senseless. Nevertheless, the process of communitarian exclusion took on a collective dimension that did not proceed randomly. In July 1975 the Christian leaders Pierre Gemayel, Camille Chamoun, and Father Sharbil Qassis accused the Palestinian resistance of "occupying" certain parts of the eastern outskirts of Beirut where the refugee camps were. Gathered around President Frangieh in January 1976, they suggested that unitary Lebanon be transformed into a federated Lebanon, which would allow the communities to organize themselves separately and independently. The attacks of their militias were thus to follow this twofold logic of forming homogeneous cantons and rejecting the Palestinian "occupation": expulsion of the Muslims of Antelias and Sebnay in the eastern edges of Beirut in December 1975, a blockade of the large Palestinian camp of Tel al-Za'tar, the seizure of the Christian Palestinian camp of Dbaye, and the total destruction and massacres in the shantytown of Qarantina in January 1976. In retaliation, following the same logic of communitarian exclusion, the Palestinian and leftist "Joint Forces" besieged and pillaged the Christian villages of Damur and Jiyeh south of Beirut, forcing several thousands to escape by sea. In August 1976 the last Muslim and Palestinian enclaves of the northern part of Beirut, Nabaa (100,000 Shi'is), Jisr al-Basha (6,000 Palestinians), and Tel al-Za'tar (50,000 Palestinians and southern Lebanese) were totally eliminated: Nabaa after an agreement between the Shi'i and Maronite leaders, followed by a massive exodus of families; the others, after interminable shellings and combats into which the Christian militias threw nearly 4,000 men and 100 armored vehicles. Women and children were evacuated in the final days. No prisoners were taken.

Sporadic in the spring of 1975, the participation of the Palestinian militias in the war became general, and then in 1976 decisive. The need was pressing to respond to attacks and defend civilians as well as to show solidarity with their Muslim and leftist allies in confronting the "Christian conservatives." Some of the Sunni leaders openly considered the Palestinians the "armed wing" of their community, while Jumblat repeatedly demanded that Arafat commit his troops on the side of the National Movement.[3] The decision was made in March 1976, after the Lebanese army broke up, when the prospects arose of President Frangieh's early departure from office and Lebanon's transformation into a progressive state supporting the armed struggle against Israel. At this time, the firepower and military preparedness of the Palestinian groups in Lebanon seemed more than adequate to ensure the military victory of the Palestinian, leftist, and Islamic "Joint Forces" over the Christian conservatives. In less than two months, the Christians lost ground in Beirut and the Mountain. Soon they controlled only a fifth of the country.

Syria Intervenes

The prospects for the Palestinians' and leftists' military victory were clear. Less clear were the political prospects. Would several hundreds of thousands of Christians, whose leaders—despite the counsels of the American mediator Dean Brown in April 1976—were unwilling to come to terms with their adversaries, have to pay for the settlement of the Arab-Israeli conflict in Lebanon with their exile? Or would their leaders launch them in the adventure of secession by resorting to an alliance with Israel? Would the new leaders of a revolutionary Lebanon long put off an attack against the Jewish state? Or would Jerusalem not allow a radical regime to be set up on its northern border without intervening? Could Yasir Arafat's PLO, with its base in Lebanon, totally free itself of Arab tutelage and become a rival or even a danger to Syria and Jordan? Finally, would the Arab countries, threatened by national revolution and a new outbreak of the conflict in the Near East, tolerate this firebrand at their flanks?

The Syrian army's entry into Lebanon was an immediate answer to these questions. Neither the Syrian foreign minister Abdul Halim Khaddam's mediation between the Christian and Muslim leaders, nor the obstinate meddling of the Sa'iqa and combatants from the PLA, infiltrating in growing numbers each month, managed to slow down the ever more dangerous developments in the Lebanese conflict. In February 1976, urged by Damascus, Suleiman Frangieh presented a plan for balancing political power in the Muslims' favor; the LNM, headed by Kamal Jumblat, declared the plan already outdated. In April, an attempted ceasefire that Syria had proposed to the Palestinians failed. In May, two-thirds of the deputies—the Lebanese Front and the "Muslim patrons" against the National Movement and Raymond Eddé—secured the presidential election of Damascus's candidate, Elias Sarkis, a former adviser to President Shihab; the "Joint Forces" completely rejected the truce he offered and continued their advance on the peaks overlooking the Matn and Kisrawan.

On June 1, 1976, several thousand soldiers from the Syrian regular army entered Lebanon through the Akkar and the international Damascus-Beirut highway. Their goal was to interpose themselves between the belligerents and thus to prevent a rout of the Christian militias. Energetic resistance by the Palestinian-leftist forces halted their advance, first at Sofar and then at the entrance to Sidon. After incurring some heavy losses, the Syrian army took control of the Matn and the Beirut road (starting in Zahle) in September and the Jezzin-Sidon axis in October. By the end of November, it was in a position to occupy nearly the whole of Lebanon after the Palestinians, the LNM, and the Lebanese Front agreed to a ceasefire in recognition of the arbitrating role it had just assumed.

Though relations between Hafez al-Assad's regime and the LNM and PLO had deteriorated since the start of the war, the opposing Lebanese Front had only limited confidence in Syrian intentions. In March 1976, Pierre Gemayel sent an emissary to Israel,[4] and in August Camille Chamoun met with Prime Minister Yitzhak Rabin. Paradoxically, yesterday's allies and today's protégés of Damascus, who had called for Syrian intervention against their adversary, shared the same suspicions and the same anxiety concerning Syrian intentions and goals. The apparent contradictions of an extremely patient strategy fueled accusations as extreme as they were incoherent: sometimes Damascus was suspected of wanting to annex Lebanon, sometimes of intending to share it with Jerusalem whose "objective" ally it was. For some, Syria wanted to crush Israel and dominate the whole Mediterranean Near East with the support of the Soviet Union; others were convinced that behind its militant rhetoric it was merely seeking an honorable and well-remunerated peace under the aegis of the United States.

Syria's Lebanon policy is based on three elements: the pan-Arab ideology of the Baath Party, the geographical and historical continuity of Greater Syria, and the strategic imperatives in the region since 1948. Since 1963, the Damascus regime's pan-Arab ideology has been not merely the official rhetoric of an ad hoc justification for the interventions of the Ba'athist officers. It effectively spurred Syrian civil servants, military men, and members of the Baath concerned for the future of their region, particularly of the neighboring countries of Lebanon, Jordan, and Palestine. At the pan-Arab level, the unitarian ideology has had, if not a mobilizing effect, at least one of legitimation. One of the principles of the unitarian ideology is the legitimacy of intervening in a brother Arab country (less readily, the intervention of a brother country in one's own territory), relativizing the notion of a border between Arab states. A corollary of this principle is that it is inappropriate to put Israeli aggression or occupation and the armed Syrian presence in Lebanon on the same level.

Nevertheless, the unitarian ideology by itself was threadbare owing to its failures, weakened by the consolidation of states in the Near East, and could not be used to further Syrian goals. It was overtaken by a second set of arguments: the natural unity of the "Greater Syrian" region (between the Taurus Mountains, the Mediterranean, and the Sinai and eastern deserts), a geographical and cultural unity, a historical unity (until the division imposed by the mandatory powers), economic unity (illustrated by the traditional communications network between the large cities of the region)—all features pointing toward political unity, or at least supporting Damascus's ambitions in the region, its efforts at rapprochement and coordination with Amman, its desire to control the Palestinian national movement, and its actions to determine Lebanon's destiny.

Syria's aims in Lebanon did not include either balkanization or annexation. Although the Syrian military has been stationed in some areas of the
country—precisely the ones taken away from the province of Damascus to
form Greater Lebanon in 1920—since 1976, the Baathist regime has shown
no indication of wanting to annex these areas—the Bikaa, Tripoli—to the
Syrian state; on the contrary, it fears the breakup of Lebanon would pave the
way for Israeli domination of more Arab regions and could by contagion
divide the Syrian Arab Republic whose population is also made up of several
religious (Muslim and Christian) and ethnic (Arab, Kurdish, and Armenian)
communities.[5]

Syrian policy toward Lebanon has often been explained by a solidarity
among minorities.[6] In 1976, Hafez al-Assad, who had been ruling in Damascus for six years, justified his troops' intervention on the side of the conservatives by the need to defend the Christians whose "confidence" he desired
to "earn." This thesis of solidarity among minority groups is fragile, however, and was in turn used to justify the rapprochement between the Syrian
Alawis and the Maronites, and between the Alawis and the Lebanese Shi'is.
It is true that the Syrian leaders approached the Lebanese crisis with the
vision of a minority group and that they preferred to intervene in Lebanon
through sectarian channels: they supported individuals, negotiated with the
clan heads, and played factions and families against each other—the Frangiehs
against the Gemayels, and Rashid Karameh against Saeb Salam. Nevertheless, they also felt compelled to deal with the legitimate power, within the
constitutional framework of the communitarian system, as long as Lebanon
did not carry out the political deconfessionalization that they would have
preferred.

Thus, it is necessary to consider General Assad's subtle formula of "Two
independent states, one people,"[7] a slogan that should not be too quickly
shelved as mere ideological rhetoric. Syria had indeed recognized the independent Lebanese state when they both joined the Arab League in 1945;
since then, the two countries had had extensive official contacts (particularly
at the ministerial and presidential level), whether good or bad. Since 1920,
and especially since 1943, the two nations, Syria and Lebanon, went on to
differentiate themselves and develop their own personalities on the international scene, but this separation did not obliterate the profound similarity in
their political cultures, a similarity that General Assad, while recognizing
before the international community that there were indeed "two states,"
asserted by saying that they still housed "one people." But since that one
people had not succeeded at becoming a single Syrian nation on the dissolution of the Ottoman Empire, the Syrian leadership applied itself to at least
placing the Lebanese state under Syrian tutelage *(himaya)* through the av-

enues of a military intervention, political pressures, and close coordination of the two countries' economies, which were considered complementary.

As regards Syria's strategic interest in Lebanon, General Assad's goals are easier to spot. Looking at a map of the Arab-Israeli conflict reveals more than the repeated assertions of the Syrian president that: "Lebanese and Syrian security are interdependent."[8] Since Israel's capture of the Golan Heights in 1967 and above all Egypt's disengagement in 1975, only Syria itself has ensured the defense of Syrian territory, and it has done so partly on Lebanese territory because the Bikaa Valley forms a natural corridor of access to the central Syrian cities of Damascus, Homs, and Hama for an Israeli army that has gained a foothold in southern Lebanon. Certainly, the Golan Heights is still the chief area of dispute between Syrians and Israelis, whose forces have since May 1974 been separated only by a narrow cordon of observers from the United Nations. In a strictly military sense, however, the Bikaa front forms the western part of the Syrian lines of defense. From a wider strategic perspective, military control of Lebanon is a trump card for Damascus in any future negotiations, while Syria is opposed to any attempt by Israel to get Lebanon to break with Arab solidarity. The competition between Syria and Israel is a case of a zero-sum game: any advance of the one is a retreat for the other.

Arab and International Guarantees

Although the deployment of nearly 30,000 soldiers on Lebanese territory roused strong emotion and was considered a bold ploy on the part of the Baathist regime, the Syrian intervention in Lebanon was part of a complex process of regional and multilateral reactions and interventions. Very quickly indeed, while it essentially set Lebanese factions to fighting among themselves, the *civil* war had some decisive consequences for the Palestinian national movement. Already, the interstate negotiation, initiated by Henry Kissinger after the October War of 1973, implied the sacrifice of the PLO's goals to those of Egypt, Jordan, and especially Syria. Now the "Christian conservatives," allied with Israel, threatened the PLO's sole remaining area of political and military autonomy. The radical Arab states known as the Rejection Front refused to participate in what seemed to them a betrayal of the Palestinian interests. Iraq, mainly, as well as Libya and Algeria supplied arms to the Palestinians and leftists.[9] At the same time, Libya and Algeria devoted themselves to reconciliation missions: aware of the Palestinians' precarious position and the danger of Syria's dominating Lebanon at a time when Egypt was opening to the "American peace," seasoned diplomats like the Libyan prime minister Jallud and the Algerian ambassador Yazid negotiated extensively. In June 1976, Tripoli even sent 500 men to Beirut to partici-pate at the side of the Syrians in what it considered a mission of pacification.

The Rejection Front scarcely had any means for applying pressure on the "Christian conservatives." But neither did it have any influence on the Baathist regime in Damascus since the latter, anxious about the progress of the Israeli-Egyptian negotiations, claimed to be the final bastion of resis-tance to Israel and invited the other Arabs, including the Palestinians, to take its side. Without openly criticizing Syria, the leftist Arab countries kept up their financial and logistical aid to the PLO and the LNM. On the other hand, the conservative states of the Arab peninsula, which backed the new pragmatic and pro-Western policy of the 1970s, were able to make them-selves heard, for they spoke a language understandable to all the protago-nists of the war in Lebanon. Because of the decision of the Arab Summit of Algiers in 1973, Syria and the PLO each received annuities of nearly a billion dollars as reparations and provisions for the war effort. As for Lebanon itself, its prosperity depended more than ever on the implementation of am-bitious economic plans in the Gulf region.

Though General Assad was obliged to take into consideration Saudi Arabia's appeal for a ceasefire at the end of the summer of 1976, the latter in turn respected Syria's interests in the Mediterranean Near East. Several ele-ments went into the Saudi strategy for handling Damascus: anxiety about the mounting ambitions of Iraq's Saddam Hussein, a concern not to favor Soviet influence in the region, relief at seeing the PLO's revolutionary might thwarted, the need to display solidarity with the Arab states of the Front, the satisfaction of making Egypt its obligee, and hostility toward Israel. Ever unequal and the object of endless mutual extortion, relations between the Saudis and the Syrians have become a central axis in the political configura-tion of the Middle East since 1973.

At the Arab Summit of Riyadh in October 1976, the "Syrian solution" to the Lebanese problem was thus adopted and set in motion under the pa-tronage of Saudi Arabia and Kuwait. While presenting itself as a safeguard for the PLO and confirming its rights obtained through the Cairo Accord of 1969, the solution ratified a balance of power favorable to the Syrian troops by organizing the Arab Deterrent Force (ADF) whose mission was to deploy over the whole of the Lebanese territory with the exception of the south. President Elias Sarkis, who had just assumed office in the shadow of the Syrian tanks, was theoretically in command of this force, which included contingents from Saudi Arabia, Sudan, North and South Yemen, Libya, and the United Arab Emirates. Three-quarters of the fighting men of the ADF, however, were none other than the Syrians who had already been in Leba-non for several months. Less than three years later, these men were the sole remaining representatives of the Arab force.

The major powers chose to remain in the background. After the French president's envoy Maurice Couve de Murville's successful mission of information in November 1975, France prompted a general outcry the next April by proposing direct intervention. The Soviet Union, sensitive to the presence of more than 50 million Muslims in its Asian republics, was in an awkward position with regard to the communitarian clashes. In a period in which American policy in the Near East was proving dynamic, the USSR included among its allies the PLO, which received messages of firm support from Moscow, and the various groups of the Lebanese left, of whose dispersion and fragility it was well aware. Faithful to its policy of respect for the political entities of the Near East, the Soviet Union was content to denounce foreign meddling in the conflict, while shipments of arms from the Eastern Bloc countries were being unloaded in Syrian ports. The problem came mainly from its Syrian ally, which the Soviets had made the leading Arab military power in the region in 1973 and whose massive incursion in Lebanon took it by surprise and provoked a stern editorial in *Pravda* on September 8, 1976 insisting on both the need for the Lebanese themselves to settle what was chiefly a domestic controversy and the autonomy of the Palestinian national movement. Moscow's disagreement about the Damascus initiative even provoked a temporary suspension of cooperation between the two countries. All in all, however, Lebanon came under the American sphere of influence, and the aging Soviet leadership favored maintaining the international status quo in the Near East, particularly in the Lebanon of the National Pact, which the Soviet leaders were quite content to live with.[10] Above all, the Soviet Union granted priority to an international meeting in Geneva during which the Lebanese dossier would be examined together with the other dossiers of the region.

The Soviets' reluctance concerning a Syrian solution in Lebanon tied in with the quiet satisfaction of the United States at Damascus's taking charge of a situation that the Americans thought was dangerously turning in favor of the PLO. They themselves could not think of intervening the way they had in 1958, since their sponsorship of the Arab-Israeli negotiations in Geneva after the 1973 war. The Syrian operation allowed for a reestablishment of the balance of power that the intransigence of the Christian leaders had driven to the brink of an unequal combat and also dampened the revolutionary ambitions of the LNM and the Palestinian national movement. Moreover, to reach a solution to the Arab-Israeli conflict, Washington judged it necessary that Israel deal with reasonable government representatives and not a revolutionary liberation movement. For Secretary of State Henry Kissinger, the Syria led by Hafez al-Assad was a pragmatic partner, reliable and effective, whose role in Lebanon he described as "moderate." The Arabization of the Lebanese crisis with the creation of the ADF in October 1976 seemed to him a fitting solution, on condition that it not endanger Israeli security. American intervention mainly consisted in acting as mediator between Israel and Syria to fix the southern limit of the ADF's advance.

The "red line" not to be crossed by the Syrian army was flexible. After a march toward Jezzin and Nabatiye, where the partisans of the Lebanese Front were battling with the Palestinian forces, the ADF took up a position from the mouth of the Zahrani River to the north of Hasbeya in the Bikaa. The war in Lebanon thus met several Israeli goals: it dealt a blow to the Palestinian resistance on which Syrians and Lebanese imposed restrictions of movement and action through the Shtaura accord of July 1977; it tarnished the image of the pluricommunitarian state that the Palestinians opposed to the Jewish state; and it bogged down the most threatening of the Arab armies in an expensive occupation—nearly a million dollars a day. In sum, "Syria does Israel's work in Lebanon," and Israel seized the chance to get a foothold in the country by secretly agreeing to outfit and train the forces of the Lebanese Front, and above all by initiating collaboration with the part of the Lebanese army that was holding the border zone.

Does this mean there was connivance between Syria and Israel in Lebanon, a convergence of goals, or collaboration? In reality, the mutual ignorance of the populations and even of the leaders of the two countries produced mutual distrust, with consequences far deeper than those between Israel and Egypt. Though Israel was delighted to see the Syrian troops weaken the LNM and the PLO, the "convergence" ended there. Israel did everything to prevent Syria from dominating the situation, from extricating itself from the "Lebanese quagmire,"[11] and from becoming able to coordinate a dynamic strategy with an allied Lebanon and friendly Palestinians. As for the Syrian-Israeli "collaboration," it consisted in receiving and transmitting their respective security needs through the channel of the United States, which saw to it that nothing interfered with the Camp David peace process: thus it was that Lebanon's air space was de facto recognized by Syria as belonging to Israeli security.

A Divided Country

The Syrian military intervention as well as Arab and international pressures imposed the return of a very relative calm thanks to which Lebanon enjoyed a semblance of normalcy between 1977 and 1981. Its prosperity seemed to hold up despite the war: the reserves of the banking sector increased by nearly 50 percent in 1977 alone, owing to shrewd transfers of activity to Athens, Amman, and Paris; the money sent back by emigrants further increased with the breathtaking rise in the price of oil; above all, nearly a fourth of the whole population took refuge abroad, in Europe or the neighboring Arab countries, proportionally reducing domestic needs. But the unbalanced economy was weakened by the destruction of the port of Beirut, the industrial infrastructures, and especially housing and living conditions, the sector most affected by the bombardments.[12] There was even a precarious political truce: the new president's assumption of office, the nomination of a cabinet, and the meetings of parliament that in March 1979 voted a law reorganizing the army and providing for it to be sent to the Israeli border—all of these poorly masked the disintegration of a state that was powerless to get the least of its decisions in matters of defense and taxation respected, and subject to censorship by Damascus.[13] More seriously yet, these measures could not slow down the geographical breakup of the country.

The fate of war had divided Lebanon into several zones distinguished by their populations' sectarian identity and by the realities of power exercised there. Tiny Christian Lebanon represented a fifth of the country's surface area and included about 500,000 persons in a quadrilateral extending from the mountain ridges to the Mediterranean shoreline, bounded in the north at Batrun and in the south dividing Beirut into two cities: Christian East Beirut and Muslim West Beirut. Several factors contributed to the cohesion of Christian Lebanon: the creation of an administration and a taxation agency parallel to those of the state; the homogeneity of the population consisting chiefly of Maronites and Greek Catholics, but also Orthodox and Armenians—for a long time the Christians still went to the "other side," particularly the business section of Hamra, while danger kept the Muslims from crossing the "green line"; the intensification of the allegiance to the ideology of the Kataeb and the "Lebanist" intellectuals of the University of Kaslik; and above all, the unification of the militias under the Lebanese Forces, commanded by the young Bashir Gemayel who began to put into effect his strategy for the conquest of whole Lebanon from the Christian Mountain.[14] A rivalry concerning the distribution of powers, spheres of influence, and profits from racketeering of the militias led to the murder of Tony Frangieh and his family in June 1978, after which his partisans from Zghorta definitively quit the Lebanese Forces. Two years later,[15] Bashir bloodily crushed the wishes for autonomy of the militia of the National Liberal Party and proclaimed: "For the first time in fourteen centuries, the Lebanese Christians are finally militarily united."

Nevertheless, more Christians lived in parts of Lebanon other than those controlled by the Lebanese Forces. The Syrians occupied the Bikaa, Hermil, the Akkar, and Tripoli; the mountain of Zghorta was held by the Frangiehs; and the plain of Kura by the SSNP. Damascus did not control the south, though it had close allies there, such as the pro-Syrian Baath and *Amal*. West Beirut and its suburbs, Sidon and its environs, Nabatiye and the Jabal Amil—that is, a major part of the country south of the capital—were under the domination of the Palestinian organizations which subordinated Lebanese interests to those of the resistance but exercised only minimal political authority. Because the state was the great absentee, the Sunni patrons had lost their legitimacy, and the LNM was weakened by its defeat in 1976 and the assassination of its chief Kamal Jumblat in March 1977, anarchy and insecurity held sway in those areas where the alliance between Palestinians, Muslim militias, and leftist parties continued to deteriorate.[16] Despite everything, certain basic features of the Lebanese identity—freedom of expression, pluralism, and even social interaction—survived until the savageries of 1982.

The worsening of the crisis between irreconcilable factions was not the only factor to deepen the gulf separating the Lebanese from each other. The Middle Eastern regional context too was disastrous. Anwar Sadat's journey to Jerusalem in November 1977 and the conclusion eighteen months later of a peace treaty between Israel and Egypt overturned the Lebanese chessboard. Faithful to its tactics of never allowing an ally to become too strong, or an adversary to be totally eliminated, Syria chose to reconcile itself with the PLO and in 1979 returned it to its former positions south of Beirut. On the other hand, its intense bombardment of East Beirut and the Christian Mountain in July and October of 1978 did not end the insubordination of the Lebanese Forces, which, reinforced by Egypt's decision, preferred to fall back on a narrow territory and tighten their cooperation with Israel. With the support of the Arab governments that were financing the ADF, especially Kuwait and Saudi Arabia, President Sarkis criticized the presence of the Syrian army as oppressive. Nevertheless, the Lebanese army was unable to replace the ADF when the latter fell back to the Bikaa in 1979 and 1980.

While Syria was losing ground and worried about its isolation in the Near East, Israel was becoming increasingly present next to the Lebanese Forces, especially in the south where bombing and incursions were a daily occurrence under Menachem Begin's new tactic of "preventive war" against the Palestinian fedayeen. In this devastated area, an air and land operation of several days in March 1978 led Israeli forces as far as the Litani River. It produced dozens of civilian victims, destroyed the homes and infrastructures of several villages, and triggered the flight of more than 200,000 Lebanese toward Sidon and the capital. By withdrawing in July,[17] the Israeli army created an obstacle to the deployment up to the border by the United Nations Interim Force in Lebanon (UNIFIL), which had just been created to restore the authority of the Lebanese state.[18] It confirmed the Army of Free Lebanon of Major Saad Haddad in its mission as guardian of a "security zone" a few miles wide, from the coast to Marjuyun.

The Lebanese lost control of the war being waged in their country under reprieve. The initial stakes—the transformation of their political system, the challenge to the distribution of powers and benefits among Christians and

Muslims, the choice between the country's Arabization or isolation—all were nearly forgotten, though in any case overshadowed by the urgent question of the fate of hundreds of thousands of Palestinians, a murderous war between Israelis and the PLO on the national soil, and the threat of a new episode in the Arab-Israeli conflict that would take Lebanon as its battlefield. At the first signs of war, the Lebanese, conditioned by their state's vulnerability and a long history of foreign interventions, turned to all sides looking for sponsors and allies. Seven years later, they were the impotent witnesses to clashes between the "protectors" of whom they were the first victims: the president took his orders sometimes from Damascus, sometimes from Bashir Gemayel; the LNM could do nothing without the PLO, and many heads of militias were Syria's henchmen. As for the Lebanese Forces, they were preparing the way for Israel's intervention. As though these divided and bleeding groups no longer belonged to the same homeland.

10

One War Hides Others (1982–1990)

T HE fifth Near Eastern war, the deadliest and most destructive in the whole Lebanese crisis,[1] was unleashed by the Israeli invasion of June 1982. It confirmed Lebanon's sense of impotence and dependence: the Israeli-Palestinian and Israeli-Syrian clashes on its territory were followed by the creation of a Multinational Force led by the United States—a brief interlude between successive invasions and occupations, for the Israeli army pulled out in 1985 only to make way for Syrian forces. The most disastrous effect of the war of 1982 was the chain reaction of confrontations between and within communities in the wake of the Israeli army: a new outburst of civil war that was to leave Lebanon wounded and bled white.

Israel in Lebanon

Like Syria, Israel had formed an ambitious strategy in Lebanon. It was separated from it by an international frontier defined at the time of the Mandatory division, confirmed by the Armistice of 1949, and overseen by a Mixed Commission assisted by officers of the United Nations. In 1968, Israel began waging a daily cross-border war against the PLO in southern Lebanon. The arrival of the Syrian troops of the Arab Deterrent Force in 1976 did not end this war, which merely changed form and scale, to the point of leading the Israeli army to an attack on Beirut in 1982. Nevertheless, Israeli policy in Lebanon involved more than the struggle against the Palestinian "terrorists." Even before 1970, when their northern border was relatively peaceful, the Israeli leaders had adopted an ambiguous strategy toward their neighbor, consisting of attempts at seduction and a patient, insidious process of undermining.

Searching for a weakness in the opposing Arab community, the Israelis claimed not to know which would be the first nation to sign a peace. Hashimite Jordan? Egypt? But they were sure that owing to its inability to take the first step, Lebanon would be at least the second. Before and after the creation of Israel, secret contacts with Lebanon's political bosses—particularly its Maronite leaders, Emile Eddé in 1937 and Camille Chamoun in 1955[2]—favored two complementary propositions among the civilian and military leaders. The Lebanese state was considered unique in the Arab political community, because it had been created around a Maronite nucleus, for the Maronites (and other Lebanese Christians), and was based on the principle of the primacy of the Maronites. In the principally Muslim East, which was rocked by military takeovers, Israel and Lebanon were generally thought of as exceptions, whose shared democratic values and ties to the West should bring them together and even make them allies against their hostile neighbors. It was in Israel's interest to get along with the Lebanese state, to build up Lebanon's military might for its defense against any foreign and particularly Syrian hegemony, and to check any attempt at domestic subversion, whether from pan-Arabists as in 1958 or, later, Palestinian militants. The other proposition underscored the state's artificial and fragile pluricommunitarian character, its demographic course that was inescapably unfavorable to the Maronites, and its possible splintering into easily manipulable entities.

Both contentions were articulated in ways relevant to Israel's definition of its two aims regarding the Arabs: to weaken and divide a generally hostile community by looking for its weak links and encouraging minority separatism (among the Kurds, Lebanese Christians, and Christians from southern Sudan) and to enlarge its own territorial base whose limits had never been fixed. In the 1950s, a debate took place between Prime Minister Moshe Sharett and his predecessor David Ben-Gurion about the value of encouraging a Lebanese officer to assume leadership of a "Christian regime allied with Israel," the viability of a state reduced to the borders of the pre-Mandate smaller Lebanon, and the risks and advantages of conquering southern Lebanon up to the Litani River, 55 percent of whose water Israel could then harness. Soon, their hesitations about the strategy to adopt with regard to Lebanon—the encouragement of a strong Maronite state or destabilization—were swept away by the new deal represented by the settling of the Palestinian resistance in that country.

From then on, Israeli policy was dominated by two primary concerns: first, to ensure the security of Galilee and the Hula basin, areas bordering Lebanon. In need of a firm defense were both the agricultural settlements established before Israel's creation as well as the populations of the northern towns in which Jewish immigrants from the Arab countries predominated. The Israeli army, by far the most powerful in the Middle East, was somewhat ineffective against a guerrilla war conducted from across the border and in the hilly, compartmentalized, and sparsely populated areas. While the prospect of living under the constant threat of shelling or hostage-taking reinforced Israeli cohesion, it undermined popular confidence in the wisdom of a repressive or "preventive" military solution. The other Israeli preoccupation was political. Since 1973, the PLO had not figured at all in the plans for a negotiated settlement between Israel and the Arab states. While the 1973 summit in Algiers of the heads of state in the Arab League recognized the PLO as "the sole legitimate representative of the Palestinians," Israel considered it the chief obstacle to peace, and sought to discredit and if possible eliminate it from the Near Eastern scene. Henceforth the issues in Lebanon were defined by the two imperatives of the pursuit of security and the undermining of the PLO.

"Peace for Galilee"

The first incidents in the Lebanese crisis gave Israel a chance to reinforce its positions: after the war of 1975–76, the Israeli government prevented the Syrian army of the ADF from penetrating southern Lebanon. In 1978, it refused to yield to UNIFIL the border area it considered its "security zone" and preferred to support the Army of Free Lebanon and to put up a costly electrified fence. In 1979, it bombed a contingent of the Lebanese army outfitted by the United States, which was proceeding to Marjuyun for the purpose of repositioning itself in the south. Nevertheless, neither Israel's assumption of direct control of Lebanese territory, its house-to-house searches, its arrests, nor its bombings prevented the fedayeen from reaching the interior of Israel by sea, or from shelling Galilee and the Hula across the security zone.[3] In June 1981, the escalation of the Israeli-Palestinian skirmishes was such that, in reprisal for the lethal bombing of Beirut's popular district of Fakhani by Israeli planes, tens of thousands of Israeli civilians at Kiryat Shmonah and Nahariya had to flee the shelling the PLO rained down on their area.

The Israeli security policy failed, only partly achieving its other goal of weakening the PLO and thus expediting a separate peace process with each Arab state. In 1978, Egypt signed the Camp David agreement, but in reaction, Syria again became allied with the Palestinians and once again granted them its support. By common consent, the two allies kept quiet about the contradictions between the Syrian interests and the Palestinian plans on which their respective strategies were based, invoked Arab "national" interest, and revived the resistance in Lebanon, thus strengthening the "hawks," the Israeli partisans of a military solution against the PLO. A first serious clash pitted Syrians against Israelis in the battle of Zahle in April and May of 1981, then, the following month, Palestinians against Israelis. The American green light for the great offensive launched by Menachem Begin and Ariel Sharon[4] was given the following year, once the Israeli-Egyptian peace was in effect. While Soviet protests against the disturbance of the status quo in the Near East had little effect—Moscow lacked the means for pressuring Jerusalem—Israel had at its command an immense capital of Western indulgence concerning its aggressions against Lebanon, which were presented as necessary for the defense of a democracy in the face of terrorism.

It took six days to reach Beirut in June 1982, which was then besieged for three months. The Shuf was occupied for a year (until September 1983), the western Bikaa and the south for three years (until June 1985). The war in Lebanon was one of the costliest for Israel since that of 1948–49 and the October War of 1973: heavy human losses[5] in an army of up to 100,000, a trauma for a society shaken in its certainty of being the "only true democracy" in the Near East, horrified by massacres of civilians perpetrated by militiamen because of the war, and questioning itself about its army's strategy and methods in light of the questionable results. After conquering more than half of Lebanon, the Israelis could neither prolong their occupation nor obtain any political capital from their military victory. All in all, the gains Israel made in the "Peace for Galilee" operation were incommensurate with the devastation it wreaked on Lebanon.

From the first day of the invasion, the inadequately prepared combatants of the PLO suffered heavy losses; they abandoned all of southern Lebanon and withdrew to West Beirut, where more than a month's intense bombardment[6] forced them to agree to an American evacuation plan: nearly 15,000 fedayeen were ordered to scatter to several Arab countries at the end of August 1982. Two hundred thousand people without electricity and often water suffered, with no panic, the siege of their city, the deluge of shells, and the advance of the Israeli army. The ever present memory of the trauma of 1948 dictated this fitting response: not to flee under threat, for fear of never being able to return. To remain was to resist, even passively, and to indicate one's solidarity with other besieged civilians.

At the same time, despite assurances from the American emissary Philip Habib, the Syrian army was swept north of the Bikaa. In five days it lost hundreds of tanks, more than eighty fighter planes, and all its batteries of ground-to-air missiles. A third matter of short-lived satisfaction for Israel was that the Lebanese Forces gave the conqueror an enthusiastic welcome, although they refrained from joining it in the fighting. Their head, Bashir

Gemayel, was elected president on August 23. The signing of an Israeli-Lebanese peace treaty was the order of the day, all the more so as the United States, like the heads of member states of the Arab League meeting in Fez in Morocco, agreed to a pullout of *all* foreign forces from Lebanon, meaning the Syrian army as well.

In a few months, however, a glaring discrepancy became apparent between the goal and the results of Israel's "Peace for Galilee" campaign. Their designated ally, Bashir Gemayel, was assassinated before assuming office. The first armed engagements between the Lebanese National Resistance Front and the Israeli soldiers covering West Beirut occurred at the end of August; they increased in the fall and were followed by the ever more numerous ones with Shi'i militant organizations galvanized by the revolution in Iran. Harassments and attacks by the secular or Islamic organizations on the occupying army and its allied "South Lebanon" militia escalated the state of latent war that had prevailed before 1982. The peace treaty of Naqoura, arduously extracted from Lebanon in May 1983, was not ratified, for Syria arranged for a wide front uniting Lebanese Muslims and leftists to refuse to sign it. Finally, when the Israeli army unilaterally pulled out from most of the south in 1985, the Palestinian fedayeen had already recaptured the camps on the edge of Sidon and resumed their commando activities, while the Syrian army reestablished itself on the heights of the Matn, from which it once again dominated Beirut and the coast.

Conquerors, Yes . . .

Operation "Peace for Galilee" was a shock primarily to the Lebanese. A salutary shock, many of them thought, that would enable them to extricate themselves from a situation of "neither peace nor war" that had now lasted for seven years, to overcome the de facto split between the area dominated by the Lebanese Forces and the rest of the country, and to reestablish a unitary state under the authority of a responsible president. But the Israeli invasion drove the moderate forces out of all parties and all communities, which were then battered by the extremists. Without its being explicitly stated, the National Pact was once again called into question: in 1958, the clashes between Lebanese had ended with a return to the traditional balance, a return symbolized by the slogan "Neither conquerors nor conquered." In 1982, the Christian conservatives, headed by Amin Gemayel who had been elected president to replace his brother, and backed by the militia of the Lebanese Forces, considered themselves the winners in the war conducted by Israel in their country. Nevertheless, no Lebanese took part in this war, apart from militants of the leftist or Islamic parties who in early June resisted at the southern access to Beirut, and the unit of the Lebanese Forces led by Elias Hobeika, who entered the Palestinian camps of Sabra and Shatila, encircled by the Israeli army, and in thirty-six hours triumphantly defeated its enemy: the bodies of several hundred women, children, and old people (almost all the men had gone into exile) lay in piles at street corners.[7]

To tighten their hegemony over the whole of Lebanon, the "conquerors" were counting chiefly on the support of the United States. Amin Gemayel had never had the same close relations with Israel as had his brother Bashir, but his advisers were such Americanophiles that they were said to dream of making Lebanon the fifty-first state of the Union. For its part, Washington wished to believe that Gemayel and Gemayel alone represented all of Lebanon. America contributed reconstruction loans and new materiel for the army and its advisers, as well as the policy of negotiating with Israel, and probably also its splendid ignorance of Lebanon's regional environment, particularly Syria—the treaty of Naqoura made provision for the Syrian army's pullout from Lebanon while it guaranteed Israel "security arrangements," recognizing its right to police the south.

After a brief interval of euphoria came the rude awakening.[8] The American, French, and Italian units of the 6,000-man Multinational Force sent in August 1982 to oversee the peaceful evacuation of the fedayeen, and suddenly recalled a month later to protect Lebanese and Palestinian civilians in Beirut, were unable to avoid being party to Lebanon's internal conflicts. Preferred to a United Nations force of which the leading Western powers could not be a part and about which the Soviet Union would have had a say, the Multinational Force stirred Lebanese memories of the French Mandate and the American landing in 1958. Even France, which in July had proposed, together with Egypt, a reasonable and generous solution of the Lebanese and Palestinian problems,[9] progressed, following the United States, from peaceful control of Beirut's populations to clashes and search operations, then was forced to pull back to entrenched positions, until it and the United States were the target of suicide bombings in October 1983 that killed 56 French paratroopers and 239 American marines; and the following month the French carried out an abortive aerial bombing of the barracks of Islamic militants in Baalbek. After clashes with heavy artillery against the Druze and the Syrian forces, the Multinational Force ingloriously pulled out of Lebanon in February 1984.

. . . But a Failed Conquest

Following the war of 1982, the blunder of the Lebanese "conquerors" was not only to shelter their power under the umbrella of the Western powers. It was primarily to misuse the Israeli victory by trying to reverse the delicate equilibriums that still prevailed in the country, to reunify the Mountain by force, and to subjugate the populations of West Beirut and its suburbs. In principle, their plan for the country's reunification and the withdrawal of foreign troops was acceptable to all Lebanese. But it would also have to be implemented, if not in some indefinable general interest, at least out of respect for the particular interests of the various groups.

On the heels of the Israeli armies, the Lebanese Forces hastened into the mountains of the Shuf, most of whose population was Christian but whose security had for the past seven years been provided only by the Druze militiamen of the Progressive Socialist Party. They had taken up positions in the coastal regions south of the capital, where a large part of the population was Christian but whose Communist and Muslim militias had provided security since the tragic massacre at Damur in 1976. They were anxious to retake the villages on the road from Jezzin to Sidon, which until then had been under Palestinian control. An ephemeral victory for the men of Samir Geagea who, despite their boasts, failed the test of arms: at each stage of the Israeli pullout between the summers of 1983 and 1985, the adventure turned into a debacle; they were unable to keep the zones "conquered" in 1982 and had to beat a hasty retreat to the Matn and Kisrawan. "Debacle," however, is too weak a word to describe what the local Christian populations had to suffer by way of reprisals for the adventure of the Lebanese Forces, the massacres and hasty flight of several tens of thousands of newly homeless people seeking refuge in Jezzin or the Matn, thus marking a new stage in the division of the country into quasi-sectarian cantons. The Druzes, who up to then had stayed oddly clear of the fighting and put up no resistance to the Israelis' foray into their mountain (possibly owing to assurances sent by representatives of the Druze community in Israel), led the triumphant reconquest of the Shuf. Once again, the vendetta produced devastation while Walid, the young Jumblat leader, failed in his responsibilities.

Amin Gemayel's attempt to impose his authority at Beirut was equally a failure: in the west, and only the west, the army, newly reorganized by close associates of the president, multiplied its search operations, its massive raids, its destruction of the flimsy shantytowns of the refugees from the south, and soon its indiscriminate shellings of the impoverished, overpopulated areas on the city's outskirts. In February 1984, the mostly Sunni Muslim and Orthodox Christian heart of the traditional city was sucked into the maelstrom of the revolt of the new city dwellers—several hundreds of thousands of Shi'i refugees left on the scrap heap of the "Lebanese miracle," deprived by the Israeli occupation of the resources of their land, repeatedly hounded out of the south toward Beirut and from Beirut toward the south to the beat of bombings, and for whom the only thing their state had to offer was to send in the troops. Galvanized by the legacy of Musa Sadr who had founded it and who since had vanished in Libya in 1978, the Amal movement, joined by the disenchanted followers of the National Movement and by all those who believed only in sectarian solidarity, led them to victory over the Lebanese army, a whole Shi'i brigade of which joined the ranks of the insurgents. The fracture of Beirut was reopened and the bombings resumed on both sides of the line of demarcation, symbol of the country's division into two camps: on one side, Amin Gemayel's government which controlled barely 10 percent of the national territory, the "Christian" regions where the Lebanese Forces dominated, and the south which was occupied by the Israeli army; in the rest of the country, a host of leftist and Islamic groups, allies of Syria or the Palestinians, and of Iran too, from which emerged the two forces of the PSP and Amal.

The "conquerors" created the illusion of reopening a national dialogue, and the "conquered" of accepting it, by meeting in two conferences, one in Geneva in November 1983 and one in Lausanne in April 1984, and later by sitting together in the government. But the Lebanese Forces' proposal to establish a territorial federalism enshrining the country's division, and Amal's proposal to have done with political confessionalism through the adoption of a majoritarian system, ran into symmetrical vetoes. In fact, this "dialogue" was merely a new chapter in the competition of the patrons defending their rival interests. In the conference hall at Geneva where Syrian policemen required, not without difficulty, that everyone enter unarmed, the patrons, now "warlords," were counting not their electors but their militiamen. Two newcomers to the club marked the rejuvenation of a system that ensured its own perpetuation: Amin Gemayel, who represented the middle Maronite stratum mobilized by the Kataeb, and Nabih Berri, the Shi'i lawyer who had led Amal since 1980. In terms of the balance of power, practically all Lebanon found itself in the "national union" government that Amin Gemayel entrusted to Rashid Karameh at the beginning of May: Camille Chamoun and the son-in-law of Suleiman Frangieh, Walid Jumblat and Nabih Berri. The government, however, was unable to supply either management for the country or the search for a political solution, as though by acknowledging insuperable disagreements, it quit taking responsibility for them.

Military Strongholds (1988)

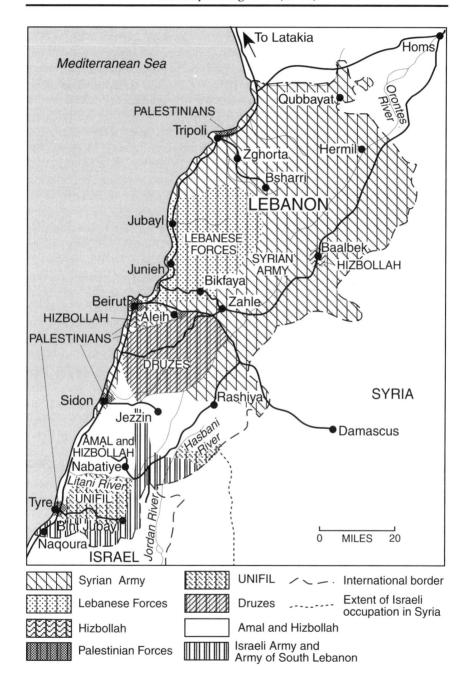

Mediterranean Sea

To Latakia

Homs

PALESTINIANS

Tripoli

Qubbayat

Orontes River

Hermil

Zghorta

Bsharri

LEBANON

Jubayl

LEBANESE FORCES

Baalbek

SYRIAN ARMY

HIZBOLLAH

Junieh

Bikfaya

Beirut

Zahle

HIZBOLLAH

Aleih

PALESTINIANS

DRUZES

SYRIA

Sidon

Rashiya

Jezzin

Hasbani River

Damascus

AMAL and HIZBOLLAH

Nabatiye

Litani River

UNIFIL

Jordan River

Tyre

Bint Jubayl

0   MILES   20

Naqoura

ISRAEL

Syrian Army	UNIFIL	International border
Lebanese Forces	Druzes	Extent of Israeli occupation in Syria
Hizbollah	Amal and Hizbollah	
Palestinian Forces	Israeli Army and Army of South Lebanon	

Joined Interests?

After the upheavals of 1982–84, Lebanon found itself again confronting its two ambitious neighbors, Syria and Israel. These countries were no longer content to threaten prompt interventions. Since the Golan Heights front had been fixed since 1974, they took Lebanon as a battlefield, set the rules for their game, and imposed their goals. In Lebanon, they seized strategic positions, attacked the allies of their opponents and even each other. In sum, the Arab-Israeli conflict—limited to the "eastern front" since peace had been concluded between Israel and Egypt—was now confined to the Bikaa and South Lebanon, which were burrowed with trenches, plowed by tanks, furrowed by barbed wire, and watered by bombs. Whether the prize was winning the war or winning trump cards for some international negotiation, Lebanon had become the battlefield of the Near Eastern conflict.

Does this mean that Syria and Israel were tacitly carving up the country, that the principle of a double occupation was accepted by both sides, and that only the line of demarcation changed? In 1982, the Israeli army pushed back the Syrian army north of the Damascus highway in the Bikaa; starting in 1985, the Syrians advanced toward the south simultaneously with each Israeli pullout toward the "security zone." In fact, though the two adversaries had to accept tacit arrangements and limit the intensity of their clashes because of pressure from the United States, the strategies of Damascus and Tel Aviv remained strategies of mutual exclusion.

For lack of a strong government in Lebanon that would have signed a peace treaty, Israel reverted to its tactics of division, supporting the local groups, providing them with arms and lavishing them with advice. Each stage in its retreat to the south stirred up a war between local factions, thus providing proof in the eyes of international opinion, and some Lebanese themselves, that the country was merely an agglomeration of hostile clans. The Israelis were unable to impose their own solution to the Lebanese crisis, but they did have the means to prevent the Syrian solution from succeeding: encouraging the most radical Christian conservatives to oppose and boycott any plan for national reconciliation that had been mapped out in the shadow of Damascus. Officially, the treaty of Naqoura was abrogated, the Israeli mission in the Christian area was sent packing, and no Lebanese party maintained relations with the Israelis. Nevertheless, there remained partisans of the "Israeli option": the military chiefs of the Lebanese Forces, the ideologues of the Maronite University of Kaslik, and the veteran Camille Chamoun, who until his death in 1978 refused to yield. Every time, the plans for a coordinated intervention by the Israelis and the Christian conservatives fizzled: in 1978, the defenders of Ashrafiyeh waited in vain for an Israeli landing; in 1982 General Ariel Sharon was disappointed by the passivity of Bashir Gemayel and the Lebanese Forces. Nevertheless, the latter continued to respond to incitements to rebellion and received logistical aid that enabled them to block the attempts at negotiation among the Lebanese: two months after Amin Gemayel had broken off his talks with Jerusalem in January 1985, a coup made Samir Geagea, an intransigent partisan of the separation of communities and alliance with Israel, the head of the Lebanese Forces. And when in May 1987 the president attempted a reconciliation with his prime minister Rashid Karameh, the latter was assassinated. Every overture by the Maronite leaders to their compatriots in the other communities was met by Israeli-backed extremists ready to scuttle it.

In the south, the goal of "security for Galilee" served as a pretext for manipulating local militias. Amal, which had become the most powerful social and political force of the Jabal Amil and Tyre after the PLO fedayeen had been evicted, adopted a moderate plan: to assure complete evacuation of the Israeli army from Lebanon, but to prevent the fedayeen from rekindling the cycle of triangular conflicts of which the local population had been victims for years on end. For several months, certain Israeli leaders saw in the Shi'i movement a trump card for reconstructing a new Lebanon at peace with Israel and counted on Amal's branch in the south, directed by Daoud Daoud, to ensure the security of the border areas. The failure of the government of "national union" at Beirut in 1984, however, marked the end of the "tacit collaboration": the Amal militants rejoined those of the National Resistance Front (the Communist Party, the SSNP, the Baath Party, and so on) which were harassing the Israeli troops to get them to respect their pledge of evacuation,[10] while imposing severe controls over the Palestinian camps at Tyre and Sidon. As for the UNIFIL forces, discredited by their ineffectualness during the 1982 invasion and caught in the crossfire between Lebanese factions, the Israelis found them something of a nuisance and wanted them stationed north of the Litani River, to form a first barrier before the "security zone."

Just as the Israelis used the Lebanese Forces to block Lebanese political developments, so they also used the fiction of the "Army of South Lebanon" (ASL)—the new name of the "Army of Free Lebanon"—to intervene beyond their border. A fiction of representativeness: the vast majority of the Army of South Lebanon were Christians, including militias that had landed by sea from Kisrawan and Matn, while the local populations it claimed to protect were 80 percent Shi'i. A fiction of independence: the ASL was outfitted, trained, and paid by Israel. A fiction of security: headlong flight and desertions in its ranks forced the Israeli army itself to fight the Lebanese resistance with ever-growing ferocity.

The intensity of the resistance in the south once again challenges the image of a symmetrical occupation by Syria and Israel in Lebanon. It illustrates the difference in the Lebanese appraisals of the presence of the Syrian army, which though loathed has often been recognized as necessary and never as totally foreign, and the occupation by the Israeli army, which was judged unacceptable. It certainly surprised the Israelis, who had been combing through the West Bank and Gaza since 1967. Unlike the Palestinians from the occupied territories, the Lebanese of the south had behind them a country that armed them and ten years of training in warfare. Furthermore, the Iranian revolution had encouraged the Shi'i resistance: since 1980, several hundred Iranian religious leaders, missionaries, and militants had spread through the Bikaa, then the region of Tyre, by coming through Syria and had trained combatants, prepared suicide commandos, and organized mass demonstrations. Their often spectacular operations combined with those of Amal and the organizations of the National Resistance Front; all were supported by a population mobilized against the occupation. Olive trees cut down, citrus harvests lost, the dumping of Israeli imports—for three years economic activity came to a virtual stop in the region. Moreover, the occupation troops hampered its relations with Beirut. After the war of 1982, several thousand men were arrested and detained for several months in internment camps near Nabatiye and even in Israel, without trial or investigation.[11] As in the West Bank and Gaza, their villages were subjected to curfew, searches, and raids; the houses of suspects were dynamited. Except for the unreliable collaboration of the ASL, the Israeli occupation met with universal condemnation.

Simultaneously, Syria reactivated its plan for controlling the PLO and the Lebanese state. It had been unable to realize it in 1976–78; but the upheavals following "Peace for Galilee" gave it new wind. Damascus at first supported the dissidents of al-Fatah in the Bikaa and fought at their side until the ouster in December 1983 of the partisans of an autonomous PLO who struggled under Yasir Arafat's command to hold on to their bases of operation in Lebanon. The Syrian army's siege of Tripoli in December 1983 was strikingly similar to the Israeli army's siege of West Beirut in the summer of 1982: both featured destructive bombing that strew thousands of civilian casualties and both ended in the pullout of Arafat and his men under France's protection. This similarity allowed the Israelis to congratulate themselves for Syria's "finishing off" the task that they themselves had undertaken. Everywhere in Lebanon, the Palestinians were deprived of organization and protection, threatened, and forced back into the refugee camps. From June 1985 to January 1988—thirty months that yielded more than 2,000 dead—the Amal militia conducted a pitiless siege of the camps of Beirut and Tyre to secure the surrender of the PLO combatants who had returned to Lebanon through Damascus or by sea, because they were a threat to its hegemony in West Beirut and the south. All during the "war of the camps," Palestinian Syria's allies and Arafat's partisans together defended some tens of thousands of refugees driven to the brink of famine, while Israeli planes bombed their bases in the Bikaa and the area of Sidon. Concluding the era of Palestinian liberties in Lebanon, the parliament voted in 1987 to abrogate the Cairo Accord of 1969.

Wasn't it an illusion, however, for the Israelis, Syrians, and all parties, Christian or Muslim, striving to push the Palestinians out of the way and to separate the Lebanese question from the Arab-Israeli conflict so as to resolve it to their advantage, to deny the participation of nearly 400,000 persons in the social, economic, and necessarily political life of a country with close to 3 million people? Furthermore, wasn't it vain to believe that the Arab states would allow, without reacting, the Palestinian cause to become an appendage or, worse, a tool of the ambitions of the Syrian state? Wasn't it premature to forget the solidarity between the Sunni and leftist Lebanese and the Palestinians while the conflict over the internal balance of Lebanon went on? During the "war of the camps," Libya and Egypt, the PSP and the Nasserists of Sidon, each pursuing its own goals, helped the Palestinian combatants to return to Lebanon. The Lebanese Forces themselves facilitated the transit of dozens of fedayeen through the port of Juniyeh because they were coming to fight their enemy, Amal. When Syria decided to subdue the last bastions of the PLO in Lebanon, it met with condemnation by the leftist Arab states and even its Saudi financial backers, not counting the USSR. Besides, the Baathist leaders knew that it was good to weaken their adversary, but not too much, so that another contender, the Lebanese Forces, did not take advantage of the situation. They could thus once again choose reconciliation, a tactical truce between two rivals pursuing irreconcilable goals, enabling them together to tip the scales in concert at the next presidential election.

While the Israeli occupation lasted, Syria gained a central position in the heart of the Lebanese system. Its aim was political. It presided over the meetings at Geneva and Lausanne, then at the negotiations in 1985 and 1986 between the three principal militias: the Lebanese Forces, Amal, and the PSP. No institutional formula could be adopted without the agreement of Syria, and Syria served as the venue for the signing in December 1985 of the tripartite accord on communitarian rebalancing, the division of executive power between the president and the prime minister, and future political deconfessionalization.

Above all, Syria imposed itself militarily; rapidly and abundantly re-equipped by the USSR, which the major destruction of 1982 had foiled but which stood by its 1980 treaty commitments of cooperation, it consolidated its positions in the Bikaa where it positioned new batteries of ground-to-air missiles; it emplaced guns on the heights of the Matn and provided arms to the opposing Lebanese groups, particularly Amal, its main ally. When in 1983 the clashes between the Lebanese resumed, Syria fired at the Lebanese Forces and the Lebanese army units that supported Amin Gemayel, and then at the

American and French troops of the Multinational Force, while it drove Yasir Arafat's PLO out of the Bikaa and Tripoli. This audacious strategy enabled it to advance in rhythm with the pullouts of the Western powers and the Israeli withdrawals—on the international Beirut-Damascus highway, in the western Bikaa as far as Lake Qaraoun and on the heights of the Baruk—to send "observers" to West Beirut in June 1985 and still others a year later, until the return of the Special Forces, its elite units, to Beirut in February 1987, and their positioning around the Palestinian camps on the edges of the city and at the northern entrance to Sidon in April. At least 35,000 Syrian soldiers once again controlled more than 60 percent of the Lebanese territory.

The silence of the international community at the new takeover of Lebanon amounted as much to an admission of impotence as to the certainty that order, even if Syrian, was preferable to dangerous and contagious anarchy. This silence modestly hid the deals proposed to General Assad: the Soviets expected him to improve his relations with the PLO and Iraq; the Western powers expected him to have a positive influence on the terrorists and hostage-takers; and the Arabs expected him to make his Iranian ally listen to reason. On the other hand, the Syrian army evoked distrust and ill feeling among the Lebanese parties—even those it had saved from defeat and the populations to which it brought some relative security. Everywhere it went, it aroused Lebanese feelings of humiliation in the face of the "savior" that had been scorned for decades. Above all, Syria's opponents and allies realized that Assad's tactics—which they saw as parallel to Israeli tactics—of playing factions against each other, of favoring certain ones, and even of sending combatants had ended up prolonging the conflict, marginalizing the state, and fueling to his advantage the "little wars" in which Lebanon was exhausting itself.

Little Wars

The shock of the summer of 1982 shattered an already sorely afflicted Lebanese society and provoked rivalries and clashes among several dozen military organizations concerned only with the autonomy, security, and material benefits of the group they represented. Thus, in the city of Tripoli, with its Sunni majority, some district organizations, federated under the banner of Sheikh Said Shaaban's Islamic Unification Movement and supported by the PLO and the Muslim Brothers who had fled Aleppo and Hama in 1982, stood up for several years to the Syrian army and its local allies of the National Movement (the Communist Party and the SSNP), and the Alawi militia of Ali 'Id. In December 1986 a massive bombardment by the Syrian Special Forces destroyed the center of the city, leaving more than 100 people dead and temporarily putting an end to the clashes. Between the mountain of Zghorta and the hills of Kura, another war pitted two groups of Christians against each other (both allied with Syria, however), the SSNP and partisans of Frangieh, for control of the region's economic interests, such as the Chekka cement works.

There are abundant examples of local groups that fell back on sectarian solidarities, the breakdown of agreements between parties with identical platforms, the clashes between allied militias. The divisions between the allies of Syria were particularly disastrous: the coalition of the National Movement and the Muslim parties was unable to weather the assassination of its leader Kamal Jumblat in 1977, the centrifugal tendencies, rivalries between leaders, conflicts of interests, and, after 1982, the pullout of the constraining but unifying force of the PLO. In May 1985, Amal overpowered the Sunni Murabitun militia in Beirut. In November, militiamen of the PSP fought Amal for the control of neighborhoods west of Beirut where both were interlopers. January 1986 saw a wave of assassinations of leaders of the Communist Party of Lebanon and of the pro-Iraqi Baath Party. In June and the following January, the streets of West Beirut were again ablaze with fighting as Amal attempted to take over there at the expense of all the other political and military forces. All during these episodes, in which the chief victims were civilians, the heads of the militias and the parties were in Damascus, convened by Syrian vice president Khaddam for endless negotiations and reconciliations. The National Salvation Front of the democratic opposition (1983) and the National Union Front (1985), whose births were successively announced, were united only in their opposition to the power of the Christian leaders, symbolized by Amin Gemayel, and their dependence on Syria, which destroyed their leaders' legitimacy and discredited their platforms. The conclusion of these divisions, struggles, and pseudonegotiations was precisely the return of the Syrian army to Beirut in February 1987.

Moreover, one new element hastened the disintegration of these opposition parties, dispersed their forces, and challenged the program of deconfessionalizing the political system, as opposed to the unjust system of the National Pact: the rise to power of the Shi'i Islamists. For the failure of the leftists in 1976, the excesses of the Palestinians toward the populations of the south—more than ten years of violence, invasions, and exodus—and later the compromises of Amal leaders more than tried the Shi'i community's patience. The clerics, who always had held an essential place in this community, were strengthened by its enormous frustration. They offered a familiar and structured framework, met the economic and sanitary needs of the population, restored dignity and gave people reason to fight, and promised victory with the help of God. With the tolerance of its Syrian ally, and by means of generous subsidies, the Islamic Republic of Iran transformed Baalbek into a stronghold of militant Shi'ism in which the Pasdaran, arriving by air from Teheran, trained combatants of Islamic Amal and Hizbollah (Party of God), and imposed on the local populations, including Christians, their revolutionary order. In the south, they were the spearhead of combat against the Israeli occupation and even against UNIFIL, whose role they wanted to end.

The rivalries and frequent shifts of alliance among the Islamic movements, secular parties, and Amal explain the diversity of tactics employed to achieve the common goal of liberating Lebanese territory as far as the international border. Combatants transferred their allegiance on the spot from one group to another, depending on circumstances and opportunities. The conflictual relations among Shi'i organizations also reflected heated competition for power between secularists and clerics, old elites and new leaders, civilian and military leaders. But soon, with Iranian encouragement, the Islamic movement bested its rivals in prestige and financial resources. Already weakened by three years of calamitous warfare in the Palestinian camps, Amal lost dozens of militants who defected and joined ranks with the Hizbollah. After Amal's military defeat in the suburbs, its leader, Nabih Berri, announced its dissolution in June 1988. In Beirut, where more than 300,000 Shi'is had lived in the 1980s, Hizbollah, after triumphing over Amal and the leftists, carved out a fiefdom in the southern suburbs,[12] in Bir al-Abed, Bir Hassan, and Ouzai, which had escaped the control of both the Syrian army and the Lebanese state. In these areas, inhospitable to both Christians and foreigners, Islamic customs ruled: women wore the *hijab*, men let their beards grow, banners bore Islamic inscriptions and Khomeini exhortations, loudspeakers broadcast continuous sermons and slogans, and armed militants assiduously policed the area to protect the population from racketeering.

But leadership conflicts did not cease. In the following two years, the Islamic Resistance, Hizbollah's armed wing, conquered first the hills around Sidon and then the villages around Nabatiye. From clashes to truce, Amal's zone of influence shrank while Hizbollah's expanded until it gained hegemony over the plethora of political and military Muslim, Palestinian, and leftist forces. The fratricidal struggle struck village after village, moving from neighborhood to neighborhood, in the end causing more casualties (but less destruction) than had the Israeli enemy. In November 1990 a ceasefire between Amal and Hizbollah ended the inter-Shi'i warfare and established Islamic supremacy in Beirut and southern Lebanon. The vanquished political parties and militias decided then to cast their lot with those who favored the restoration of state sovereignty. Communists, Nasserites, and other leftist parties joined Amal in supporting the Taif Accord (approved by fifty-nine of the seventy-two surviving deputies), which had been concluded on October 22, 1989, and favored a unified national government.

Hizbollah's victory over Amal gave new impetus to the resistance against Israel and the Army of South Lebanon. Rather than make local agreements with Zahal, as Amal had done since 1985, Hizbollah adopted the tactic of deploying dozens of commandos against ASL in the Israeli-occupied "security zone." These operations, so costly in human lives, more showy than substantive, only deepened the frustrations of the southern Lebanese without winning them over to the Islamic militant cause. Israel responded by carrying out vast bombing raids with infantry and helicopter support in Sidon and Bikaa. Guerrilla operations of this type were unable to alter the local interplay of forces. At most they helped to keep the Israeli-Arab, or more exactly, the Israeli-Syrian front active while awaiting negotiations, which seemed imminent. Syria, together with Iran a sponsor of the Amal-Hizbollah Accord, intended to play the Islamic Resistance card in its confrontation with Israel. Syria closed its eyes to, and even facilitated, the armed clashes to underline its opposition to Israeli occupation of Lebanon and the Golan. Yet Syria never ruled out the possibility of ordering a freeze on resistance operations if necessary to provide guarantees to the United States and thus progress toward peace with Israel. Above all, Syria would not allow Hizbollah to interfere with the secular and military order it wanted to impose throughout Lebanon.

The series of wars and local clashes following the 1982 Israeli invasion plunged the Lebanese political system into complete disarray. From that time on, having assigned priority to the resolution of the Palestinian question, enflamed since 1987 by the intifada, the great powers refused to intervene, and Syria was able to cash in its chips. The moreso because a parallel process of disintegration and confrontation embroiled the Christian side.

From the Christian Militia to Aoun's Adventure

Despite the military unity Bashir Gemayel had imposed on the Christian region, the competition among his lieutenants was fierce. In a climate of intrigue, opposition, and insurrection, the population was subjected to a war of succession by the chiefs of the Lebanese Forces, his militia. Fadi Frem succeeded him in 1982, followed in 1984 by his nephew Fuad Abu Nader. In 1985 a triumvirate of Samir Geagea, Karim Pakradouni, and Elias Hobeika decided to seal an alliance between the Lebanese Forces and the Syrian regime by signing, together with Walid Jumblat and Nabih Berri, the Tripartite Accord. But the project failed and Hobeika, ensconced in Zahle with several hundred men, became one of Damascus's ally-clients. Samir Geagea retained leadership of the Lebanese Forces. In the late 1980s he came close to realizing what had once been Bashir Gemayel's goal, to establish in the so-called liberated zone (the region untouched by the Syrian army, where the LF had uncontested control) a military and civilian administration to replace those of the Lebanese state. On the one hand, he transformed the militia into a veritable army, complete with intensive training, rank designations, barracks, and heavy equipment (supplied by Israel and by Saddam Hussein's Iraq, who wanted by any means to weaken his rival Hafez al-Assad).[13] On the other hand, the militia built up the public service—surveys, taxes, transportation— as well as social and medical services by heavily taxing all the region's inhabitants.[14]

However, the separatist option was only a second alternative for Geagea and Gemayel. Despite an apparent prosperity, which contrasted with the ruination of the rest of the country, East Beirut and the little enclave controlled by the Lebanese Forces could not flourish if their trade with the rest of Lebanon was cut off. They derived some of their revenues from abroad, but some also from trade in foodstuffs and oil products with neighboring regions, and even Syria. Far from negligible were the revenues furnished by illegal trafficking in arms, drugs, and even passports for Palestinians seeking to return to Lebanon. In order to become, as some dreamed it might, the Singapore of the Mideast, "Little Christian Lebanon" had to engage in trade with its neighbors, and these consistently opposed the separatist option.

The Lebanese Forces' first objective, then, was to reconquer all of Lebanon. They could not do so militarily, since the previous routs in the Shuf in 1983 and Iqlim al-Kharroub in 1985 and the redeployment of the Syrian army around the "free" zone effectively eliminated this option for Samir Geagea and Fuad Malik; but they sought a political reconquest: to seize control of the Kataeb Party and so mobilize Christians around the Lebanist ideology. Above all, they hoped that such a strategy would lead them to ascend to the presidency of the Republic. Boycotted by his Muslim ministers, harassed by Syria, discredited by financial scandals and the plummeting Lebanese pound, Amin Gemayel and his disputed presidency came crashing down. Rather than accept a pro-Syrian, Washington-approved successor, his only choice was to transfer power to a member of the Lebanese Forces or to Michel Aoun, Commander in Chief of the army. He chose the latter.

As interim prime minister, Michel Aoun had a rival in the person of Salim al-Hoss, who refused to step down as prime minister and claimed executive power. In September 1988, Lebanon's legal status was for the first time riven by the same evil divisiveness that had plagued the country for thirteen years. Two sharply demarcated zones, two governments, two civilian administrations, two regular armies coexisted, but only one central bank, which strangled the Christian region. To resolve the impasse, in March 1989 Aoun initiated a "war of liberation." He was right in identifying his enemy, adopting the LF slogan "Know your enemy: the Syrian is your enemy." He was also right in identifying his objective, since the reestablishment of unity, sovereignty, and the rule of law won the enthusiastic support of the Christian population and gave Muslims cause for hope. But in his political analysis the ambitious officer made two fatal mistakes. First, he believed that the Western powers, specifically the United States and France, would fly to his side in a battle against Syria which his weak army could never win unassisted. Yet the United States, convinced of Syrian efficiency, remained cynically silent; France, whose domestic disputes spilled over into Lebanon, made nothing but vain gestures. Then Aoun made the mistake, in response to Syrian shelling of East Beirut, of bombing economic targets and civilian populations in West Beirut. Originally seen as a national savior, General Aoun thereafter was widely perceived to be yet another militia chief concerned with his own community and the preservation of his own power. The logical and terrible consequence of his militaristic behavior was the "inter-Christian" war (January-July 1990) in which he fought the Lebanese Forces for leadership control over the tiny "liberated" territory between Beirut and Jubayl. The result was one thousand deaths, three thousand wounded, and the worst destruction of the entire war.[15]

Taking advantage of the diversion of the Gulf War, on October 13, 1990, Syria sent its land and air forces to intervene briefly and put an end to Aoun's adventure. The Lebanese army and government were then reunified, and after many long months in the French embassy, the general went into exile. The war was over. In March 1991 a decree dissolved the militias. The Lebanese Forces, deprived of their illegal resources and despised by their own people, survived as a political party until it was banned for security reasons in April 1994.

Yes, war was over. Now Lebanon was to draw up a balance sheet of confrontations and defeats, and to build peace.

11

A Consensus Destroyed

Bᴇᴄᴀᴜsᴇ of extensive media coverage of the war in Lebanon, for fifteen years the world was able to follow in weekly installments the various stages of destruction and the widespread suffering of the populace. The shock value remains for those who revisit the country, for it is beyond recognition. The road from Damascus to Beirut, once brilliantly lined with opulent summer resorts and the soaring panorama of a modern, dynamic capital cradled between sea and mountain, is now heartwrenching at every turn. Savage attacks disfigured the landscape modeled by an ancient civilization; in Beirut, the blind fury of indiscriminate shelling and machine-gun fire is everywhere apparent. After years of horror, these now-common sights have lost their power to perturb the Lebanese. Ruins have become an everyday sight, and many Lebanese have known no other. Deeper yet than the country's devastation has been the havoc wreaked on individual lives: the slide into violence and poverty has been unrelenting.

A Devastated Country

Each phase of the war brought in its wake new destruction in downtown Beirut and the industrial areas on the outskirts. Tripoli, repeatedly besieged, emptied of its inhabitants, was given over to combats between rival militias; Sidon was conquered, then retaken and bombed; Zahle, crisscrossed by the militias of the Lebanese Forces, was encircled in the spring of 1981 by the Syrian army. In the villages of the Shuf and the coast between Sidon and Beirut, houses were systematically destroyed to discourage their owners from ever returning. The villages of the south were sacked and abandoned and the fields left fallow. Interventions by foreign armies added to the damage of the civil war: during the summer of 1978, the ravaging of Ashrafiyeh by Syrian artillery; in 1982, the siege of West Beirut and the continuous bombing of apartment houses by the Israeli air force; in December 1983, the firing from the American battleship *New Jersey* on the Shuf and the heights of the Matn; and last but not least, the barrage of shellings in 1989 between East and West Beirut.

The severity of the destruction was of little concern to observers of the Lebanese economy who had long admired the vigor of its financial networks, the gratifying behavior of the Lebanese pound, and the sizable remittances of Lebanese emigrants, at least until the sharp decline in oil revenues in the mid-1980s. Nevertheless, Lebanon lost nearly a third of its fixed industrial capital and its infrastructure greatly deteriorated. War and neglect eroded roads, ruined hospital equipment, the ports, water mains, electricity, and the telephone network to such an extent that experts from the World Bank, on the basis of studies by the Lebanese Council for Development and Reconstruction, estimated the cost of repairs at more than $10 billion. The reconstruction of Lebanon would require $4.5 billion, or more than one year's gross domestic product, to which another $6 billion must be added to rebuild housing and private industry facilities.[1] The Beirut area, in which more than two-thirds of the country's population resides and an equal percentage of its activity is concentrated, has been devastated. Its downtown, hub of commercial and banking activities, was destroyed in the first two years of the war and now epitomizes all the challenges and promises of reconstruction. Despite a sizable banking sector, Lebanon requires a huge influx of funds, in the form of foreign aid and loans, to promote reconstruction and inspire the confidence of private Arab investors and most especially, that of the Lebanese themselves.

Because Lebanon's economy is concentrated in the service sector, the loss of human resources has been utterly catastrophic. Death and disablement have struck down tens of thousands. Emigration, which was temporary in the early phases of the war, has now drained off more than a fourth of the labor force. Ever since the final upheaval and the division of the country, the exodus has tended to be permanent: the most highly skilled and educated—scholars and professionals—settled in Europe and North America; merchants, along with bank and service employees, took themselves and their businesses abroad. Moreover, Lebanon endured the departure of so many skilled workers in the industrial and construction trades that it is now deemed a "developing" country.

Appearances are deceptive, for half the personal income in the country still derives from remittances from abroad, so that the maintenance of a certain standard of living for many Lebanese masks the downturn in economic growth. Building and real estate ventures in which the oil fortunes were preferentially invested enjoyed nearly a decade of uninterrupted boom: in 1980, the cost per square meter of land in the village of Bikfaya was more than $3,000. Until 1982, a great deal of money was circulating in Lebanon, invested in prestigious and sometimes profitable projects. After years of economic priority for Beirut and Mount Lebanon at the expense of other areas, the division of Beirut and mounting insecurity caused a counterexodus and a redistribution of economic activity. This movement brought new prosperity to both the eastern and the western suburbs, revived many mountain villages that had been all but abandoned by their inhabitants, and transformed former summer resorts into places of permanent residence. Commercial, banking, administrative, and university centers were created or enlarged; soon leisure complexes and industrial areas accommodated the activities that had been concentrated in the capital, now divided between East and West by an almost uncrossable and always dangerous "green line," periodically the scene of lethal encounters. Juniyeh, which became the country's third port, administrative capital, and luxurious commercial center for the residents of "Christian Lebanon," and Sidon, where the Saudi-Lebanese businessman Rafiq Hariri invested billions to reconstruct the roads, hospitals, and universities after the war of 1982, illustrate in the east as in the west a process of broad, spontaneous, and dynamic decentralization, a model of Lebanese boldness and adaptability. Other examples are Jubayl, Zghorta,[2] or the peaceful rural town of Zahle, which in ten years grew to some 130,000 inhabitants and was equipped with nine banks whose customers included the major traders of Damascus.

The war, moreover, was not a calamity for all. Those who in Lebanon or from a European refuge controlled the arms market or hashish trade,[3] had holdings in currency, or imported foodstuffs and basic commodities, became highly prosperous. Because Lebanon was isolated, the smuggling of petroleum products into Syria and Israel, where the price was several times higher, left the Lebanese stranded but lined the pockets of the businessmen allied to militia leaders. A wartime monopoly in sugar, flour, or cement distribution was an automatic moneymaker. The hierarchy of the great fortunes was upset by a new criterion: armed force. Domination by an intercommunitarian bourgeoisie, exiled while waiting for the storm to pass, gave way to domination by militia leaders, the "warlords," who seized control of the economic networks in their territory, levied their own taxes, and directed both the redistribution of income and social advancement. The new Shi'i fortunes in the banking and real estate sectors were particularly spectacular. Surely not everyone profited by the war, but those who did rose to a position of considerable power.[4] After several docks in the port of Beirut were knocked out of commission in 1976, the state proved powerless in preventing the militias from taking over half a dozen makeshift piers that dotted the Lebanese coast, thereby gaining a monopoly over customs duties, as occurred, for example, in the port of Tripoli, controlled by militants of the Islamic Unification Movement until December 1985 then by Syria; the pier of Khaldeh, profits from which Walid Jumblat used to finance the PSP; the port of Juniyeh and the fifth dock in the port of Beirut, which remained under the exclusive control of the Lebanese Forces until the final days of the war. The latter even tried, unsuccessfully, to open an international airport in the area they controlled.

The new apparatus for domination was financed through customs duties, taxes on gas, restaurants, dwellings, and a panoply of illegal taxes levied by the political-military organizations divvying up Lebanon. Militia money was used to build clientelist networks by means of social redistribution, assigning top priority to remunerating members of the militia on a regular basis. At the end of the 1980s, as much as one-third of the total domestic product was linked to militia activities.[5] As the Lebanese economy was delivered into the hands of the militias, the great loser was, of course, the state. Lebanon's expenses, which before the war had been modest, took a growing share of the GNP (up to 45 percent in 1985) because of its employment policy—no interruption of salaries for 60,000 civil servants—and state subsidies for staples like flour and gasoline. Twice over, in 1979 and again in 1983, the state made large military outlays[6] to purchase American and French equipment, after which the newly reconstituted army of some 36,000 men split up, leaving the president in command of only two brigades. One after another, plans for reconstruction were abandoned for lack of credit authorization. For though its outlay increased, the state's revenue shrank by half in ten years; the losses in customs duties amounted to 80 to 85 percent,[7] which resulted in indebtedness increasing at a breathtaking rate. The state's fiscal incompetence and its inability to fulfill basic functions (public safety and social services) continue to plague the early postwar period, when foreign debt is estimated at nearly $600 million.

In the early years of the war, the Bank of Lebanon had great reserves of gold and currency which it could liberally draw on to support the Lebanese. Until the shock of 1982 the treasury had held up well with regard to the slowdown in growth. Afterward, to cope with its expenses, however, the state resorted to increasing the money supply, thus encouraging the banks to speculate. The country thereafter lived to the beat of inflation and even hyperinflation;[8] between the summers of 1984 and 1987, prices increased eightfold and the Lebanese pound, which between 1975 and 1982 had depreciated by only half, lost thirty times its value in relation to the dollar. But that was nothing in comparison to the ruination of the immediate postwar period. Lebanese banks and capitalists had no confidence whatsoever in the fragile political regime. In the early 1990s, the pound lost ten times its value, and then as much as twenty times its value in 1992 when discontent was at its peak due to rigged elections. It took a wad of banknotes to purchase a pack of cigarettes, and most transactions were carried out in dollars.

Stripped bare by the drying up of its foreign financial resources, the Lebanese economy reacted dynamically: thanks to a highly favorable rate of exchange, exports rose modestly starting in 1985 and sent the balance of trade into the black. Agriculture once again crossed the threshold of profitability. But these successes could not make up for the country's overall pauperization, which can be seen in two figures. Forty percent of the employable population—more than half a million persons—were jobless and prices in Beirut between 1984 and 1987 increased three times as quickly as wages. In September 1987, spontaneous hunger riots shook the capital, with widespread looting and bank robberies. Except for a minority whose resources were held in dollars, most of Lebanon's inhabitants had suffered a dramatic reduction in their standard of living: in 1987 it was estimated that more than 600,000 people—nearly a fifth of the population—were living in poverty. The consequences of the war have been long-lasting since the country has not experienced true economic recovery five years after ceasefire. While the most dynamic firms and a great part of the public sector have left Beirut, the city inherited the homeless, the jobless, and war victims, who suffer from the combined problems of overpopulation and increasing urban impoverishment. In a country where the social security system is not available to all and education is for the most part private, the result is a general lowering of health standards and cultural literacy. In May 1992, for the first time in Lebanon's history, a general strike and street demonstrations brought down the government—the one appointed by Omar Karame in December 1990—because the distress had become as intolerable as war.

An Exhausted Population

The human cost of the war, impossible to fix in numbers, has been frightful. One person in thirty has been killed, an equal number gravely wounded;[9] victims have been overwhelmingly civilian. The rationing of water and electricity during the fighting (particularly in 1976 and 1982) together with the difficulty of obtaining oil, the scarcity of medicine, and the destruction of hospitals, fomented epidemics and the spread of contagious diseases such as cholera, poliomyelitis, and measles, which UNICEF and the World Health Organization have attempted to stem through a campaign of emergency vaccinations. In the winter of 1987, besieged for months in camps on the outskirts of Beirut, many Palestinians starved to death. Buried under the admirably maintained texture of everyday life, psychological trauma ran deep in much of the population, stirring an ardor for living, and the need to forget for a moment and compensate for misery through pleasure. But at what cost! No one in Lebanon was spared; all witnessed or were victims of bombing, assault, torture, or extortion. Every family was affected by the kidnaping of at least one member. Nearly 20,000 people were abducted, including two dozen Western hostages, diplomats, journalists, and university professors. Every night pierced by the sound of shelling, every day shattered by explosions of boobytrapped cars, no child has had a full year's schooling or any memory of peace. In the minds of many, the overconsumption of tranquilizers and other drugs was a lesser evil in the face of criminality, psychic wounds, and despair:

> "No longer was the war an idea in the air, a distant roar. The war had killed off a good many of Ahmad's friends; it disfigured the daughter of the neighbors across the street as well as a journalist I'd once read. In his article he had talked of the blazing sniper fire that spared nothing, not even the watermelons. Outside our window they paraded dozens of young men, blindfolded, prodded by the Kalshnikov rifles whose butts had beaten them earlier." [10]

The very structure of society was overturned: the patriarchal head of the family and the familiar presence of state representatives gave way to the reign of the militias. The militias, unified in East Beirut and in "Christian Lebanon," were often enemies in West Beirut, the south, the north, and the Syrian-controlled Bikaa; but they all recruited from the same pool of unschooled, unemployable youth swollen with hatred. Membership in a militia not only assured families of a regular income, but also guaranteed their security, at least in the area under the militia's control. In the disadvantaged areas on the western edge of the city, it was not unusual to find within a Shi'i family an Amal adherent, a member of the Communist Party, a Hizbollah *mujahid* (guerrilla fighter), and (let's be provident) a soldier in the Lebanese army. The law of the militias permanently subjected civilians to crossfire, shelling, snipers (whose mission was to stir up the conflagration), sudden arrest by flying roadblock, blind vengeance for crimes of the night before, the taking of an entire village or neighborhood hostage. Militias did not often distinguish between political goals and the material cravings of their people in arms: not content with heavily taxing their "protectees," gang members carried out requisitions and looted abandoned dwellings in which refugees cowered.

Exploiting their control over most of the country, officers of the Syrian army ran large-scale smuggling operations to move stolen goods and merchandise from Lebanon to Damascus, where they fed a flourishing private market.[11] They also encouraged opium cultivation in Bikaa and organized heroin trafficking in collusion with various militias. While attributed by some to the pernicious influence of a disintegrating Lebanese society, the behavior of the Syrians of the ADF should be seen as a reflection of the Damascus regime: a military-mercantile coalition for which power was a source of personal enrichment. It is certainly no consolation to know that the Israeli soldiers were not to be outdone in the business of looting and smuggling.

All the years of war have also spurred exoduses to the rhythm of battles and changes in the front lines. The rural population crowded into large cities, camping in public parks, living in schools, or squatting in the apartments of city residents who took refuge in the Mountain or abroad. Other groups, hounded out of their neighborhoods by sustained bombing, or expelled by direct force, could not return to their native villages and uncultivated lands; now, poor and illegal and threatened constantly with new reasons to flee, they settled in makeshift towns. The intensity and duration of the population displacement during the war served as a barometer of the political and military situation. Early on in the war, some people were permanently expelled, particularly Palestinians and Muslims of the poor eastern suburbs of Beirut. Most of the civilians risked returning home during lulls in the fighting, but more often, rising intolerance, together with wholesale massacre and destruction, caused temporary absences to become prolonged and finally permanent. Several hundred thousand Shi'is from the south fled Israeli bombardments in 1978, 1982, and again in 1993. They settled in the pulverized center of Beirut or on vacant lots in the southern suburbs, creating a "temporary" situation that by now has persisted for nearly twenty years. Another large group of refugees was made up of hundreds of thousands of Christians who fled the Shuf and the Sidon area after the Lebanese Forces were defeated from 1983 to 1985. In total, over a third of the country's population has been displaced, cut off from its resources and roots. The Ministry of Displaced Persons has a gargantuan problem on its hands that will require foreign aid. In addition, the state has to guarantee the protection of the minority groups in every region. Most of all, the Lebanese will need to have confidence in the fragile peace that was initiated in 1990.

A Divided State

As the conflict intensified and violence swept away reason,[12] adversarial positions became more polarized, and one concern dominated all others: the preservation and security of the individual group, and the expulsion of non-members. Syria and Israel encouraged and aggravated this tendency, for they feared a Lebanese reconciliation at their expense. Meanwhile, the warlords saw a way to strengthen their hold over their own communities: Samir Geagea of the Lebanese Forces went off in conquest of the Shuf, which he wanted to use as a springboard to dominate the south; Walid Jumblat wanted to protect the Christians in *his* mountain, but not to share power.

Every region in Lebanese territory underwent a radical transformation in the direction of sectarian group homogeneity. Many Christians lived in the northern city of Tripoli, and they gradually left the city to escape the pressures from Islamists and their incessant clashes with the Syrian army. The same process occurred in the Bikaa north of the Beirut-Damascus highway, where Christians regrouped around Zahle and Muslims in Baalbek, with economic and administrative trade heavily controlled by the Syrian army. The mountain of Jubayl, the Kisrawan, and nearly the whole of Matn, as well as the coastline between Shiq'a and East Beirut, became exclusively Christian. Though the region of Baabda remained mixed owing to the presence of several official and governmental organizations, the exodus of Christians from West Beirut after the war of 1982 grew more acute with each new clash, until by 1987 there were no more than 50,000, a third of what they had been ten years earlier. When the hostilities ended, Christians returned in limited numbers: with some dwellings destroyed, and many others inhabited by squatters from the south, many Christian families chose to remain in East Beirut rather than return to their former often unrecognizable neighborhoods. In the western part of the city and its outskirts, the new Shi'i residents—nearly 300,000 of them—greatly outnumbered the Sunni population. In the southern areas, where in the late eighteenth and early nineteenth centuries the Maronite peasantry had settled and bitter communitarian clashes had occurred in 1860-61, there were dramatic regroupings: several hundreds of thousands of Christians fled Aleih, the Shuf, western Bikaa, and the coast up to Sidon, where the Druzes lived on the heights and the Sunnis in the plains. Jabal Amil and the *sahel* (seashore) of Tyre were Shi'i, whereas the strongholds of Hermon were Druze. Only two regions remain mixed, both areas dominated by foreigners during the war: the "security belt" where Christians and Shi'is lived side by side under Israeli occupation, and the Akkar, on the northern edge of the Syrian border. Even the Palestinians were forced out of the scattered sectors they had lived in since 1948; they resettled in the refugee camps on the outskirts of the large cities.

The war abruptly cut off the trade that had developed between communities, and interrupted a flourishing Lebanese artistic and political culture, causing a dramatic regression. Whatever the wealth and diversity of their backgrounds, social status, profession, class, ideological or political orientation, individuals came to be identified exclusively by membership in a particular communal group. Geographically, an already tiny national territory was reduced to cantons surrounded by unknown and hostile areas; for ten years, it was risky to cross the demarcation line in Beirut. People could work and move about only within their area of residence: a Maronite from Zghorta, for example, had problems teaching Arabic literature at the Lebanese University of West Beirut; even less could he teach "in the East," which was under the control of the Lebanese Forces. Businesses retrenched and geared down. Each canton had its own network of foreign relations. Only the banking system resisted "cantonization"—money crosses communal lines. Radio stations, television channels, and information agencies proliferated, as did the development of mutually alien cultural references. The prewar diversity of views in the press had represented a democratic asset; the news media during the war reinforced exclusivity and hostility, as can be gleaned from the station names themselves: the Voice of Lebanon, the Voice of the Mountain, the Voice of Truth, the Voice of Free Lebanon, and so on.

The various and separate Lebanese groups shared a great heritage, but not a state, since after 1984 the president's authority extended over only a minuscule territory around the presidential palace in Baabda and the ministry of defense in Yarze, while the two prime ministers were embroiled in legitimacy battles. There was no minimal consensus over Lebanon's foreign relations, the Syrian protectorate, or the peace with Israel, and still less over the nature of Lebanon's political regime or future reforms. Only the desire to preserve the country withstood all the rifts of war; the ordeal eventually ended several decades of "Syrian temptation," among Sunni leaders who claimed some "participation" in the management of Lebanese affairs. Above all, it rallied a silent majority against the warlords' rule of might and exploitation. Pacifists, families, and militants alike attempted to protest militia roadblocks. Tragically, no authority could mobilize and organize these people and give voice to their aspirations; the communitarian authorities took no interest in "civil society" since they were directly engaged in political competition; the unions had no power, and the intellectuals were for the most part prisoners of their community membership. It was only in the final years of the war, after the ceasefire moreover, that intercommunitarian nongovernmental organizations were formed to deal with social, cultural and ecological questions, but they are still rather ineffective. The everyday heroes during the war were the ones who repaired electric lines, managed water distribution, endlessly negotiated local truces and the freeing of hostages, continued to teach and dispense medical treatment, and above all, resisted the dominant atmosphere of hatred and fear of the Other. Yet the international media too often ignored these resistance forces, as the Jesuit André Masse noted before he was assassinated in Sidon in September 1987: "Whole pieces of political, economic, cultural life in the broadest sense have been passed over in silence."[13]

Militias and New Social Forces

It was Lebanon's good fortune and also its curse that, contrary to the image promoted by extremist and simplistic clichés, a solid Christian bloc was not confronting a solid Muslim bloc: diversity persisted in the east, the west, the "liberated areas," and the "national areas," a heterogeneity that was one of the reasons for the state's creation. Nevertheless, each faction ignored this diversity by imposing group hegemony through its militia.

In the eastern zone controlled by the Lebanese Forces, it was unclear whether the Maronites represented the demographic majority, or whether the other communities, Greek Orthodox and Greek Catholics, Armenians, and Catholic minorities taken together, were not more numerous. The warlords claimed to speak in the name of all Christians, but any monolithic view was purely mythical. True, the Maronite community is a beacon for the Christian communities of the Middle East, and its patriarch's strength and independence from governmental authorities guarantees the survival of Christian minorities in nations with Muslim majorities, such as Turkey and Iraq. But the Maronites' central role must be seen in the context of the rich history of the Eastern churches and their coexistence with the dominant religion in each country: whereas the Maronites were isolated from the Druzes and the Shi'is, the Greek Orthodox, for example, have lived since the birth of Islam in symbiosis with the Sunnis; what differentiated them from the Maronites is less a matter of doctrine than of political culture and mode of relating to their environment—the choice of a future.

Many Christians lived outside the area controlled by the Lebanese Forces. Several tens of thousands of them remained in West Beirut because for generations it had been their city, their neighborhood, their home, and their Sunni neighbors had guaranteed their security, or because they rejected the monolithism imposed in "the east." There were Christians in the Bikaa as well, and Maronites in northern Lebanon, not just in the area of Zghorta, whose population was homogeneous and whose chief, Suleiman Frangieh, was both a Maronite patron and an ally of Syria. Maronites also populated villages and towns of the mixed Akkar region that thirteen years of occupation by the Syrians had kept relatively free of conflict. In the "liberated" areas of central Lebanon, violence silenced dissent. The "Lebanists" of the Maronite University in Kaslik imposed their views by gagging liberal intellectuals and political nonconformists. An inordinately powerful militia that eluded constitutional authority and civil justice maintained order through dictatorial methods and terrorism, as in neighboring Syria,[14] but did nothing to forestall clashes between rival factions or the succession of bloody coups. Behind the apparent unity of the movement around a hard Maronite core, these factions reflected the diversity rooted in Lebanon's history: the perceptions of a northerner like Samir Geagea were different from those of someone like Amin Gemayel, a bourgeois raised in Beirut, or from someone like Danny Chamoun, heir of the National Liberal Party, whose family traditionally had coexisted with the Druzes in the heart of the Shuf. Chamoun's assassination in October 1990 was the last episode in the bloody struggle of the Christian patrons, whose attempt to unify the "Christian areas" proved that they cared less about the future of Lebanon than the entrenchment of individual power in certain territories.

By wiping out the higher and lower strata of society, the war engendered a schematic and impoverished notion of Christian identity, thereafter reduced to Maronitism and controlled by the Lebanese Forces. The wealthy bourgeoisie went into exile. The mixed working class vanished. Industrial wage earners, left jobless, volunteered for positions with the local and communal militias. There remained the middle strata whose ambition was to supplant the traditional elites in managing the country. When war broke out, hard hit by the crisis, they threw in their lot with their own community, viewing demands by other communities, particularly the Sunnis and the Shi'is, as obstacles to their own advancement. The Lebanese Forces proposed a moral, economic, and military order that basically set the putative unity of the Christians against a hostile outside world. But the price they paid to safeguard and defend their interests grew ever higher with the isolation of "the east": the military defeat of the Lebanese Forces compelled tens of thousands of Christians to take refuge in the "Christian stronghold," where their presence aggravated economic conditions. The regime imposed itself by force. Shakedowns increased as the demand rose among the small ruling class for real estate, luxury goods, and foreign capital accumulation.

General Aoun, who became prime minister in September 1988, owed his immense popularity to his radical condemnation of the militias and his opposition to the division of Lebanon, as well as to his oft-proclaimed desire to reestablish state authority and sovereignty throughout the country. His war against the Lebanese Forces (February–March 1989 and January–July 1990) gave people great cause for hope, despite the acute destruction it caused, especially in the northern suburbs of Beirut. But after fifteen years of division, this last attempt to reestablish legality was doomed to failure, first because Aoun never received the international support from the United States or France that he expected when he attacked Syria in 1989; and second, because his own army was only one among many, composed of ill-equipped brigades uncertain whether to go along with his program. Above all, by shelling civilians under the pretext of attacking Syrian forces, Aoun made his "national liberation" objectives less credible. Despite his stated interest in "national" unity (Bashir Gemayel had a similar posture in 1982), his strategy was that of one warlord in competition with others, his objective to preserve the interests of his Christian constituency. Banished in 1991 for five years, Michel Aoun has no future in Lebanon except as a representative of Christian interests in the face of new demographic and regional balances, but he is more and more estranged from the Lebanese postwar scene.

Another attempt at forced unification took place in "the west," where the rise of the Shi'i middle strata, modest in the 1960s and spectacular in the 1970s, has been the most noteworthy phenomenon in the social history of independent Lebanon. Until then, the Shi'i community had been organized around two poles: an aristocracy made up of tribe chiefs in the Bikaa and great estate owners in the south, which ranked among the largest fortunes of Lebanon and was accustomed to an inferior rank in the political system and state apparatus; and the lower peasant strata, greatly affected by the rural exodus, whom one writer not suspected of radicalism described as the "proletariat of the earth."[15] When the Shi'i middle and lower middle class emerged owing to professional and scholastic advancement as well as income from emigration to Africa, they became eager to win their share of economic and political power. Just as the Kataeb and then the Lebanese Forces organized and represented the middle strata of the Maronites, Amal, —both a political movement and a militia,— organized and represented the new middle strata of the Shi'is.

Under the direction of Nabih Berri who gave it a modern face, Amal proposed a nationwide plan to rebalance and gradually secularize the political system. At first it had a more specific goal: to replace the National Pact, which represented a Maronite-Sunni compromise, with a Maronite-Shi'i compromise reflecting the country's new balance of power. In the government Berri became the interlocutor of other warlords. On the battlefield, his militia took advantage of the turmoil following the Israeli invasion of 1982 and tried to establish its hegemony over the "national" zones, particularly West Beirut, its outskirts, and the south. Amal's Syrian protectors encouraged the undertaking and in 1985 provided combatants with materiel including T-54 tanks. In this way, the Damascus regime hoped to achieve two goals: to crush the forces of the PLO loyal to Arafat and reduce the Lebanese political landscape to a minimum of players with real power. Amal engaged in more than three years of fighting and even then did not succeed in eliminating its rivals: the Druze PSP, forced to lower its profile in Beirut, withdrew to the Shuf mountain but refused to knuckle under. Reminiscent of the bedouin attack against the cities of North Africa in Ibn Khaldun's time, the Sunnis of Beirut and Sidon, with Palestinian support, mobilized to resist the conquest of their city by these country people. Secular intellectuals were assassinated for denouncing the Shi'i movement's intolerance, hardly masked by its universalist rhetoric. Then, in 1988 after thirty months of bombardments and an extremely cruel siege, the Palestinian camps in Beirut and Sidon were crushed. Communitarian gangs, subsidized and prodded by Syria, had destroyed the "national" ambitions of the 1975-vintage militants.

In the late 1980s, Hizbollah owed its rise to power primarily to the rejection of Amal's corrupt practices and Amal's compromise with the Syrian forces and Israeli forces in the south. The Islamic Republic of Iran lent Hizbollah's rebellion an Islamic ideology, rooted in the Shi'i culture of political martyrdom and submission to the clerics.[16] Iran sent several hundred armed Pasdaran—guardians of the Revolution—and paid them a regular salary. In exchange, it used Hizbollah to conduct terrorist operations against western targets, seize hostages, and attack the Israeli armed forces. In the face of state inaction and Syria's exploitation of intercommunitarian rivalries, Hizbollah pitted itself mainly against its rival Amal, concentrating its efforts between 1988 and December 1990 on taking control of most of the Shi'i community.

The fratricidal combat between Hizbollah and Amal did as much as the Israelis to wreck the economy of southern Lebanon. Later Hizbollah ensured its domination through aid distribution, an authoritarian framework, and the "re-Islamization" of society. Thus the evolution of the Muslim regions, like that of the Christian, was grist for the mill of the radical ideologies, whose new Lebanon was a thousand miles away from the old Lebanon of consensus.

12

Which Lebanon?

Toward the latter part of 1990, when the weapons fell silent due to the utter exhaustion of all military forces and the collapse of the social structure, the hostilities ceased as illogically as they had begun. The urgent tasks requiring new rules and new commitments were now those of maintaining order and ensuring economic survival.

But could the vicious circle of war produce a nonvicious environment? Wedged in a region upset by the Gulf War and soon after by the Arab-Israeli negotiations, a new Lebanon was born in the 1990s. To evaluate the Lebanese crisis and the country's future prognosis, we will need to examine Lebanon's characteristics, identify its weaknesses, and draw some comparisons. Lebanon in the past was a model of prosperity and intercommunitarian balance; now "Lebanonization" denotes a state in disarray, marked by ethnic conflicts. In the post–Cold War period, when the very existence of the nation-state is being called into question, many countries in the Mediterranean and the Mideast and indeed throughout the world are facing the same problems that led to Lebanon's downfall and are trying to resolve the same questions surrounding reconstruction: how can a small, weak country find its rightful place in a regional context; and how can diverse communal group identities be honored and respected without undermining the democratic functioning of the rule of law?

Taif and the Second Republic

Without a president since Amin Gemayel's mandate ended in August 1988, lacking a unified army or a unified government, the Lebanese turned, as they often had in the past, to foreign powers in an attempt to find a compromise solution. With U.S. encouragement, negotiations took place under the aegis of the Arab League, which appointed a tripartite committee composed of Saudi Arabia, Morocco, and Algeria. Syria, to be sure, kept a close watch on its work, and when in June 1989 the committee criticized Damascus, it was called to account. Syria and Saudi Arabia eventually proposed a solution to the Lebanese. In October 1989, summoned to a conclave to Taif, summer capital of Saudi royalty, and generously subsidized, fifty-eight of the seventy surviving deputies approved at a comfortable margin the Document of National Reconciliation, which contained various amendments to the constitutional system. A few days later they elected René Moawad as president, and two days after he was assassinated on November 22, the national holiday, they elected his successor, Elias Hrawi, a Zahle Maronite with even closer ties to Syria. On September 21, 1990, the same deputies approved the constitutional amendments adopted in Taif and the Second Republic was born.

The new Lebanese political system—the Taif Accord—was at once a return to and a restructuring of the National Pact of 1943. It was the final incarnation of many preceding drafts: in September 1975 the National Committee for Dialog had debated constitutional reforms, and President Frangieh had proposed these in February of the following year; the Lebanese Front (January 1977) had followed suit; then had come President Sarkis's Fourteen Points (March 1980); the Druze High Committee Document (May 1983) and the Amal Movement draft plan (November 1983); later had come the conclusions of the Lausanne Conference (March 1984), the Damascus Militia Agreement (December 1985) and finally, President Gemayel's proposals (March 1987) and those of Rafiq Hariri (November 1987). Thus the restructured National Pact emerged from previous commitments stated at one time or another by most of the country's leaders. While guaranteeing the permanent institutions that most Christians wanted, the Taif document responded to the Muslim elites' demands for "participation" in exchange for their acceptance of Lebanon's status as a "definitive" and independent country. This principle had been accepted by Saeb Salam, although he had been the main architect of the 1958 Revolution. It had been advocated by Rashid Karane when, at Amin Gemayel's behest in May of 1984, he had headed the "national unity" government. In addition, a similar formula had been backed by two militia chiefs, Druze Walid Jumblat and Shi'i Nabih Berri, when they agreed to the solution which Abdel Halim Khaddam, the Syrian vice president, imposed at the March 1984 Lausanne Conference.

The most salient feature of Lebanon's postwar political system is the solidification of political communitarianism. Although the specter of its elimination still hovered, the deputies preserved the famous article 95 of the constitution, which stipulates that "in the transition period [which has persisted since 1926] . . . the communities shall be equitably represented in the ministries."[1] Communitarianism has not only been reinforced but enshrined. For while the National Pact of 1943 only evoked the unwritten rule of communitarian coexistence, now a "pact of shared existence" was made explicit and the power's legitimacy was based on this new pact.[2] At the same time the principle of political communitarianism was somewhat modified, since the 54:45 balance of parliamentary seats was split evenly 50:50 between Christians and Muslims and generally extended to high-ranking posts in government and the public sector.

The political avatars of the prewar period, Pierre Gemayel, Rashid Karameh, Camille Chamoun, and Kamal Jumblat, all of whom perished during the war, would have been surprised to see that the Document of National Reconciliation in no way abolished "confessionalism"—which had always been the apple of discord, along with the question of the Palestinian presence—indeed, its future abolition now appears most improbable. Such a reversal can be explained by looking to how choices were made at Taif and by whom. Those who signed and supported the Document of National Reconciliation were deputies, the true representatives of the sectarian groups. Miraculously rehabilitated as decision makers after having been totally discredited and having lost their ability to influence the state's future, these deputies would hardly fail to seize the opportunity to restore their own legitimacy and power. Yet the perpetuation of communitarianism was also in the interests of the two regional powers who were its solid supporters: Saudi Arabia, for whom a political regime in the Arab region founded on faith—albeit Christianity—was preferable to a secular regime; and Syria, whose hegemony has been built on its role as official arbiter of Lebanon's communal group conflicts.

The Taif decision reflects a radically new, war-induced notion of communal identity. In the 1970s, secular customs and demands had become more widespread as standardized urban culture had developed. Today, collective cultural identities are acknowledged and celebrated, group particularities defended. The failure to abolish confessionalism not only lifted the taboo against communal socialization but presented it as the norm. Insecurity, dispersion of families, generational differences, the loss of socioeconomic criteria at a time of disintegration, the paralysis and subsequent breakup of the state structure—all contributed to the reevaluation of the religious community as final molder of identity. Communal differences became the guiding principle of political analysis as immediate realities were the most pressing in the wake of ardent ideological warfare and wasteful wishful thinking. The new constitution reflected the resilience of the communal groups as the most immediately operative part of the Lebanese social structure and thus codified the elements of communal group interaction. Finally, it should be borne in mind that though the war was the principal motor of change, the changes of the postmodern world also played a part: Replacing bipolar conflict as the dominant global dynamic was what Samuel Huntington called the "clash of civilizations" in which ethnic groups draw together to form communities and demand political representation or even a territorial homeland.

The second important feature of Lebanon's postwar political system is that presidential supremacy has been replaced by a triumvirate regime in which power is shared by the president, a Maronite; the prime minister, a Sunni; and the president of Parliament, a Shi'i, each of whom has veto power over the other two.[3] Executive power, then, passed from the hands of the president to the collective authority of the Council of Ministers, whereas parliament, whose president is now elected to a four-year term, acquired increased powers to draft and administer laws. Notably, it must approve by a two-thirds majority any decisions affecting national security. In practice this carefully calibrated system transforms the business of government into an endless game of negotiations and rivalries, which often ends in a stalemate. Most likely to win any impasse is the one of the three presidents with the most forceful personality, and more significantly, with the closest ties to Damascus, the final arbiter of Lebanese politics. At any rate, the triumvirate system is symptomatic of the dangerous absence of a national consensus for political reconstruction.

Indeed, at the time of the French military conquest in 1920, the controversy between the Maronite patriarch, who wanted a Christian Lebanon, and the new modern-leaning elites, who advocated the development of an intercommunal political culture, had been decided in the former's favor.[4] Greater Lebanon's reason for being was less to satisfy the search for communal harmony than to assign pride of place to the Christians, the Maronites in particular, who alone represented half of the Christian population. In territory (the coast and its ports and the interior fields of grain joined to the Mountain), identity (markedly Christian, whereas all the Arab states are mainly Muslim), and geo-political position (Western-leaning), Lebanon was conceived as a "country for Christians, and for others, too, if they so desire,"[5] even though great numbers of Muslims lived there and soon became a majority. Maronite hegemony was secured by legal means (article 17 of the constitution) and above all by a regime that leaned toward presidentialism. From that time on, national politics was for or against, revolving around, and centering on, Christian preeminence. The postwar state, on the contrary, has been characterized by a lack of higher authority and the rejection of communal group preeminence. Now under threat of structural upheaval, no one group can assert itself over the others; but neither is any authority in a position to regulate the competition. Actually, the state is not derived from national consensus: yet, rather than having a desire to live together, as holds in the consenus democracies such as Switzerland or the Netherlands, the Lebanese communal groups have an obligation to live together, an obligation which arises neither from idealism nor ideology.[6]

The third important feature of the Taif document is that while it only alludes to the potential for reform, it contemplates the creation of new institutions in the areas of constitutional oversight, judicial independence, economic regulation, social protection, and administrative decentralization in order to strengthen the state and encourage power sharing. Clearly, a sufficiently autonomous political authority would need to be motivated enough to risk undertaking such reforms and honest enough to refrain from interpreting the spirit and letter of the law to the exclusive advantage of one group. Several years after the Taif Accord was adopted, the government is still concentrating on the immediate problems related to administration and the daily management of intercommunal relations. Most of the contemplated reforms have remained a dead letter. Those that have been undertaken, such as the reorganization of civil service, have been dominated by factional disputes between communal groups, or, as in the case of the new electoral law of 1992, are in flagrant contradiction to the constitution. It is probably too soon to tally the successes and failures of postwar Lebanon. But the success of the reforms depends on domestic conditions and regional circumstances, neither of which gives great cause for optimism.

The fourth and final feature of Lebanon's new political system is its structural alliance to Syria.[7] In May 1991—there was no dallying on reforms in relation to Syria—the Friendship and Cooperation Accord between Damascus and Beirut, followed soon after by the establishment of a mixed Higher Council, prompted intergovernmental cooperation on economic, defense, culture and energy issues, among others. If any state has taken advantage of the latent confliction of the Lebanese system, then, it is Syria, exerting external pressures in the absence of Lebanese consensus. Every communal and military group has been affected by Syrian leader Hafez al-Assad's strategy of ethnic consolidation. The paradox of Syria, a regime that trumpets itself as a secular state with the utmost respect for its smaller neighbor's sovereignty, is that by promoting sectarianism and manipulating the balances of local populations, its presence in Lebanon is at once indispensable and sorely resented.

Between Consensus and Confrontation

Syria remains indispensable because the Lebanese Second Republic was born under extremely precarious conditions. When Amin Gemayel's rule ended, two separate governments vied for national legitimacy. Prime Minister Salim al-Hoss, who for several months had been in the process of resigning, backed the Taif Accord. He organized the presidential elections carried by René Moawad from Zhgorta, a sincere nationalist who also favored constitutional reforms, two reasons for which he was considered dangerous and promptly assassinated. Next, in 1990, the year of Lebanon's vertiginous decline, Salim al-Hoss became prime minister under President Hrawi. His rival, General Michel Aoun, whom Amin Gemayel had named prime minister on the day he left office, was an implacable enemy of the Taif Accord, which he rightly saw as a bid to institutionalize Syrian ambitions over Lebanon. After an initial attempt to prevent the deputies by force from participating in the Taif meeting, Aoun had turned to the militias in the Christian areas, intending to unify the Christians under the leadership, then rally all Muslim regions in support of his administration. In 1989, still seeking domestic and international legitimacy, he had become embroiled in an unequal war against Syria and its Lebanese allies around the demarcation line and especially Suq al-Gharb, and then had clashed with the Lebanese Forces in an indecisive and destructive battle.

When in October 1990, abetted by the Gulf War, an assault by the Syrian armed forces put an end to Aoun's venture, the eastern regions had been bled dry and the country's infrastructure lay in ruins. The population was frustrated and impoverished, in theory hostile toward the reconciliation agreement but in reality starved for the promise of peace and safety that its provisions offered. The situation was no less clear in the Muslim areas in which the population had been victimized by the escalating competitive violence between Amal and Hizbollah, the former avid to obtain a new legal framework and the latter eager to reap the benefits of a prolonged armed struggle. In December 1990, after Aoun's defeat, Syria once again showed the extent of its influence in Lebanon by conniving, together with Iran, to suspend inter-Shi'i hostilities and liberate the last of the Western hostages.[8]

In contrast to the prolongation and factionalism of the war, the reestablishment of Lebanese rule of law was a relatively rapid affair. In March 1991 all the militias were dissolved, except for Hizbollah, which carried on its "liberation struggle" against Israel in the south. The assault weaponry that the militias and the Palestinians had amassed was collected with the help of Syrian troops. By July the reconstituted and reunified Lebanese army, with significant assistance from Syria, had been deployed throughout the country, except in the "security zone," which Israel controlled. Parliament had a total of 108 members, including 40 new deputies who were nominated in June 1991 to fill vacant seats and ensure parity between Christians and Muslims. Political maneuvering intensified when in response to massive popular protests Rashid Karameh's administration resigned in May 1992. A new electoral law, tailor-made to ensure certain candidates' ascension to power, was approved and legislative elections quickly followed that summer. Roundly rigged by the government, closely "supervised" by Syrian forces, and boy-cotted by nearly 80 percent of the electorate—especially by Christians whose leaders exhorted them to abstain—the elections produced 128 deputies,[9] many of them faceless names whose only merit was their support of the Taif Ac-cord, their dearth of contestants, or their status as clients of one of the new regime's patrons or the new political movements.

The manner in which Shi'i deputies were elected in 1992 will illustrate how the political system in Lebanon developed. The Amal movement, pillar of the Second Republic, had obtained in June 1991 two out of the three new seats assigned to Shi'i deputies (of which one was reserved for Nabih Berri). In summer 1992, Berri was busy gaining for himself the great Shi'i *za'ama* of south Lebanon (leadership), previously held by Kamel al-As'ad. Pressing into service an impressive electoral machine, he ran a campaign that was a suc-cessful feat of electoral engineering. Nabih Berri led a coalition list made up of 4 Amal members, of candidates of Hizbollah and of the leftists parties, as well as of some notables and members of prominent families. According to Nabih Berri, who won three times the votes that Kamel al-As'ad did, his list's crushing victory "enables us to turn the page of four hundred years of political feudalism in Lebanon." Berri, who as a result of his election as a speaker of the parliament became the number two figure in the Republic, had no political platform and practically no autonomy from his Syrian god-father. Yet he cleverly turned As'ad's clientelist practices to his own advan-tage. Interestingly, his Hizbollah adversaries also fared well. They dominated electoral operations in the Bikaa and the southern suburbs of Beirut by providing disciplined militants and effective transportation and security services. Running on common lists with Christian candidates, they won eight seats in Parliament. Thus, Hizbollah entered the Lebanese political arena without having to make any major concessions. It became the most cohe-sive and active opposition group and a player to be reckoned with in the country's future.

The government's activities did not slacken after the rigged elections. In October 1992 the Saudi-Lebanese billionaire, Rafiq Hariri, was put in charge of maintaining public order and was handed an agenda that included: reor-ganizing the civil service, maintaining public order, equipping the army, ne-gotiating with Israel, rebuilding downtown Beirut, and restoring fiscal bal-ance. Modest progress was made on all these fronts, despite obstacles and constraints.

The resumption of governmental activity and solidification of political communitarianism might have created the illusion of continuity from the prewar to the postwar period—thus enclosing fifteen years of war into a parenthesis of silence. Yet, as we have seen, the constitution was not the only thing that had changed: the practice of politics was also keenly affected.

Politics was seriously infected by a militaristic spirit. Most of the key prewar leaders were dead or in exile;[10] and the new political class belonged to a new social strata. The change was not merely generational, as exemplified in the young Minister Suleiman Tony Frangieh, grandson of President Suleiman. Nor was it solely attributable to the fact that representatives from a new, urbanized social class entered the political arena. It was principally a question of the militia leaders' cooptation, first into the government, then into Parliament, and finally into the higher executive levels. There, in addition to Nabih Berri, Walid Jumblat, Elias Hobeika and briefly, Samir Geagea, former leaders of the three large community militias, Amal, PSP and LF, one might also find Marada representatives from Zghorta, representatives from the "Greater-Syrian" SSNP, the Alawite militia of Tripoli, the chief of Saida's Nasserite popular organization, an Ashbash—Islamic Sunnis from Beirut— leader, and of course, Hizbollah higher-ups. The March 1991 amnesty law, generous though nonbinding, enabled the whole cast of characters to parade in civilian garb in the corridors of power. By imposing collective amnesia of wartime events, the law precluded the rehabilitation of the Lebanese citizenry and might, as the former Prime Minister Salim al-Hoss noted, "penalize those who refused to bear arms."

These militiamen, newly anointed in politics, have a different concept of *res publica* from that of the traditional *za'ama*. Their objective is not to build consensus among the elites but to ensure that their solidarity group interests prevail. For example, in 1991, Walid Jumblat demanded that a "Ministry of the Mountain" be created, from which the Druze under his jurisdiction could derive benefits as great as those that Nabih Berri had obtained for the Shi'is through his "Ministry of the South" created in 1984. In October 1992 he was appointed Minister of Displaced Persons in the Hariri government, in other words, he aquired control over a portion of public and private monies to resettle Christians in the villages of the Shuf.

Furthermore, these former militia leaders have little civilian or technical competence and their presence in the highest levels of public service is simply frightening. They were granted sinecures in return for partisan affiliations and feats of arms, after bitter bargaining among the presidential troika— Elias Hrawi, Nabih Berri and Rafiq Hariri—with each one seeking to position his own men and reward his own people. The list of new civil servants appointed in May 1993 reflects, beyond community balances, the respective weight wielded by each of the militias within the state apparatus. It mixes a few competent technocrats of integrity with former gang leaders and other apparatchiks who have more in common among themselves than with the traditional leaders of their respective communal groups. The rapidity with which they distanced themselves from violence is, in itself, to be commended, though they might just as quickly revert to their old ways in a crisis. At the apex of the state, interminable negotiations between traditional elites have given way to thinly disguised pressures, aggressive statements, and futile power plays. Since no one constitutional mechanism exists to keep the players in check, each has become everyone else's potential rival. The interplay of forces in the crude military sense, a dynamic which should have been quickly transcended, has now proven an unassailable fact of life of Lebanese politics.[11]

A Rampart Against Totalitarianism

After years of division, ignorance and mutual distrust, it is difficult to see how Lebanese society might acquire a political culture secure enough to serve as the new foundation for Lebanese identity, not to mention a national state. The restoration of the communitarian system under the aegis of the militias begs the question of the state's future identity. It was a conservative choice, partly attributable to the strategies and ambitions of the state's new leaders, whom it serves. Those who established it justified their decision by arguing that secular representation based on demographic majority would entail the serious risk of a slide into totalitarianism.

The proponents of communitarianism oppose the constitutional means by which most of the Arab successor states to the Ottoman empire crafted their institutions. Whereas Lebanon gave communal groups access to political representation, the other states rejected this "traditional" mode of organization. In their embrace of modernity, they theoretically chose the path of secularization and national integration according to which equally empowered citizens of equal rights would interact with the state. In principle, then, the political majority of these countries is determined strictly by the law of numbers. In practice, however, secularization was never fully realized since the *shari'ah*, the Islamic law, affected in one way or another all the constitutions of the Arab world. Moreover, most of these political systems, far from ensuring equal competition, enshrined the domination of one communal group (either ethnic or religious segment of the population) over the others.[12] Thus, the so-called secularization of states such as Syria or Iraq masks a system of communal exclusion more virulent than that of institutionalized communitarianism because it escapes constitutional regulation.

In denouncing the dictatorial nature of "modern" secular regimes and in going so far as to declare that Lebanon has been the only state in the region to escape totalitarianism, the proponents of political communitarianism highlight another problem: the lack of democracy in the neighboring Arab countries. However, these Arab regimes are not dictatorial because they are secular[13] but rather because they are merely secular on the surface, for in essence they are profoundly communitarian. They have warped the principle of the separation of religion and state by identifying the state with a single communal group, have transformed the "one man, one vote" rule into a plebiscite without choices, and have delegitimized their opponents, excluding them from public life by accusing them of sedition.

However acute the problem of a democratic deficit may be in patrimonial, militarized regimes, it afflicts communitarian regimes as well. The communal group tends to impose on the individual its own type of totalitarian isolation, as developed in Lebanon in the war between militias. The most glaring example of this drift was the strategy of territorial withdrawal and homogenization implemented by Bashir Gemayel and his successors at the head of the Lebanese Forces: the institutionalization of a "state within the state" with its own police, army, privately owned radio and television, legal and administrative services, and above all, economic regulations. For this "state" the young chieftain developed a kind of corporatism associated with the desire for political decentralization and the idea of the "plurality of civilizations" in Lebanon. Isolation of the Christian stronghold and conquest of the whole country were the two prongs of an unrealistic strategy in the name of "Lebanonism." Disseminated through imagery and symbolism combining paramilitary order and the Catholic faith,[14] this ideology was conceptualized and given expression at the Maronite University of the Holy Spirit at Kaslik (Junieh), where certain monks were the powerful architects of the radicalization of the Lebanese Forces.[15] Under the banner of Christian unity, the Lebanese Forces' militia oppressed the populations it claimed to be defending via censure, physical threats against clerics and intellectuals, forced conscription, indoctrination of youth, heavy taxation for the war chest, and at the same time, siphoning funds for lucrative private investments in Europe and America. And finally, rivalry among warlords, through assassinations and carbomb attacks, was rampant in the very heart of Christian areas forcing thousands of people to expatriate. Such excesses in the defense of communalism are alien to democratic pluralism.

The Rising Tide of Islam

In addition to the desire to avoid dictatorship, there was yet another reason why political communitarianism persisted into the postwar period. Many Lebanese feared that calls for secularization would pave the way for intolerant majorities, especially, through the rising tide of fundamentalism.

In Lebanon itself, radical Islamic groups developed in the wake of excesses and failures by leftist and nationalist Arab groups in the earliest years of the war. The collapse of Arab nationalism, which had been the great Near Eastern ideology of the 1950s and 1960s, and later disillusionments in the struggle for the liberation of Palestine—the mobilizing mythology of the 1970s—left entire generations feeling frustrated and tormented by war, betrayed by their leaders. The National Progressive Movement proved incapable of drawing up a blueprint for government or of stopping the desertion of militants to other organizations whose leaders were concerned primarily with the defense of their own communities. The deconfessionalization of the political system as advocated by Jumblat's National Movement might pave the way for political democratization, but only if steps also had been taken to separate the individual's status from faith, in recognition of the rights of secular Lebanese.

If these two processes—deconfessionalization of the state and secularization of the society—are not carried out simultaneously, the first alone, if a majority system were adopted, would essentially impose on everyone the political vision of the demographically dominant group: thus, the Muslims could demand that the Christians submit to a state based on Islamic law and the Shi'is could prescribe a government of their religious leaders.[16] The Sunni leaders and new Shi'i elites brandished this possibility as a lever for gaining acceptance of their minimal demand for rebalancing and "participation." However, Hussein al-Quwwatli, director of Dar el-Fatwa, the legal authority of the Sunni community, in an article much discussed early in the war declared that an Islamic government was not only theoretically possible but also ideally desirable: by so stating he did not help the cause of deconfessionalization.[17] Musa Sadr contributed to the ambiguity in the Amal movement, which vacillated between advocating a secularization program with intercommunal cooperation on the one hand, and an ahistorical admixture of politics and religious beliefs on the other, thereby promoting, in accordance with Shi'i doctrine, a return to government by descendants of the Prophet. The Hizbollah spiritual leader Sheikh Muhammad Hussein Fadhlallah has preserved the same ambiguity, holding that Lebanese society is not ready for an Islamic state, yet not ruling out the possibility of one.[18]

The Islamic revival in Lebanon is supported most of all by the Shi'i community. Islamic movements in the Sunni community are many but splintered: Tripoli's Movement for Islamic Unity was powerful in the mid-1980s until it was crushed by the Syrian army. The *Jama'a islamiyya* is an extended network of Sunni *'ulama* (Islamic scholars), mainly from the coastal cities. The most organized and highly motivated group is Ashbash, a Beirut-based movement. As a whole, the Sunnites are leery of any tendency that garners Shi'i support.

Hizbollah, on the other hand, has succeeded remarkably in the last ten years in establishing itself in the Shi'i community among the popular masses as well as in religious, political, and intellectual circles. Hizbollah has as many followers in the rural region of Baalbek as it does in the huge southern suburb of Beirut with its problems of underdevelopment, or in the border villages along the "security zone" controlled by Israel. Of course, Hizbollah greatly profited from the influence the Iranian Islamic Republic has exerted on Islamic movements throughout the world, especially in the Shi'i community. It also benefited from the generosity of various state authorities in Teheran.

But Hizbollah's popularity is owed mainly to a combination on the one hand of social, educational, and charitable programs which, despite their archaic religious doctrine, have proven exceptionally dynamic and modern, and on the other hand, to an audacious harassment strategy carried out against Israeli forces, which made the Islamic Resistance (Hizbollah's military wing) the main armed force of southern Lebanon. Whereas in the 1980s Hizbollah was most active in the anti-Israeli and anti-Western struggle in Lebanon, notably via terrorist bombings and hostage taking, in the 1990s its armed combat role has had mainly a symbolic value, because military operations are mostly manipulated by Syria, Iran, and Israel, each using Hizbollah as the local instrument of its regional political aims.

However, many social institutions in the Shi'i regions are linked to Hizbollah and are engaged in long-term activities ranging from Islamic instruction to martial arts centers, the establishment of radio stations, newspapers, television, libraries and professional schools, not to mention the sorely needed hospitals and dispensaries. One such institution, Jihad al-Bina' ("reconstruction effort"), a tentacular organization tied to the Foundation of Martyrs and dependent on Iran, has organized committees and cooperatives, spearheaded reconstruction efforts, and initiated water and electricity access projects with an efficiency that contrasts markedly with the state's negligence and Amal's political clientelism.[19] As a result, Hizbollah's legitimacy has been enhanced in the Shi'i community.

Not surprisingly, many Lebanese suspect that despite demands for deconfessionalization and the adoption of majority rule, the Shi'i community is ambitious enough to seek to impose its legal system and orientation on the entire population. All controversy and statistical analysis aside, the Shi'is are unanimously recognized as the most numerous; they are the majority group in sociological terms, although not demographically, since they represent less than 50 percent of the population. Hizbollah leaders feel free to insist on the demand for deconfessionalization, confident that with their military victory over Amal in 1990 and the legislative successes of 1992, they have won hegemony in the Shi'i milieu. Naturally, Hizbollah's plans fluctuate; they vary according to the interplay of forces within the *majlis al-shura*, its governing council, and the strategy of its Iranian protector. The fact remains that everywhere in the Mideast, "Islamism" means the enforcement of *shari'ah* and an inferior status for the Christians and Jews. If majority rule were followed, secular Lebanon would run the risk of waking up one day as an Islamic republic.

There is no satisfactory solution to this disquieting possibility, since the development of the Islamic movement in Lebanon depends on various internal and external factors. Nevertheless, to understand how the future relationship between Islam and the state in Lebanon will take shape, two additional factors need to be taken into account. First, there have been visible changes in the Shi'i community, which due to developments in education and professional training has experienced mass urbanization and rapidly increasing social mobility. Two dynamics, more complementary than contradictory, are at work: one enforces group cohesion and the stress on collective identity; and the other enforces the splintering of traditional structures in favor of individual aspirations and development. Whereas the first dynamic tends toward the re-Islamization of the society, the other tends powerfully toward secularization. Second, there is great diversity within the Shi'i community, which it would be just as foolish to characterize as monolithic as it would be to condider the "Muslim world" as a single political entity: regional diversity from Bikaa to Beirut and southern Lebanon; religious diversity between quietists and radicals, between the followers of one *marja* (religious referee) or another; political diversity among leftists, communists, Greater Syrian nationalists, prominent family loyalists, Amal adherents, and so on; growing differentiation among social strata, and finally, a multitude of centers of economic power, given the undeniable effects of emigration. The Shi'is more than any other community might reject the Islamic movement's tendency toward totalitarianism and work for genuine secularization.

Necessary and Fearsome Peace

In these early postwar years the Lebanese have not had much of a choice between the pernicious effects of the communitarian system and the dangers of abandoning it. In order to halt the hostilities, their leaders legitimized, solidified, and prolonged Syria's control over the country. The Document of National Reconciliation followed the name of the intrusive protector a formula of allegiance that rattles the ear of many: "May they [the Syrians] be thanked!" In its economic, domestic, and international policies, Lebanon must now avoid any action harmful to Syria.[20] In fact, as regards opening the Lebanese market to Syrian products, jointly exploiting hydroelectric resources, awarding contracts for the reconstruction of public works—not withstanding the profits made by hundreds of thousands of Syrian workers in the country— Lebanon must comply with Syrian interests. In a regional context, Lebanon is profitable to Syria not only as a source of revenue, for which the oil monarchies will pay to keep the peace, but also as a card to play in Syria's confrontation with Israel.

Even more damaging than Syria's exploitation of a country it has helped to ruin is the military and political control it has exercised over Lebanon since the war ended. Although its armed forces are less visible since the Lebanese army has been in position, it is no secret that there is close cooperation between command posts and information networks, and that many Lebanese officers are now trained in Syria. In addition, no governmental decision of political importance is made without the acquiescence of a high-ranking Baathist leader—generally, Vice President Khaddam—whom the Lebanese ministers and three presidents must seek out in Damascus.

In the process of strengthening its grip on Lebanon, Syria has benefited by divided regional politics and above all, by the Arab-Israeli conflict, since Syria's intervention in Lebanon was aimed at preventing Lebanon from entering an alliance with Israel or falling under Israeli influence. From 1980 to 1988 Syria made the most of the war between Iran and Iraq. Adhering to the old rule of alliances, "My enemy's enemy [is my friend]" Syria supported Iranian influence in Lebanon and the Islamic Republic's mobilization of Lebanese Shi'is. Thus, Teheran was able to enforce its international terrorist strategy from Beirut, with the Lebanese Shi'is as go-betweens, while fanning the fires of armed struggle against Israel in the south. Damascus remained master of the game, as could be seen when the hostages were liberated and Lebanon's Shi'is pledged allegiance to the new legal government at the very time that Syria joined the international coalition in the Gulf War. But the relationship between Iran and the Lebanese Shi'is predated the civil war and will continue in times of peace. The emigration of religious Persians and the financing of Islamic organizations such as Hizbollah did not stop at the war's end, even though they have diminished considerably due to the economic crisis and internal dissension in Iran. Syria has also benefited by Iraq's misadventure in Kuwait. Hafez al-Assad was able by improving his image in the international community and sending a contingent to Saudi Arabia in October 1990 to drive Saddam Hussein out of Lebanon (the ambitious challenger had been generously supplying Lebanese Forces with sophisticated weaponry since 1987) and once and for all to crush General Aoun.

Caught up in the destructive cycle of "war for the sake of others," Lebanon had placed great hopes on the Arab-Israeli negotiations that got underway at the Madrid conference in October 1991. The resolution of the Palestinian question, an end to Syrian and Israeli presence in Lebanon, the opening of regional markets: all must have seemed bright possibilities. However, bitter experience has taught leaders and the populace alike to be deeply skeptical. Lebanon's issues, unlike possible Palestinian and Jordanian resolutions, cannot by treated independently of Syro-Israeli negotiations; indeed, Lebanon has become a bargaining chip between Damascus and Jerusalem, and Beirut is rightfully concerned that the price of any future peace will be high.

The Lebanese are confronting a reality that they have always tried to deny and that even now many still refuse to believe. The Israeli-Palestinian accords of 1993 contemplated a limited return of "displaced" Palestinians from the war of 1967, but not of those from 1948–49; the fate of those refugees will not be discussed until after 1996 at best. Together with their descendants, these refugees in Lebanon represent a population of at least 250,000, predominantly Sunnis who were left in financial shambles when the PLO was expelled from Beirut in 1982 and the Gulf monarchies took economic reprisals against Arafat's organization in 1990. Except for a minority, the approximately 400,000 Palestinians living in Lebanon have no future outside of Lebanon. Even without Lebanese nationality, they are an integral part of the country's social structure and economic life, and will probably be given some sort of residency status. In the flourishing 1950s the Palestinian presence was well accepted; but in the 1990s Palestinians have become a thorny problem for Lebanon: they are an economic burden, target of communal discord, subject to political manipulation, and possibly also a source of instability on account of their frustrations. In other words, after fifteen years of war, they have ended up in a position much worse than the one they occupied in 1969 or 1973.

Moreover, the Lebanese fear that foreign armies will not retreat completely. It is quite possible that Syria and Israel will reach a security agreement whereby Hizbollah will be disarmed and the control of southern Lebanon turned over to the Lebanese army with Syrian "assistance." In short, this would be an extension and legitimation of their tacit "red line" agreement reached under the aegis of the United States in 1976. Then the Israeli Defense Forces, and with them hundreds of the ALS militia who would be undesirable in a reunified Lebanon, might leave Lebanese territory. Yet such an arrangement would probably impose Lebanese-Israeli coordination on security, and above all, the granting to Israel of rights over the Hasbani and the Wazzani, the two tributaries of the Jordan that spring from Lebanese territory, which Israel has always coveted and has controlled since 1967.[21] Likewise, Lebanese sovereignty will remain limited for as long as Syria retains a military presence. Not only is this presence dependent on the improbable secularization of the domestic political system, but Israel and the international community may want to assign Damascus a security role in a new regional order and thus reward Syrian participation in the peace process, giving short shrift to Lebanon's independence.

Further, the Lebanese fear they are not equipped to profit economically from a new mideastern market or to confront the pitfalls it represents. The country's infrastructure is in ruins, skilled labor has fled, capital remains sluggish. The Gulf is no longer the resource it was when for three decades

Lebanon enjoyed seemingly unending wealth by catering to unlimited service needs. Surely the ambitious reconstruction projects in downtown Beirut are aimed at preparing the country for the coming peace process. Despite the advantage of its intimate familiarity with the Arab region, Lebanon is now well behind Israel, who is already exporting agricultural goods and material to its neighbors, initiating economic and technical cooperation with some countries of the Gulf and the Mahgreb.

It remains to be seen whether in the new context of peace Lebanon will receive Western support to help reestablish its sovereignty. One may well imagine that after Israel and Syria sign formal accords, countries like the United States, because it has global political responsibilities, and France, on account of historical and emotional ties, will revisit the Lebanese question, long since shelved while awaiting a solution to the Palestinian question. Any political interest shown by the West would have the double effect of tempering the ambitions of the regional powers and restoring Lebanese confidence in their own country. However, throughout the fifteen-year war, in the name of global balance in the Near East, Washington showed a growing disinterest in the country of the cedar tree. France, on the other hand, made a show of vain promises and puffing; not only was Paris unable to act independently of its Western allies but at the same time it managed other interests (Syrian, Iraqi) in the region. Lebanon was cynically bandied about in an internal French dispute between right and left, and the instances of French intervention, from the rescue of the PLO in 1982 to the asylum it granted General Aoun in 1991, were more symbolic than substantive. The possibility or threat of Western intervention that haunted the war in effect only encouraged extremism and paralyzed a local search for solutions. Past instances of indispensable and destructive intervention by foreign powers linger in the minds of the Lebanese. Is it reasonable, then, to hope for intervention when the problems of the Near East will become less acute? And would such intervention benefit Lebanon?

Small and Pluricommunitarian

As we have seen, the reconstruction of Lebanon is taking place in a particularly strained context. The implosion of the Soviet Union produced a series of breakups and realignments in the Mideast, of which the Gulf War was the most obvious. Lebanon's two powerful neighbors, Syria and Israel, each cashed in on dividends from the collapse of Iraq, thereby reducing Lebanon's autonomous space. Moreover, recently, new religious and ethnic forces are being unleashed, especially east of the Mediterranean, which further complicates the chessboard of the country's domestic politics. Added to these complications are the new facts of the global economy: the relative impoverishment of the oil-exporting countries, the delocalization of service activities, and the development of a parallel cross-border economy that only a minority profits from. It is tempting, as it was early in the war in 1975, to attribute the critical state of Lebanon's stagnation to uncontrollable circumstances, to blame foreigners for the misfortune, and to await unlikely assistance from abroad.

However, Lebanon's structural problems are manifold and revealing. Lebanon is a young, small, multiethnic state, qualities that are perilous at best in a post-Cold War world characterized by the delegitimation of states and the rise of nationalist passions. The sacrosanct respect for states that threw off the yoke of colonization is now subject to change. Iraq's attempted annexation of Kuwait, even though it ended in a burning rebuke, illustrates the fragility of international borders in the Mideast and the shattering of the taboo against inviolability, respected since World War II. What Syria had never dreamed of doing formally in Lebanon has now become feasible, even if blameworthy. After the Gulf War, military incursions and humanitarian operations across borders framed the Kurd question in a regional context, thus signaling both the end of dogma regarding state sovereignty and the growing importance of sub- and trans-national actions. Elsewhere, while the press refers to the "lebanonization" of the ex-Soviet Caucasus and the former Yugoslavia, there are many examples of federations breaking up and new states being created along ethnic lines. These examples may provoke yet another temptation for disgruntled Lebanese.

What the Lebanese state has in common with many Third World countries who are facing the difficult task of "inventing" a state on the basis of common identity and compatible interests, is youth. To undertake a process of nation building, a country's small size is no obstacle if its population is homogeneous, as is the case with Tunisia, for example. Where the population is not homogeneous, secession—such as occurred with the Czech Republic and Slovakia—is a partial solution, although no panacea. Yet Lebanon's territory is too limited and its population too into a mosaic of intermingled communal groups for the separatist option ever to become a wise option.

The need remains to acknowledge ethnic and religious differences (without pretending particular groups retain immutable identities) while securing communal representation under the authority of a lawful state held accountable by a responsible citizenry. In matters of creating and overseeing such a hybrid polity, however, law and political science are still in their infancy. Since the fall of the great empires at the turn of the century, international law and human rights have been codified; but the rights of communities, ethnic groups and nations have remained undeveloped. What needs to be forged is a form of federalism that leaves room for individual options and acknowledges communal identities while enhancing state-citizenry relations. This federalism should not be territorially based; in this way, further population displacement will be avoided. This is why the creation of a senate organized along communal lines, so long as it is not a disguised return to political communitarianism, might be a salutary complement to the eventual deconfessionalization of the Lebanese Parliament.

The major problem remaining is the authority of the state and especially the exercise of executive power. The Lebanese experiment has amply shown that a political system based on communal consensus can end in paralysis and distort political purpose. In the decades following independence, the programs indispensable to the country's development—highway construction between Beirut and Damascus, exploitation of the lower Litani valley, and educational reforms—were all postponed for lack of a responsible executive authority acting in the national interest. Now in the reconstruction period, although the spirit of the times favors giving private entrepreneurs great latitude, infrastructure rebuilding and market regulation require an effective and independent state. It may seem old-fashioned to deplore persistent underdevelopment in Lebanon and the fact that the revenue gap grew wider during the war, that provisions for the minimal nutritional and sanitary—not to mention educational—needs of whole sectors of the population were further eroded; but it bears repeating that the "market" scarcely profits by impoverished consumers or an unhealthy, uneducated work force. Likewise, "security" is endangered when a growing percentage of the population has nothing to lose, for stability is a mirage when entire groups are tempted to operate and place their hopes outside the political system. To address all these problems, the state must assume a role in Lebanon—that much is indispensable. On the other hand, the development of a state requires stronger civilian organizations, for they are the only ones who can hold the state accountable. They alone can convey social demands, direct efforts, and attract individual loyalties. Crushed during the war by communal organizations that claimed to speak and act in Lebanon's name, civil society only rarely and timidly showed its face. In order for Lebanese society to move beyond the rancor of communitarian wound-licking, common rules should be laid down and generally followed in the realms of intellectual, material, and symbolic interchange.

Epilogue

Who bore the heaviest responsibility in this affair? The Egyptian pasha, certainly, who set the mountain dwellers against each other. We also, British and French, who came here to prolong the Napoleonic wars. And the Ottomans, in their negligence and fanaticism. But to my mind, since I have come to love this Mountain as if I'd been born here, it is the men of this country: they alone cannot be forgiven.

In Lebanon today, as after the dramatic events of the nineteenth century, it is less important to assign blame than to find the basis on which the "people of Lebanon" can build a future. In the mid-1990s the Lebanese are facing major obstacles to national reconciliation. In order to overcome these obstacles, they have to succeed in the following three major trials.

The first issue relates to the reconstruction of downtown Beirut. The Hariri government decided in 1993 to assign this ambitious project to a private company, Solidere, in an effort to restore life to the merchant city and enable the country to face new regional developments. Beyond architectural choices and financial results, the downtown reconstruction project raises the key question of the connection between the future prosperous center and the impoverished, underequipped urban periphery (not to mention the rural areas that have experienced significant demographic decline), and between high performance entrepreneurs linked to the world economy and the unemployed masses. While it has become the symbol of economic recovery in Lebanon, downtown Beirut will be the litmus test for seeing if effective interchange among the different sectors of the population can take place.

The second issue is Christian participation in the new republic. Christian Lebanese have become a demographic minority, militarily defeated, and sometimes suspected of political treason. Former members of the Lebanese Forces are now being prosecuted for crimes and bombings that in no way pale in comparison to those committed by the militias of all the other communities. Former leaders are being denounced for having collaborated with Israel at a time when every faction had been seeking foreign patronage. Although a banal politician, General Michel Aoun is still considered a dangerous outlaw. This unequal treatment, justified by shortsighted security interests, must be weighed against the rise of Islamist movements and Christian uneasiness throughout the Arab East. However, beyond the need to disarm the militias and keep the peace for the good of all, what is at stake is Lebanon's very identity, its preservation as a distinct and independent entity within its surroundings.

The third issue revolves around preserving freedoms without compromising Lebanese security. Governmental authority is still shaky, legitimacy weakened by dependence on Syrian power, the army still exercising precarious control over the country. The prolongation of Elias Hrawi's presidential mandate for three more years because of alleged "exceptional circumstances," announced in Damascus in October 1995, will not modify Lebanon's global policy. Nevertheless, it is an indication of little concern for the country's institutions and national independence. The temptation is great for the government, in the name of efficiency, to revert to coercion, multiply prohibitions, and stretch the law, as Lebanon's neighboring states are in the habit of doing. Thus, in the reconstruction period, amid a "new order" in the Mideast, Lebanon's judicial independence and freedom of the press are particularly endangered. Historically Lebanon's prosperity was tied to its atmosphere of freedom and creativity. Fortunately, for decades, all the communities have tested their right to criticize and their right to choose, and they all have in common the desire to protect those rights.

After fifteen years of destruction, Lebanon is encountering serious impediments to preserving its essence and correcting the excesses that undermined it. In confronting these problems and the complexity of current issues, the Lebanese sometimes hark back to the time when peace was a dream and the will to survive a source of strength. Yet to build the future they will have to overcome their bitter experience.

Appendix

Presidents of the Republic of Lebanon

Charles Dabbas	1926–1933
Habib al-Saad	1933–1935
Emile Eddé	1936–1941
Alfred Naccache	1941–1943
Ayyub Thabit	1943
Petro Trad	1943
Bishara al-Khuri	1943–1952
Camille Chamoun	1952–1958
Fuad Shihab	1958–1964
Charles Helou	1964–1970
Suleiman Frangieh	1970–1976
Elias Sarkis	1976–1982
Bashir Gemayel	1982
Amin Gemayel	1982–1988
René Moawad	1989
Elias Hrawi	1989–

Military Forces Engaged in the War, 1976–1982

Lebanese Army

Lebanese Front (founded in 1976)
  Lebanese Forces (Kataeb/Phalange Party)
  National Liberal Party (Camille Chamoun)
  Guardians of the Cedars (Etienne Saqr)
  Liberation Army of Zghorta/Marada (Suleiman Frangieh)
  Order of Maronite Monks (Sharbil Qassis)
  Tanzim (Fu'ad Shimali)
  Army of Free Lebanon (Saad Haddad)

Lebanese National Movement (founded in 1973)
  Progressive Socialist Party (Kamal Jumblat; Walid Jumblat)

Murabitun (Ibrahim Quleilat)
Lebanese Communist Party (George Hawi)
pro-Iraqi Baath Party (Abdel Majid Rafii)
Organization of Communist Action (Muhsin Ibrahim)
Syrian Social Nationalist Party (Inam Ra'd)

Allies of the National Movement Aligned with Syria
National Front
pro-Syrian Baath Party (Asim Qansuh)
Union of the Toiling People's Forces (Kamal Shatila)
Syrian Social Nationalist Party (Ibrahim Qnayseh)
Amal/Movement of the Deprived (Musa Sadr; Nabih Berri)

Syrian Army
Palestinian Forces of the Sa'iqa (Zuhayr Muhasin)

Palestine Liberation Organization
Militias of the Resistance Organizations
Palestine Liberation Army

Major Dates in the War in Lebanon

April 13, 1975	Beginning of the war between the Lebanese Front and the National Movement supported by the Palestine Liberation Organization.
June 1, 1975	Entry of the Syrian troops at the request of President Frangieh in order to prevent a victory of the radicals.
April 1978	Operation Litani: 2,000 deaths and 250,000 displaced persons following the Israeli invasion. Positioning of UNIFIL in southern Lebanon.
July 1978	Beginning of clashes between Syrians and the Lebanese Front.
April 18, 1979	Proclamation of the State of Free Lebanon by Major Saad Haddad.
July 7, 1980	Forced unification of the Christian militias under the authority of Bashir Gemayel.
April–June 1981	Syrian-Israeli missile crisis.
July 17, 1981	Bombardment of Beirut by the Israeli Air Force: 300 dead. The UN arranges a ceasefire.
June 5, 1982	Operation "Peace for Galilee"; two-month siege of Beirut by Israeli forces.
September 24, 1982	Following the massacres at Sabra and Shatila, a multinational force moves into Beirut for the protection of civilians.
May 17, 1983	Signing in Naqoura of a Lebanese-Israeli peace agreement.
August 1983	Shuf war; the Druzes drive out the Lebanese Forces and clash with the army.
October 23, 1983	Suicide attacks on American and French members of the Multinational Force: 299 victims.
November 1–8, 1983	National dialogue conference in Geneva.

December 1983	The Syrian army besieges the PLO at Tripoli.
February 1984	The Amal movement and its allies drive the army out of West Beirut.
March 12–20, 1984	Second national dialogue conference in Lausanne.
February–June 1985	Operation Iron Hand of the Israeli army in southern Lebanon ending in its fallback to the "security zone."
May 1985	Beginning of "camp wars" between Amal and the Palestinians.
December 28, 1985	Damascus Accord between Amal, Jumblat's PSP, and the Lebanese Forces.
January 15, 1986	President Gemayel rejects the Damascus accord.
February 20, 1987	The Syrian army returns to West Beirut.
September 11, 1987	An agreement between Amal and the Palestinians brings the war of the camps to an end.
September 22, 1988	End of President Amin Gemayel's mandate. In the absence of a successor, he appoints General Michel Aoun to form a government.
November 28, 1988	Beginning of clashes between Amal and Hizbollah on the outskirts of Beirut and in the south.
February 1989	Clashes in east Beirut and central Lebanon between the Lebanese Forces and General Aoun's army.
March 14–September 22, 1989	General Aoun's "war of liberation" against Syria.
October 22, 1989	Taif Accord.
November 5, 1989	René Moawad elected President.
November 22, 1989	René Moawad assassinated.
November 24, 1989	Elias Hrawi elected President.
January 30, 1990	Beginning of clashes between the Lebanese Forces and General Aoun's army.
October 12, 1990	Syrian air attack puts an end to General Aoun's separatist government.
November 6, 1990	Ceasefire between Amal and Hizbollah.
December 24, 1990	First postwar coalition government formed.

Notes

Chapter 1. The Search for Origins

1. N. Wehbé and A. al-Amine, *Système d'enseignement et division sociale au Liban* (Paris, 1980).
2. *Tarikh al-Mawarina*, who draws on the apologetical work of Bishop Istifan Duwayhi, *Tarikh al-Ta'ifa al-Maruniyya* [History of the Maronite Community] (Beirut, 1890).
3. For a synthesis of the history of the populating of Mount Lebanon in antiquity, see the opening pages of Kamal Salibi, *The Modern History of Lebanon* (New York: Praeger, 1965).
4. Thus they are not feudal lords in the socioeconomic sense and especially not in the territorial sense that this term has in the Latino-Germanic areas. It is more a case of tax collectors becoming local notables.
5. Albert Hourani, "Ideologies of the Mountain and the City," in Roger Owen, ed., *Essays on the Crisis in Lebanon* (London: Ithaca Press, 1976), pp. 33–41.
6. Jouplain (Bulos Noujaim), *La Question du Liban: étude d'histoire diplomatique et de droit international* (Paris: A. Rousseau, 1908), chap. 1.
7. Kamal Salibi, "Fakhr ed-Din and the Idea of Lebanon," lecture given at the University of the Holy Ghost (Kaslik), in *Dimensions of Lebanese Nationalism*, in Arabic (Kaslik, 1970), p. 11.

Chapter 2. A Land of Communities

1. Edmond Rabbath, *La Formation historique du Liban politique et constitutionnel* (Beirut, 1986), p. 7.
2. *Statistiques scolaires 1965 à 1973–74* (Beirut: National Education Ministry).
3. Estimates for the mid-nineteenth century cited by Dominique Chevallier, *La Société du Mont Liban à l'époque de la révolution industrielle en Europe* (Paris: Paul Geuthner, 1971).
4. Claude Dubar and Salim Nasr, *Les Classes sociales au Liban* (Paris: Presses de la Fondation Nationale des Sciences Politiques, 1976), p. 30.
5. Ahmad Beydoun, *Identité confessionnelle et temps social chez les historiens libanais contemporains* (Beirut, 1984), p. 283.
6. According to Dubar and Nasr, these impositions represent a minimum of 8 percent of the land tax, that is, 25 percent of the harvest.
7. In 1860, the French consul general in Beirut pointed out the "disastrous repercussions" of the French financial crisis of 1857–58 on the country. Cited in Chevallier, *Société du Mont Liban*, p. 201.

8. See the well-known critique of the European orientalists by Edward W. Said: *Orientalism* (New York: Pantheon, 1978).

Chapter 3. The Choice of Greater Lebanon

1. Albert Hourani, *Arabic Thought in the Liberal Age, 1789–1939* (London/New York: Oxford University Press, 1962), p. 248.
2. B. Abu-Manneh, "The Christians between Ottomanism and Syrian Nationalism: the Ideas of Butros al-Bustani," *International Journal of Middle East Studies* 2 (1980): 287–304.
3. Jouplain, *Question du Liban*, p. 587.
4. Bertrand Badie, *Les Deux Etats: pouvoir et société en Occident et en terre d'Islam* (Paris: Fayard, 1986), p. 177.
5. William I. Shorrock, *French Imperialism in the Middle East: The Failure of Policy in Syria and Lebanon, 1900–1914* (Madison: University of Wisconsin Press, 1976), p. 138.
6. Stephen H. Longrigg, *Syria and Lebanon under French Mandate* (New York/London: Oxford University Press, 1958), p. 58.
7. Edmond Rabbath, *Unité Syrienne et Devenir Arabe* (Paris, 1937), p. 154.
8. *Yawm Maysalun* [the Day of Maysalun] (Beirut, 1965) poignantly traces the defeat of the Arab nationalists of the Near East by France and Britain.

Chapter 4. The Merchant City

1. Dubar and Nasr, *Classes sociales au Liban*, p. 54.
2. Longrigg, *Syria and Lebanon under Mandate*, p. 277.
3. Roger Owen, "The Political Economy of Grand-Liban, 1920–1970," in Owen, *Essays on the Crisis in Lebanon*, p. 24.
4. Ibid., p. 25.
5. Dubar and Nasr, *Classes sociales*, p. 23.
6. Carolyn L. Gates, *The Formation of the Political Economy of Modern Lebanon: The State and the Economy from Colonialism to Independence, 1939–1952* (Unpublished doctoral dissertation, Oxford University, 1985), p. 294.
7. Daoud Sayegh, *L'Exercice de la fonction Législative au Liban* (Beirut: Université Libanaise, 1985), p. 96. See also Abdo Baaklini, *Legislative and Political Development: Lebanon, 1842–1972* (Durham, N.C.: Duke University Press, 1976).
8. P. Huvelin, *Que vaut la Syrie?* (Paris: n.d.), p. 26.
9. The French Republic, *Rapport à la SDN 1929*, cited by Gates, *Formation of the Political Economy*, p. 46.
10. Amin al-Hafez, *La Structure et la politique économique en Syrie et au Liban* (Beirut, 1953), p. 46.
11. Planning Ministry, *Industrial Census 1971*, cited by *al-Nahar*, June 9, 1975.
12. Dubar and Nasr, *Classes sociales*, p. 77.
13. Ibid., p. 54.
14. Ibid., p. 60.

15. Jacques Couland, *Le Mouvement syndical au Liban, 1919–1946* (Paris, 1970), p. 133.
16. Nadim Shehadi, *The Idea of Lebanon: Economy and State in the Cénacle libanais, 1946–54* (Oxford: Centre for Lebanese Studies, 1987).
17. Gates, *Formation of the Political Economy*, p. 291.
18. Yusuf Sayegh, *Entrepreneurs of Lebanon: The Role of the Business Leader in a Developing Economy* (Cambridge, 1962), pp. 81–82.
19. Couland, *Le Mouvement Syndical*, pp. 318ff.
20. Sayegh, *Entrepreneurs of Lebanon*, pp. 81–82.
21. Dubar and Nasr, *Les Classes sociales*, p. 67.
22. Marwan Buheiry, *Beirut's Role in the Political Economy of the French Mandate, 1919–39* (Oxford: Centre for Lebanese Studies, 1986), p. 15.
23. Gates, *Formation of the Political Economy*, p. 312.
24. From 77,820 to 161,382 inhabitants.
25. *Le Commerce du Levant*, February 9, 1952.
26. Sayegh, *Entrepreneurs*, pp. 81–82.

Chapter 5. Patrons and Clients

1. "Le Malheur des uns . . . ," telecast on the French channel Antenne 2, July 7, 1982.
2. On the historical dimension and current nature of political clientelism in Lebanon, see Samir Khalaf, *Lebanon's Predicament* (New York: Columbia University Press, 1987), in particular chapters 4–6.
3. From 1960 to 1991, the total number of deputies has been 99, consisting of 30 Maronites, 20 Sunnis, 19 Shi'is, 11 Greek Orthodox, 6 Greek Catholics, 6 Druzes, 4 Armenian Orthodox, 1 Armenian Catholic, 1 Protestant, and 1 minority Christian.
4. See Chapter 6.
5. Alexander Heard, *The Cost of Democracy* (Chapel Hill: University of North Carolina Press, 1960), p. 374. The cost to Lebanon, however, is half of that to Israel.
6. Khalaf, *Lebanon's Predicament*, p. 126.
7. There has been an average turnover of 40 percent of the deputies in each new parliament since independence. Ibid., p. 132.
8. Ibid., p. 135.
9. Michael Hudson, *The Precarious Republic: Political Modernization in Lebanon* (New York: Random House, 1968), p. 268.
10. Malcolm Kerr, "Confessionalism, Public Administration and Efficiency in Lebanon," in Leonard Binder, ed., *Politics in Lebanon* (New York: Wiley, 1966), p. 180.
11. Michel Seurat, "Le Quartier de Bab Tebbane à Tripoli (Liban): étude d'une 'asabiyya urbaine," in CERMOC, *Mouvements communautaires et espaces urbains au Machreq* (Beirut, 1985), p. 146.

Chapter 6. A "National" Pact

1. Rabbath, *Formation historique du Liban*, p. 90.
2. L. Meo, "The Separation of Lebanon from Greater Syria" (unpublished doctoral dissertation, Indiana University, 1961).
3. Pierre Rondot, *Les Institutions politiques du Liban* (Paris, Institut d'Etudes de l'Orient Contemporain, 1947), pp. 28–29.
4. N. Beyhum, "Espace urbain, espaces politiques: villes, états et communautés: Beyrouth vers 1975," in N. Shehadi and D. Haffar Mills, eds., *Lebanon, a History of Conflict and Consensus* (London, 1988).
5. Rabbath, *Formation*, pp. 518–26.
6. Michel Chiha, *Politique intérieure* (Beirut, 1964), p. 303.
7. Arend Lijphart, *Democracy in Plural Societies: A Comparative Exploration* (New Haven: Yale University Press, 1977), p. 96.
8. Rondot, *Institutions politiques du Liban*, pp. 28–29.
9. Camille Chamoun, *Crise au Moyen-Orient* (Paris, 1963), pp. 335ff.

Chapter 7. The Palestinian Factor

1. Georges Corm, *Fragmentation of the Middle East, the Last 30 Years* (N.Y.: Unwin Hyman, 1988).
2. Alain Gresh, *The PLO: The Struggle Within: Towards an Independent Palestinian State*, trans. A.M. Berrett (London: Zed Books, 1988).
3. René Chamussy, *Chronique d'une guerre: Liban 1975–1977* (Paris: Desclée, 1978), p. 30.
4. According to the version published by *al-Nahar* (November 6, 1976) and authenticated by the number-two man of the PLO, Abu Iyad, and by President Charles Helou.

Chapter 8. A Society in Crisis

1. Institut de Recherche et de Formation en vue du Développement, *Besoins et possibilités de développement du Liban* (Beirut, 1960).
2. A. Khalil, "Junub Lubnan bayna l-dawla wal-thawra" [Southern Lebanon between the State and the Revolution], *Dirasat 'Arabiyya* 4 (February 1975).
3. See Chapter 4.
4. Lebanese Communist Party, *Al-Qadhiyya l-zira'iyya fi Lubnan* [The Agrarian Question in Lebanon] (Beirut, 1973), pp. 308–9.
5. *L'Economie des pays arabes*, March 1974, p. 86.
6. S. Nasr, "The Crisis of Lebanese Capitalism," *MERIP Report* 73 (December 1978), p. 4.
7. C. Henry Moore, "Prisoner's Financial Dilemma: A Consociational Future for Lebanon?" *American Political Science Review* (March 1987).
8. Nasr, "Crisis of Lebanese Capitalism," p. 11.

9. Fouad Ajami, *The Arab Predicament: Arab Political Thought and Practice Since 1967* (London/New York: Cambridge University Press, 1981), pp. 141–42.

10. Sadeq al-'Azm, *Al-Naqd al-dhati ba'd al-hazima* [Self-criticism After the Defeat] (Beirut, 1968).

11. Constantine Zurayk, *Ma'na l-nakba mujaddadan* [Meaning of the Repeated Disaster] (Beirut, 1968).

12. Nasif Nassar, *Nahwa mujtama' jadid* [Toward a New Society] (Beirut, 1970).

13. See Chapter 12.

14. Particularly the *Enquête par sondage sur la population active au Liban*, carried out and published by the Ministry for Planning in 1970; *La Famille au Liban, enquête par sondage*, published by the Lebanese Family Planning Association in 1971; and the adjustment of the investigation of 1970 by Y. Courbages and Philippe Fargues in *La Situation démographique au Liban* (Beirut: Publications de l'Université Libanaise, Librairie Orientale: 1974).

15. In 1974 a projection based on the 1932 census resulted in the following community percentages: Maronites, 23; Greek Orthodox, 7; Greek Catholics, 5; other Christians, 5; Sunnis, 26; Shi'is, 27; Druzes, 7.

16. See the first and second "principles" of the "Considerations" that follow the *Mithaq harakat Amal* [Pact of the Amal Movement] (Beirut, 1975), on the all-embracing nature of the Divine Law, on the cultural heritage, the spiritual values, and the heroic Shi'i tradition to be safeguarded.

17. Waddah Sharara, "Rabi' 1975 al-Lubnani" [Lebanese Spring of 1975], *Dirasat 'Arabiyya* 11: 12 (October 1975).

18. John P. Entelis, *Pluralism and Party Transformation in Lebanon: al-Kata'ib, 1936–1970* (Leiden: Brill, 1974), p. 160.

Chapter 9. War Violent and Rampant (1975–1981)

1. Halim Barakat, *Lebanon in Strife: Student Preludes to the Civil War* (Austin: University of Texas Press, 1977), p. 53.

2. Jonathan C. Randal, *Going All the Way: Christian Warlords, Israeli Adventurers, and the War in Lebanon* (New York: Random House/Vintage, 1983), p. 100ff.

3. Kamal Jumblat, *I Speak for Lebanon* (London, 1979), pp. 153–54.

4. Ze'ef Schiff and Ehud Ya'ari, *Israel's Lebanon War*, trans. Ina Friedman (New York: Simon & Schuster, 1984), p. 11.

5. A. Perlmutter, "Begin's Rhetoric and Sharon's Tactics," *Foreign Policy* (September 1982), pp. 67–83.

6. About 9 percent of Syria's population is Christian. The Alawis, an esoteric Shi'i community to which the main Syrian leaders belong, account for 12 percent and the Sunnis 75 percent. In Lebanon, the Alawis number about 20,000 in Tripoli and environs; they were not among the officially recognized communities, but one Lebanese Shi'is authority, Musa Sadr, acknowledged them as Shi'i in 1973. See Martin Kramer, "Syria's Alawis and Shi'ism," in Martin Kramer, ed., *Shi'ism, Resistance, and Revolution* (Boulder, Colo.: Westview Press, 1987), p. 248.

7. In an interview published in the French weekly newsmagazine *Le Point*, December 26, 1983.

8. Jumblat, *I Speak for Lebanon*, p. 188.

9. Thomas L. Friedman gave the figures of $20 to $25 million a month for the cost of the militias alone; *International Herald Tribune*, May 18, 1982.
10. Antoine Jabre (Lebanese ambassador to the USSR from 1973 to 1977), *La Guerre du Liban* (Paris: Belfond, 1980).
11. Eric Rouleau, "La Syrie dans le bourbier libanais," *Le Monde*, June 1–5, 1976.
12. Selim Turquié, "De quoi vivent les Libanais?" *Le Monde Diplomatique* (October 1979).
13. Karim Pakradouni, *La Paix manquée, le mandat d'Elias Sarkis (1976–1982)* (Beirut, 1984).
14. P. Kemp, "La Stratégie de Bachir Gemayel," *Hérodote* 29–30 (1980), pp. 55–82.
15. The day after the massacre, when he proclaimed the birth of his "July 7 Movement" (1980).
16. Rashid Khalidi, *Under Siege: P.L.O. Decisionmaking During the 1982 War* (New York: Columbia University Press, 1986), pp. 30–31.
17. Frederic C. Hof, *Galilee Divided: The Israeli-Lebanon Frontier 1916–1984* (Boulder, Colo.: Westview Press, 1985), pp. 123ff.
18. Resolution 425 of the UN Security Council, March 19, 1978.

Chapter 10. One War Hides Others (1982–1990)

1. The first four were the Palestine War (1948–49), the Suez War (1956), the Six-Day War (1967), and the October War (1973).
2. On the Israeli search for a Maronite ally in Lebanon, see Livia Rokach, *Israel's Sacred Terrorism: A Study Based on Moshe Sharett's Personal Diary and other Documents* (Belmont, Mass.: Association of Arab-American University Graduates, 1986), pp. 24–30.
3. The official Israeli count for 1980 is eight infiltration attempts and 262 attacks and bombings.
4. Perlmutter, "Begin's Rhetoric and Sharon's Tactics."
5. According to Israeli military information of June 10, 1985: 654 Israeli deaths, 3,890 wounded, and 21 suicides in Lebanon. Cost: $3.5 billion.
6. According to UNICEF, from June 4 to August 15, 1982, the war claimed 29,506 victims, of whom 80 percent were civilians in Beirut and its outskirts.
7. Israel Commission of Inquiry into the Events at the Refugee Camps in Beirut, *The Beirut Massacre: The Complete Kahan Commission Report* (Princeton, N.J.: Karx-Cohl, 1983).
8. Wadi D. Haddad, *Lebanon, the Politics of Revolving Doors* (New York: Praeger, 1985).
9. Khalidi, *Under Siege*, p. 135.
10. M. Mruwah, *Al-Muqawama* [The Resistance] (Beirut, 1985), pp. 83ff.
11. Amnesty International, *Annual Reports*, 1983–1993.
12. Elizabeth Picard, *The Lebanese Shi'a and Political Violence* (Geneva: United Nations Research Institute for Social Development, 1993) pp. 34ff.
13. More than 350 tanks, nearly 40 helicopters, 20 frigates and enough missile-launchers to constitute a third artillery battalion with missile capabilities for the war against Aoun. The data was obtained from the LF periodical, *al-Masîra*, in 1989 and 1990.

14. Raymond G. Helmick, "Internal Lebanese Politics: The Lebanese Front and Forces," pp. 306–23 in Halim Barakat, ed., *Toward a Viable Lebanon* (London: Croom Helm & Washington: Center for Contemporary Arab Studies, 1988), p. 317.
15. *Jane's Defense Weekly*, November 3, 1990.

Chapter 11. A Consensus Destroyed

1. *Nord Sud Export Consultants*, March 13, 1993, p. 46.
2. E. Longuenesse, "Guerre et décentralisation urbaine au Liban: le cas de Zghorta," in *Petites villes et villes moyennes dans le monde arabe* (Tours: Urbama, 1986), pp. 345–61.
3. Hashish cultivation covered 80 percent of the cultivated surface area in the region of Baalbek and Hermil until 1991. See *al-Nahar*, September 25, 1985, and H. Makhlouf, *Culture et trafic de drogue au Liban* (Paris: l'Harmattan, 1994).
4. S. Turquié, "De quoi vivent les Libanais?" *Le Monde Diplomatique* (October 1979).
5. Georges Corm, "Hégémonie milicienne et problème du rétablissement de l'Etat," in *Liban: Les guerres de l'Europe et de l'Orient, 1840–1992* (Paris: Gallimard, 1992), pp. 225–57.
6. Forty-four percent of the budget in 1984, the year of the reconstruction of the army; 19 percent in 1986, on a budget of $2 billion. See "Etudes et consultations économiques," *Rapport économique libanais* (Beirut, 1985).
7. Nasser H. Saidi, *Economic consequences of the war in Lebanon* (Oxford: Centre for Lebanese Studies, 1986), p. 13.
8. A. Dagher, "La Grande détresse de l'économie libanaise," *Le Monde Diplomatique* (January 1985).
9. Final calculations by the Internal Security Forces, released in June 1994.
10. H. al-Shaykh, *The Story of Zahra* (London/New York: Quarter Books, 1986).
11. Y. Sadowski, "Cadres, Guns and Money: The Eighth Regional Congress of the Syrian Ba'th," *Merip* 134 (July–August 1985), pp. 3–9.
12. During the war, there was very little original reflection upon the transformations of the communitarian society and their social cost. See W. Sharara, *Hurub al-istitba'* [The Wars of Subjection] (Beirut, Dar al-Tali'a 1979). See also the studies of Mahdi Amil (Hasan Hamdan), particularly *Madkhal ila naqd al-fikr al-ta'ifi* [Introduction to the criticism of communitarian thought] (Beirut, 1985). Among the intellectuals of the Lebanese Front, the social question remained exclusively a communitarian question. See W. Faris, *Al-Ta'addudiyya fi Lubnan* [Pluralism in Lebanon] (Beirut, 1979).
13. Letter quoted in *Le Monde Diplomatique* (November 1987).
14. Hence the simultaneity of the repeated terrorist attacks against civilians in several cities of Syria and in Beirut between March and May 1986.
15. Ghassan Twaini in *al-Nahar* (March 18, 1974).
16. E. Picard, *The Lebanese Shi'a and political violence* (Geneva: UNRISD, 1993), pp. 28–34

Chapter 12. Which Lebanon?

1. Al-Jumhuriyya al-lubnaniyya, Majlis al-nuwwab, *Al-Dastur al-lubnani* (Beirut, 1990), p. 78.
2. Eleventh and last general principle of the Document of National Reconciliation. Among the political reforms in Title II are equitable (among Christians and Muslims) and proportional (among the various sects) distribution of parliamentary seats. An English-language version of the Document of National Reconciliation was published and commented on by Joseph Maila. See J. Maila, "The Document of National Reconciliation: A Commentary," *Prospects for Lebanon No.4* (Oxford:Centre for Lebanese Studies, 1992).
3. *Al-Dastur al-lubnani*, op. cit., p. 51.
4. On the genesis of a political pluricommunitarian culture in Mount Lebanon, see: Engin Akarli, *The Long Peace, Ottoman Lebanon, 1861–1920* (Berkeley: University of California Press, 1993).
5. This definition of Lebanon's identity was devised much later by Bashir Gemayel in a speech given on the day he was assassinated (September 14, 1982). Cited in Abou, *Bechir Gemayel*, p. 301.
6. G. Salame, "Small Is Pluralistic: Democracy as an Instrument of Civil Peace" in G. Salame, ed., *Democracy without Democrats? The Renewal of Politics in the Muslim World* (London: I. B. Tauris, 1994), p. 105.
7. The Document of National Reconciliation devotes a long development in Title II (Extent of State Sovereignty) and throughout Title IV (Lebano-Syrian Relations) to Syria's role in Lebanon.
8. A. R. Norton, "Lebanon after Taif: Is the Civil War Over?" *The Middle East Journal,* Vol. 3, no. 54 (1991).
9. In 1992 parliament had 64 Christians: 34 Maronites, 14 Greek Orthodox, 8 Greek Catholics, 6 Armenians, 2 others; and 64 Muslims: 27 Sunnis, 27 Shi'is, 8 Druzes, 2 Alawites. See F. al-Khazen and P. Salem, eds., *Al-Intikhabat al-ula fi Lubnan ma ba'd al-harb [The First Election in Lebanon after the War]* (Beirut: Dar al-Nahar, 1993).
10. Kamal Jumblat was assassinated in 1977. Pierre Gemayel died in 1984, Camille Chamoun in 1988, Suleiman Frangie and Sabri Hamade in 1990. Rachid Karame was assassinated in 1987. Raymond Edde has lived in Paris since 1977, and Saeb Salam in Geneva since 1984. Kamel al-As'ad tried to stage a political comeback but lost the 1992 elections.
11. Waddah Charara, "Deux ans de réunification nationale: une libanisation gigogne," *Cahiers de la Méditerranée* 44 (June 1992), p. 168.
12. In a process shown by Michel Seurat, *L'Etat de barbarie* (Paris: Le Seuil, 1989). Thus the Alawi Baathist militants from Syria use their communal solidarity ties (*'asabiyya*) to monopolize power. In the name of national integration they forbid other communal groups from doing the same.
13. The lack of democracy in the state of Israel stems from the negation of the dual national character of its population.
14. See E. Picard, "Milices libanaises et paramilitaires nord-irlandais: De la mobilisation du groupe à l'invention de son identité," pp.115-135 in D.C. Martin, ed., *Comment dit-on "nous" en politique?* (Paris: Presses de la FNSP, 1994).
15. Among others, *I'raf haqiqat Lubnan as-siyasi* [Understand the truth about Lebanese politics]; *al-Islam as-siyasi wa wihdat Lubnan* [Political Islam and Lebanese Unity]; *al-Qadhiyya al-lubnaniyya* [The Lebanese question], a series of brochures

on the crisis of 1975–76. Also *School Curricula and Formation of the Lebanese Patriot* (1971); *Greater Lebanon: Agony of a Half Century* (1975), etc.

16. On the debate among the Lebanese Shi'is on Ayatollah Khomeini's proclamation of the *wilayat al-faqih*—the return of political power to the "just jurisconsult," see E. Sivan, *Radical Islam, Medieval Theology and Modern Politics* (New Haven: Yale University Press, 1985) and R. Norton, "Lebanon: The Internal Conflict and the Iranian Connection," in J. Esposito, ed., *The Iranian Revolution* (Miami: Florida International University Press, 1990).

17. In *al-Safir*, August 18, 1975; reprinted October 9, 1975 in the Kataeb newspaper *al-'Amal*.

18. M. Shams, *Al-Harakat al-islamiyya fi Lubnan* [The Islamic Movements in Lebanon] (Beirut, 1984) p. 263. See also his televised interview by Ghassan al-Twaini, Télé Liban, May 6, 1993.

19. See A. N. Hamzeh, "Lebanon's Hizbollah: from Islamic Revolution to Parliamentary Accommodation," *Third World Quarterly*, Vol. 14, no. 2 (1993), p. 322.

20. But the bilateral accord of May 1991 does not contemplate reciprocity. In this respect it is similar to the Lebano-Israeli "Naqoura" treaty of 1983, never ratified and abandoned in 1985, which provided for the Lebanese army to suppress all the Lebanese or foreign forces susceptible to harming Israel.

21. J. Kolars and T. Naff, "The Waters of the Litani in Regional Context," *Prospects for Lebanon* No. 7 (Oxford: Centre for Lebanese Studies, 1993).

Epilogue

1. Epigraph taken from Amin Maalouf, *Rock of Tanios*, trans. Dorothy Blair (London; Quartet Books, 1994).

Suggested Reading

The following is a list of books and articles in English with which readers can extend their knowledge of the political system and the conflict in Lebanon. This list supplements the bibliographical references given in the notes.

History

As I have mentioned, many historical works in Arabic and English have appeared since the beginning of the war. As a result knowledge of Lebanon's past, particularly the Middle Ages and the modern era, has greatly advanced. The leading historian Kamal Salibi has produced several excellent studies, particularly in *A House of Many Mansions: The History of Lebanon Reconsidered* (Berkeley: University of California Press, 1988), an exciting and accessible book, full of humor and erudition.

On the modern period, there are Albert Hourani's *Syria and Lebanon: A Political Essay* (London/New York: Oxford University Press, 1946); William Polk's illuminating *The Opening of South Lebanon, 1788–1840: A Study in the Impact of the West on the Middle East* (Cambridge, Mass.: Harvard University Press, 1963); and Leila Tarazi Fawaz's *Merchants and Migrants in Nineteenth-Century Beirut* (Cambridge, Mass.: Harvard University Press, 1983). The study of Ottoman Lebanon has been recently renewed by Engin Akerli's *The Long Peace: Ottoman Lebanon 1881-1920* (Berkeley, Los Angeles and London: University of California Press, 1993), as well as by Leila Tarazi Fawaz, *An Occasion for War: Civil Conflict in Lebanon and Damascus in 1860* (London/New York: I.B. Tauris, 1994).

The decisive episode of the Mandate is now better understood thanks to Stephen Longrigg's *Syria and Lebanon under French Mandate* (London/New York: Cambridge University Press, 1958). It can be supplemented by Meir Zamir's *The Formation of Modern Lebanon* (London/Dover, N.H.: Croom

Helm, 1985), which deals with the French Lebanese and inter-Lebanese debates at the time of the creation of the state of Greater Lebanon.

Institutions and Political Life

The political history of the independent republic is covered by two excellent books: Leonard Binder, ed., *Politics in Lebanon* (New York: Wiley, 1966); and Michael C. Hudson's synthesis, *The Precarious Republic: Political Modernization in Lebanon* (New York: Random House, 1968). Unfortunately, neither the legal analyses of Edmond Rabbath, nor the theoretical reflections of Antoine Messara on consociational democracy have been so far translated into English.

Among studies of political forces in Lebanon, three are especially valuable: John P. Entelis, *Pluralism and Party Transformation in Lebanon: al-Kata'ib 1936–1970* (Leiden: Brill, 1974); Labib Zuwiyya Yamak, *The Syrian Social Nationalist Party: An Ideological Analysis* (Cambridge, Mass.: Harvard University Press, 1966); and Michael Johnson, *Class and Client in Beirut: The Sunni Muslim Community and the Lebanese States, 1840–1985* (London/Atlantic Highlands, N.J.: Ithaca Press, 1986). Two interesting studies of the political role of the Shi'is can be added: Fouad Ajami, *The Vanished Imam: Musa al Sadr and the Shia of Lebanon* (Ithaca, N.Y.: Cornell University Press, 1986); and Augustus R. Norton, *Amal and the Shia: Struggle for the Soul of Lebanon* (Austin: University of Texas Press, 1987).

Economy and Society

Unfortunately, there is no synthesis on the economy of contemporary Lebanon. The investigation of the Institut de Recherche et de Formation en vue de Développement which has served as a reference for many economic analyses up to now dates from 1960. The doctoral dissertation of Carolyn Gates, *The Formation of the Political Economy of Modern Lebanon, the State and the Economy from Colonialism to Independence, 1932–1952,* is to be published by the Centre for Lebanese Studies (Oxford). She already published *The Historical Role of Political Economy in the Development of Modern Lebanon* (Oxford: Centre for Lebanese Studies, 1990). One can read with profit Youssef Sayegh's *Entrepreneurs of Lebanon: The Role of the Business Leader in a Developing Country* (Cambridge, Mass.: Harvard University Press, 1962).

In addition to the studies of the sociologist Samir Khalaf, *Persistence and Change in 19th Century Lebanon: A Sociological Essay* (Beirut: American University of Beirut/Syracuse University Press, 1979); and *Lebanon's Predicament* (New York: Columbia University Press, 1987), a collection of articles with an emphasis on the relations between society and politics, communities and politics, there is also Fuad Khuri's excellent monograph *From Village to Suburb: Order and Change in Greater Beirut* (Chicago: University of Illinois Press, 1975). Published at the outbreak of the war, Khuri's study prefigures the power struggle between older urbanized and the recent immigrants. On the other hand, at the beginning of the war, Halim Barakat published a study based on an investigation of the students of Beirut, *Lebanon in Strife: Student Preludes to the Civil War* (Austin: University of Texas Press, 1977).

Political Thought

Special mention must be made of works published since 1973 by the Centre d'Etudes sur le Monde Arabe Moderne at the Université Saint Joseph in Beirut, the *Ceman Reports* (Beirut/Washington, D.C.), which contain analyses of and statements by the protagonists of all sides of the war in Lebanon, as well as valuable documents from the communitarian and religious authorities and political parties.

To these must be added the *Papers on Lebanon* series published since 1986 by the Centre for Lebanese Studies at Oxford; and *The Beirut Review*, a quarterly university review founded in 1989 that publishes the best English-language experts on Lebanon.

Personal Accounts

There are few English-language political memoirs or memoirs translated into English, except for Kamal Jumblat's *I Speak for Lebanon* (London, 1982) and one of Amin Gemayel's numerous defense pleas, *Rebuilding Lebanon* (Labham, Mass.: Center for International Affairs, Harvard University, 1992). See also Karim Pakradouni, éminence grise of the principal leaders of the Lebanese Forces, generally compelling in his revelations but to be taken with a grain of salt due to his political ambitions and changing convictions, *Le Piège: De la malédiction libanaise à la guerre du Golfe* (Paris, Grasset, 1991).

The reader may skip over Barbara Newman's *The Covenant: Love and Death in Beirut* (New York: Crown Publishers, 1989) on Bashir Gemayel, which lacks both information and sincerity.

In the context of an endless war in which ideologies and subjectivity play an essential role, novels and stories make up more than a personal account, a participation in this conflict. On this score, the contribution of women writers is remarkable, as Miriam Cooke shows in *War's Other Voices: Women Writers on the Lebanese Civil War* (Cambridge/New York: Harvard University Press, 1987). Particularly worth reading are Lina Mikdadi Tabbara, *Survival in Beirut: A Diary of Civil War*, trans. Nadia Hijab (London: Onyx Press, 1979); and Hanan al-Shaykh, *The Story of Zahra* (London: Quartet Books, 1986), as well as *Beirut Blues* (London: Chatto & Windus, 1995).

Jean Makdisi's journal, *Beirut Fragments* (New York: Persea Books, 1990) accurately depicts the mixture of banality and horror marking the fifteen years of war in the capital.

International Aspects

The long war in Lebanon is the subject of more or less extensive discussions in many works about the Middle East in general. One memorable one is George W. Ball's scathing analysis, *Error and Betrayal in Lebanon: An Analysis of Israel's Invasion of Lebanon and the Implications for U.S.-Israeli Relations* (Washington, D.C.: Foundation for Middle East Peace, 1984).

While Rashid Khalidi treats the Palestinian aspects of the Lebanese conflict in *Under Siege: P.L.O. Decision-making During the 1982 War* (New York: Columbia University Press, 1986), Yair Evron's excellent book *War and Intervention in Lebanon: The Israeli-Syrian Deterrence Dialogue* (London: Croom Helm, 1987) puts the war in Lebanon in its regional context.

For an account of the Lebanese tragedy and its place within the Arab-Israeli conflict and the maneuvering of the great powers, required reading is Noam Chomsky, *The Fateful Triangle: the United States, Israel and the Palestinians* (London: Pluto Press, 1983). Also indispensable is *The Beirut Massacre: the Complete Kahan Commission Report* (New York: Kartz-Cohl, 1983).

Finally, Ghassan Tueni has written of his experiences as Lebanese ambassador to the United Nations from 1977 to 1982 in *Une Guerre pour les autres,* (Paris: Lattès, 1985). This subtle and well informed analysis aims to show how Lebanon was a victim of "war for the sake of others."

The War and Its Developments

Marius Deeb has given one of the first accurate chronicles of the war of 1975–77 in his *The Lebanese Civil War* (New York: Praeger, 1980). The impassioned book of Jonathan C. Randal, who was a correspondent for the *Washington Post* in Beirut, *Going All the Way: Christian Warlords, Israeli*

Adventurers, and the War in Lebanon (New York: Vintage, 1984), throws harsh light on the plans and ambitions of the protagonists.

Another war correspondent, Robert Fisk of the London *Times*, gave an impressive account of the post-1982 events, with special attention to the south: *Pity the Nation* (Oxford: Oxford University Press, 1990). A young and talented Lebanese journalist produced a well-informed and critical record of Aoun's years: Carole Dagher, *Les paris du Général* (Beirut: FMA, 1992).

Of more academic tone are Helena Cobban, *The Making of Modern Lebanon* (Boulder, Colo.: Westview Press, 1985), stressing the sectarian division of the country; and Tabitha Petran, *The Struggle Over Lebanon* (New York: Monthly Review Press, 1987), a detailed chronicle of the war years.

The following are useful as works of reference: David McDowall, *Lebanon: A Conflict of Minorities* (London: Minority Rights Group, 1983); and particularly the excellent *Essays on the Crisis in Lebanon* (London: Ithaca Press, 1976), edited by Roger Owen, whose pessimistic analyses have, alas, not been refuted.

The articles published by Ahmad Beydoun throughout the war can be consulted in a collection titled *Liban, itinéraire dans une guerre incivile* (Paris: Cermoc-Karthala, 1993), well thought-out reflections by an intellectual who understood the mechanisms of the conflict and never let himself be swayed by partisan thinking.

Rebuilding Lebanon

Since the end of the war, three books have dealt with the previous fifteen years and the problems of Lebanon's reconstruction: Theodor Hanf, *Coexistence in Wartime Lebanon: Decline of a State and Rise of a Nation*, translated from German by John Richardson (London: I. B. Tauris, 1993), interesting above all for its surveys and interviews; Deirdre Collings, ed., *Peace for Lebanon: From War to Reconstruction* (Boulder, Co.: Lynne Rienner, 1994), sponsored by the Canadian Institute for International Peace and Security; and Fadia Kiwan, ed., *Le Liban aujourd'hui* (Paris: CNRS-Cermoc, 1994), written by a dozen Lebanese university professors who lived in the country throughout the war and now occupy positions of responsibility.

Index

Page numbers in boldface refer to maps.